This Restless Life

Churning through Love, Work and Travel

BRIGID DELANEY

MELBOURNE
UNIVERSITY
PRESS

MELBOURNE UNIVERSITY PRESS
An imprint of Melbourne University Publishing Limited
187 Grattan Street, Carlton, Victoria 3053, Australia
mup-info@unimelb.edu.au
www.mup.com.au

First published 2009
Text © Brigid Delaney, 2009
Design and typography © Melbourne University Publishing Limited, 2009

Text design by Nada Backovic
Cover design by Design by Committee
Typeset by TypeSkill
Printed by Griffin Press, SA

National Library of Australia Cataloguing-in-Publication entry

Delaney, Brigid.

This restless life: churning through love, work and play / Brigid Delaney.

9780522855968 (pbk.)

Bibliography.

Quality of life.
Life skills.
Life.

646.7

CONTENTS

Acknowledgements   v

Introduction   vii

LOVE   1

WORK   81

TRAVEL   169

Conclusion   249

Notes   255

ACKNOWLEDGEMENTS

This book—while its errors are all mine, writing and researching it has felt like a collaborative effort. Firstly, thanks to all those who spoke to me on and off the record for the book's many interviews. I am grateful for your generosity with your time and your stories.

I'd also like to thank those who through many discussions helped tease out the book's themes and stress-test my arguments, those who had been published before and talked me through the process, those who lived with me while the book was being written and endured much discussion of its themes and frustrations, the newspaper editors who allowed me to explore consumer culture more fully— particularly in Sydney—and those with sharp eyes who read and edited sections at various points on the way. Basically—all of you who supported me.

In Sydney: Sharon Verghis, Patrick Muhlen-Schulte, Nick O'Malley, Adam Haddow, Stephanie Peatling, Kathleen Furey, Adam Williams, Ben Allard, Jackie Dent, Ellen Connolly, Bob Ellis, Michael Visontay, Susan Wyndham and Lisa Pryor. A special thanks to my agent Pippa Masson at Curtis Brown.

In London: Bonnie Malkin, James Button, Andrew Charlton, Ryan Heath, Tim Clelland, Alessio Fregni, Paola Totaro, Robert Wainwright, Dave Fickling, Kate Mackenzie, Annabel Crabb, Joh Leggatt, Catherine Humble, Michelle Chan, Sean Pepper, Phil Malone, Liz Colman, Penny Bradfield, Angela Dridan, Dale Ranson,

Jodie Reed, Harvey Redgrave, David Wroe and a special thanks to Lee Glendinning, who always believed that the manuscript would one day end up in book form, even when I didn't.

In Melbourne: Tom Dobson, Matthew Torney, Louisa Dickinson, Sophie Dougall, Heather Clarke, Sioban Murnane, Jo Beattie, Melissa Fyfe, Jemma Purdy and all the team at MUP, especially my editor Foong Ling Kong, who understood that writing about lives that jump around may result in a similarly fluid book.

And finally to my brothers, Michael, Justin and Matthew, and my parents Jim and Mary Delaney. The safe harbour you built allowed me to voyage out to more uncertain waters.

INTRODUCTION

When I started writing this book in 2005, I intended to focus on the strong consumer culture fuelled by the long economic boom. I was living in Sydney and noticed an emerging but distinct ascetic: a high maintenance glossy look, boys with statement hair, girls with manicures and spray-on tans. Brands were back, credit card debt had never been higher and there was a gilded age, Great Gatsby-esque feeling in the air. It was a time of champagne and parties, a mania for high-end restaurants, extravagant travel and cocaine making a comeback.

So pervasive and dominant was this new consumer culture, so little resistance was being put up, that things that had once stood outside the marketplace like love, religion and our work identities seemed to be dragged in like iron filings to a powerful magnet. To borrow from F Scott Fitzgerald, it was shaping up to be a giddy, gaudy time and I was keen to gauge what psychic and social consequences such a long run of prosperity would have on us.

I started making observations, detecting shifts in mood, interviewing the glossy boys and girls and lining up my experts: what's it all about? I asked them. Where's this going to end up? In all their answers, one word kept being repeated by my subjects—quite independently from one another, and quite unconsciously. That word was 'churn'.

The dictionary definition of churn is to 'stir or agitate violently' and also to 'produce, proceed with, or experience violent motion or agitation'. But my experts were using it in a more general, almost intuitive way to describe everything from the movement of young people through Pentecostal religions, to the reconfiguration of the labour market, immigration patterns and a rapid-turnover serial monogamy that characterised the relationships of restless singles.

The church experts described how 'promiscuous' people had become with their faith, trying out one religion for a year or so before moving on to the brighter promise of something else. The old model had not only been faith for life, but faith that was passed through generations like DNA, that had been subverted in one restless generation who were churning through beliefs.

Those studying patterns of immigration and mobility were surprised at suddenly how circular movement had become—that is, we were not just going away and staying away as was the usual pattern of migration but we were going and coming back and going again. We were churning. We were also churning through partners thanks to internet dating where high speed search engines and choice, choice, choice made the search for a mate akin to shopping. As for work, the last decade had seen an increasingly restless economy and the emergence of churn jobs—the growth of part-time, casual and contract, temporary work, where people don't progress incrementally through one workplace, but rather flit from one temporary contract to the next, churning through workplaces, projects and colleagues.

Consumer culture, many of the experts argued, was partly responsible for this restlessness. People had become used to so much choice and shopping that they unwittingly commodified things that had once existed outside the market: love online had a retail element, religion was becoming a pick 'n' mix proposition and people chose what country to move to as if selecting furniture from a brochure.

This restlessness was the new default speed. News and information was churning through powerful and popular new technologies—there was a Google churn where thousands of pages on any one topic appeared at the press of a button. The media also picked up the pace, becoming diffuse to the point of being unwieldy with hundreds of choices about where to get information, including endlessly multiplying blogs and hundreds of thousands of new clips uploaded on YouTube each day.[1]

My own life was becoming increasingly restless. My childhood was textbook stable—wonderful parents, three younger brothers and a dog, living in a large, old and interesting house in a picturesque coastal town. Yet as soon as adulthood hit, so too did restlessness. I have worked in 144 jobs. As a result I belong to dozens of super schemes. By the time I was twenty-seven I'd had three major career changes that required complete changes of skill-set. And lately, in the months between December 2007 and February 2009, I had not only moved house eleven times, but six of those moves had been to different countries.

I was bingeing on choice. I couldn't seem to settle down. I was exhausted from constantly moving (packing up the house in Bloomsbury, dropping off the Berlin keys, picking up the Brussels key, unpacking my bags in Bayswater) but each new place promised to be *the one*, so I kept moving.

During this time, I became addicted to using the internet, which only seemed to fuel my feeling of restlessness. I got anxious if I spent a day offline—my virtual world, my virtual life—didn't stop and I began to feel obscurely anxious if I spent any time away from it. I couldn't be still, even when I was sitting still in front of a screen. So many nights after I'd been online, I'd feel so overstimulated it became difficult to fall asleep.

What is this restlessness doing to us, I wondered? Does it make us feel anxious, insecure, untethered, less stable, more transitory, more superficial? Is it a kind of mania that is all sound and fury but signifying nothing? Space junk. Or has this restlessness been enriching, allowing us to sample more of the world's experiences than ever before: to travel, to live overseas, to work in many different industries, to have many different partners and sexual experiences, to learn about a lot of different religions?

And what about now—will the global recession be enough to apply the brakes to our restless, reckless ways of living and make us reassess the social and environmental costs, as well as the costs to our psyche, of restlessness?

The only thing for it was to try and fight my way through the foam the churn creates, negotiate its tides and eddies, its strange swirls, mysterious gravitational pulls and write about it. The leap from a study of consumer culture to restlessness is not a great one. Our entrenched consumer culture is built on choice and choice stimulates restlessness. It all connects.

I have focused on three areas affected by this restlessness: travel, work and love. They have traditionally provided some of the deepest wells from which we draw meaning and sustenance. In seeing how they have been changed by the churn, we can also see something of how we have changed. The book was written, researched and debated—and therefore is set—on the move: Sydney, Melbourne, Port Fairy, New York, London, Rome, Brussels, Berlin, Paris. Looking back it seems in writing this book, I did not so much as avoid the strong pull of restlessness, as submit to it.

I owe a great intellectual debt to academic and author Richard Sennett and his writing on the new economy in *The Corrosion of Character*. Sennett's ideas are throughout this book. He examined how flexibility and the new economy affect character. His question was: how do we decide what is of lasting value in ourselves in a society which is impatient, which focuses on the immediate moment?

How can long-term goals be pursued in an economy devoted to the short term?

My own questions are—in the age of restlessness is it better to live broadly or deeply? And can we do both?

Brigid Delaney

Melbourne, 2009

LOVE

The sky is darkening and the clouds are low and heavy in the sky. Leicester Square is jammed with tourists and promoters leaning against sandwich boards offering cheap theatre tickets, cut-price internet use, discount international phone calls or leather goods HALF PRICE TODAY ONLY. Fast-food wrappers blow across the street while black cabs and their drivers sit wearily in traffic. It's early on Saturday night and as good a place as any to find love. I meet my friend Amy in a pub near the tube station and we exclaim over each other's dresses and hairstyles. We down our drinks for courage before running out into the rain then up the stairs into the nightclub.

At The Penthouse we are given nametags and a number, some forms and a pen. 'Brigid 5' my nametag reads. The form lists twenty spaces where I am to grade the men I will be meeting tonight. They in turn will rate me. Speed dating works like this: twenty men, twenty women, three minutes chatting with each other before a bell rings and the man moves on to the next woman. You tick 'yes', 'no' or 'friendship' on the form provided. If you both want to be friends or you both have a match of yes, then email addresses are exchanged and you can arrange a date.

Speed dating in this context acts as a clearing house, or a vetting system for relationships. In many ways it mimics the tools used by big companies when mass recruiting—that is, to get all interested applicants together for a round-robin of testing so they can eliminate candidates as swiftly and expediently as possible.

Speed dating and mass recruitment also mimic the format of many reality TV shows such as *Australian Idol* that use cattle call auditions to vet hopeful contestants. Judges then 'thin-slice'—watching thirty seconds of singing and dancing or casting an eye over the model's weight and cheekbones or assessing the diction and poise before making their decision.

This thin-slicing process is now being applied to finding a partner—and companies have sprung up to facilitate the process. A company called X.date.co.uk, a chain of sorts, with branches in Brighton, Leeds, Manchester and London, and speed-dating functions every night of the week, is running the event tonight.

More than getting a job, more than being a top model or a singing star or being on TV—finding a partner is seen as the ultimate 'life choice'. But in our ambitions we forget there's also alchemy involved. I never thought this alchemy would sit comfortably amid the rituals of registration, displayed name badges and poised 'greeters' that meet all applicants at the door. But here I am attaching my name badge to my chest, surveying the minor squalor and sadness that is a nightclub before it gets dark and wondering if my hair looks right. I'm also feeling something I haven't felt for a long time—nervous.

I check out my competition before the whistle sounds. There's a mousy woman in the corner, who hasn't made much of an effort getting her face ready, but she's already talking to some guy and he looks really into her. Is that in the rules? Can she jump the gun? In another corner is a group of girls in their early twenties. They look tanned, bored, dismissive. They are drinking bottles of champagne. They have shiny hair and bare shoulders. Two men ask to sit with Amy and I before the whistle sounds. Neil and Richard. We answer questions like: 'Where are you girls from? Can I detect an accent there? Oh, what part of Oz?' And I am thinking: stop talking to me now because we'll be too familiar during our three minutes together.

The women running the event are Amazons. One is black, the other white. They are bootylicious—with enormous shoulders, huge breasts, rounded rumps, big hair and hoop earrings. Their presence is reassuring somehow—house-mistresses supervising a sort of randy, alcoholic version of school sports. They move from booth to booth, setting us up for the night and explaining the rules again.

The whistle sounds and I take a deep breath (although not too deep as the air in the room smells sort of beery and sour). For the next two hours there is flat-out, even exhausting, flirtation. I'm selling myself with just the right amount of sexual kick to make it interesting—and the men are doing the same. Then the whistle blows and some sort of mask slips and there is the faint but perceptible detection of coldness in the air, as we shield our scorecards to our chests and rate each other. 'Thanks, lovely to meet you.' Next.

Neil was first. Very thin with brown hair and bulgy eyes, his job is spray-painting police cars. I got excited thinking he was some sort of hoodie, but instead he's a chemical engineer. Different squads have different cars. Different colours have different meanings. Signs and signifiers. 'So how will I recognise an undercover cop car if it's tailing me?' I ask. 'Do you put a lick of secret paint somewhere, so those in the know ... you know ... know ...' He seemed affronted, rather than charmed by the question. Our time was up. I ticked no.

Mark was next. He lived in Croydon but hailed from Israel. He liked working out and watching TV. We talked about the gym for a bit, then the telly and—God—had only one minute passed? Shit— what do we talk about? What I wanted to talk about was a big iceberg I was trying to swim around. But the silence weirded me out and I found myself stumbling and asking anyway; 'So Mark—Hezbollah— you must be bummed that they are bombing your country. But I guess you guys started it ...'

I saw him tick no. I ticked no as well. Three minutes stretched out to a lifetime.

Next.

Darren wouldn't look at me. His nose looked freshly broken. He talked to the table. Even lowered, his eyes were beautiful.

Nick didn't waste time. He swaggered into the booth with a Caipiroska and a cockney accent. 'Yeah, I like 'em', he said about his green drink. 'Girls' drink but so what, yeah, go on, have a taste. Yum—eh?' Nick worked in insurance in the city. He asked about my job and was impressed. 'You're clever, yeah. I like clever girls.' He wrote 'clever' on the form next to the number five. 'I'm writing clever on my form—yeah? Let's cut this rubbish. Here's my phone number—let's go out.'

He wrote his mobile number on my form and winked before getting his straw entangled with the foliage in his drink. The whistle blew and he winked again and sauntered to the next girl. I tried to guess his age. Possibly he was as much as twenty.

His friend Ollie was next. He had red hair and liked to ski and drink Caipiroskas. But not at the same time.

Mark liked healthy eating and had fond memories of watching *Prisoner: Cell Block H* as a child. My accent reminded him of *Prisoner*, he said.

I was getting drunker. At half time in the ladies toilets the young girls drinking champagne were bemoaning the talent.

'Neil is a freak. What a drip, he is awful.'

'The longest three minutes of my life …'

'Too many guys who work as computer analysts here.'

'Bunch of duds …'

'Oh, God—have you met that awful Neil yet?'

After the break the speed dating seemed to take on amphetamine-fuelled qualities. It seemed I had barely introduced myself to the guy across the table before the whistle was blown. My notes at this stage became hazy and intriguing: 'Logan—Indian, wants to change the world. John—dad a doctor in Saudi, annoyed at gov't/taxes. José—Barcelona, wants to take me back there. Martin—acne, likes fencing. James recommends visiting Bath. Rob—astrometry, duck pancakes, Belgium(?). Paul—marine biologist—does not believe sea turtles can be saved, prefers plankton.'

The whistle blew again and it was over. I could barely remember who I had spoken to, let alone if I wanted them to be my boyfriend. In the bar José tried to talk to me about Barcelona, but Logan, who didn't feel he'd explained adequately his world philosophy to me, stood behind José waiting to chat. Oh, God—was this round two? The guy who liked *Prisoner* already had his arm around the mousy girl. Amy had bought a round of drinks and was in a booth with Zac. I tried to remember if I had speed dated him. Maybe he was in the hazy mid set of boys numbered twelve to sixteen. Zac … Zac … Zac?

Neil was nowhere to be found. Had he gone home? Already? Nick was pashing one of the champagne girls near the loos. I had to laugh. At the bar ordering more Caipiroskas he rubbed his groin into my back and said, 'Baby, you're clever, you got my number, call me'. That made me laugh even more although I wished he'd at least offered to buy me a drink. Of course people come to speed dating to get laid. He was going to get laid tonight.

Nick would be okay—people like him always are. But there were other people there who may not be. Paul, with half his life spent underwater, his passion for plankton, the way his glasses always found their way down the bridge of his nose no matter how many times he pushed them up—three minutes for him was inadequate. Any package or brand that he could hope to construct would not do him justice. He's not a salesman. Same with José, with his poor English, jaundice pallor and Barcelona lisp, or Martin, with his passion for wearing chain metal and picking up swords. How can you brand *that*?

Men who come into the city in their best shirt and just the right amount of product in their hair. Three minutes. Girls in the toilets laughing at them. A twenty year old with the right sales patter leaving with his pocket stuffed with phone numbers. And for a minute, feeling the vibration of the new Justin Timberlake song through the floor, feeling the heat of too many bodies in a too small room, I felt really sad. Sure chemistry is either there or it's not but what happened to letting things develop?

The next morning I dozed to Psychedelic Furs singing *Pretty in Pink* on the radio. My room was warm, it was raining and the music made me feel nostalgic. The song was from the 1980s movie where Molly Ringwald was in love with Andrew McCarthy and Jon Cryer was in love with Molly. The whole thing played out in the schoolyard, the drama building until prom night when sexual tension, jealousies, lust—the lot of it—had its climax. It wasn't just the song that was nostalgic—it was the movie, it was the times.

For all the fun and the flirting, speed dating is a savage playground. There is no room for mistakes or bad impressions or a romantic build-up. That's why they call it speed dating. There is something chilling and pernicious at the heart of this new style of courtship. Something detached and clinical and brutal about speed dating that rubs up uncomfortably with our idea of romantic love—with the very idea of *falling* in love. Here you do not so much as *fall*, as assess.

But with its evil twin—internet dating—speed dating has become our dominant courtship ritual, and with that, *the way* we fall in love is set to change. It's restless love for the restless generation.

In Melbourne, Sydney, Perth, Adelaide and Brisbane dozens of companies offer speed-dating nights. In London almost a hundred companies run speed-dating nights, every night of the week. It costs on average $50 for the night. The overheads are low for these companies—renting a room at a bar is a cost, but likely to be commercially advantageous for the bar itself as the speed daters down buckets of booze in order to calm their nerves. Any contact the speed-dating company has with applicants is no-cost—via email, with standard forms that are spat out in bundles.

No segment of the market seems out of reach for these companies. There is Christian speed dating, orthodox Jewish speed dating, lesbian single mothers speed dating, marketing professionals speed dating, IT workers speed dating, ethnic speed dating, black speed dating, gay speed dating, and most nights are broken down into age range, so a 40-year-old woman does not find herself trying to chat up a 19-year-old boy.

Even people in relationships are a market not immune from the lure of speed dating. When I asked my friends for someone to attend speed dating with me, those in couples seemed the keenest. Why? Maybe they wanted to prove they still had it. Maybe they wanted the flirting without the risk or vulnerability—to be able to be charming and desirable for three minutes, to get a sense of their market value and then move on. No one gets hurt that way.

The Psychedelic Furs' song finished and was replaced by Snow Patrol. Time to get up. My hair smelt of smoke. The rain kept falling. My speed-dating feedback form was covered in wine stains and scrawls. Romance was dead. The market entered our love lives when our eyes were closed. But I'm opening mine now and I'm not very happy with what I'm seeing.

Speed dating and the internet are the best—and most efficient—ways to find someone, *everyone* says. Success stories abound in this brave new world of courtship. When I tell people that I am researching internet dating they become animated—and recite the roll-call of people who have found sex, love and even marriage through the internet. These people had given up! *Given up,* I am told. Until they used the internet. There was an evangelical tone to a lot of these conversations. It was as if people were compensating for stigmatising it five years ago. 'I would do it!', say friends and acquaintances who are beautiful and desirable. 'If I were single.'

There were so many success stories, so many happy couples and so many new sites appearing on what seemed to be an almost weekly basis that I wondered if people were actually meeting *without* the internet's help.

Of course it's not just about love—it's also about money. And while you may think the players are the singles sticking their photos up and cutting and pasting their blurbs—*the real players* are transnational companies. Speed-dating events in the UK generate nearly $10 million a year with 10 000 people a month taking part.[1] But speed dating is small change compared to the global internet dating stakes.

'Online dating is a new economy success story', claims an article in the *Telegraph Magazine* about a dating site catering for married consumers who want to have affairs. Niche site Ashley Madison, an adultery website, has a turnover of around $10 million a year and boasts that its business doubles every year.[2] In 2009, membership soared from one million to 3.6 million.[3] Users must be married (to other people). Says one user: 'On joining, you are obliged to choose from a list of "encounters you'd be open to". I won't go into detail but it's like joining a giant international brothel. For the sexually addicted, it offers a quick and powerful fix; it's the crack-cocaine, trance-inducing, addictive modern version of adultery. The moment I signed up, I was so besieged by leering messages and intimidating fantasies that I couldn't log off fast enough.'[4]

Other niche sites include one for Australian millionaires, where extra services include a wardrobe makeover or even a referral to a dentist or plastic surgeon[5] or Great Boyfriends, which works like TripAdvisor (but for people rather than hotel rooms.) The software lets users write glowing recommendations of their friends, siblings and exes. 'Think of yourself as the seller or "publicist"', the site encourages. And there's a sex hook-up site called OnlineBootyCall, with a focus on anonymous sex, similar to what might happen in a haphazard way at a beat or a bar. The site founder brags of 'only one confirmed marriage among the first one million users'.[6]

Go mainstream and the number of online users swells almost beyond comprehension. Over one month dating sites like eHarmony can draw more than twenty million unique (i.e. individual, not repeat) visitors.[7] The aim is to convert these casual visitors to subscribers who usually pay a monthly fee that enables them to contact matches rather than just post a personal profile.[8] Over a six-month period Americans can spend as much as $250 million searching for a partner via the internet.[9] According to IT online magazine *Computerworld*, well-run internet dating sites can generate in excess of $200 million a year.[10]

There is an in-built churn or restlessness in the sites themselves. Customers come and go. 'A large percentage of customers fall off the love wagon after finding their "one true love"', explains *Computerworld*.[11] But many customers keep coming back. Founder of the dating site True.com, Herb Vest, says returning customers produce 'a revenue stream that has a very long tail'.[12]

While many experts now describe the market as saturated, so far online dating sites seem to be recession-proof. Match.com general manager Mandy Ginsberg says, 'People are anxious right now. They want to find someone with whom to weather the financial storm.' Online dating is cheaper, she says, than mate-seeking in a bar or even at Starbucks.[13]

So why is big business so keen on helping 'facilitate' sex and love? Why have they stepped into the role of matchmaking mothers?

There are a number of reasons and none of them are nostalgic. The first has to do with the market. There was a gap in the market and companies responded with new products and services to fill that gap. The nature of the gap was an absence of rituals around mating, and societal change, with more of us getting divorced and more of us staying single than ever before. Living alone, longer working hours and higher mobility mean we are uprooted with more frequency— and the implications for coupling are profound. It's harder to start, let alone establish and maintain, relationships when your job means you work long hours and move cities every eighteen months.

As the markets for these sites grow due to rapid social change, so grows the chance for profits. Profits in this sector come from a couple of sources. Companies make their money from subscriptions—the amount a person pays to use the site—and revenue from advertising. Banner, click-on or pop-up ads are common on internet dating sites and all generate revenue for corporations.

For big media corporations, internet dating sites can create powerful marketing synergies.[14] These synergies relate to sharing of content (i.e. a newspaper owned by News Limited or Fairfax can provide content on a second-use basis to a website free of charge) and holding consumers in the sites. So if you have a subscriber to your internet dating site, and you are a media company that also has a news website and a classifieds site—including housing and job ads—you can hold the consumer within the portal (or branches of your brand) for longer periods of time. The consumer using dating website rsvp.com. au can click through to smh.com.au, then click through to drive.com. au or mycareer.com.au, then back to smh.com.au to be entertained by the blogs, video feeds, audio files or podcasts, then traffic back to rsvp.com.au—and in the three or four hours that person has been online they have not left the host's house (which is owned by the one company, Fairfax). In the new media parlance this is called 'stickiness' and it's very important to have it. Advertisers like it—and in the transition from old media (free-to-air television, radio and newspapers) to new media (online news and entertainment), new ways of generating revenue must be created. Consumers are always one click away from another site but if you can keep them playing in your patch for a little bit longer then the more advertising a consumer will be exposed to.

Look at the web of companies associated with internet dating and you'll find there are many of these commercially beneficial associations. Interviewed in *e-commerce news*, Jonathan Gaw, an analyst with research firm IDC, said Match.com attained its large user base partially through 'a very advantageous deal with America Online'.[15] The site's wide distribution gives it what Gaw calls a critical component of internet dating success: a large member base. 'Users want to go to where there's the most choice', he says. 'Just like an online auction space, if you're a buyer, you need to go to where all the sellers are.' Word-of-mouth endorsements also help on the marketing side. 'Once [a personals site] gets to a certain size, you hardly need to do any more promotion because it just promotes itself.'[16]

The value of a large subscription base—whether it is for attractiveness to advertisers or subscription fees—has been under the spotlight in the USA where a former Match.com subscriber took the company to court. Matthew Evans, an American in his thirties, claimed that Match.com used attractive young women to take men out on 'sham dates' so members retain their subscriptions, and posted fake postings to 'falsely represent more subscriber participation than actually exists'.[17] Match.com denied the allegations and defended the action. A company spokesperson tartly stated that it doesn't need to resort to baiting individuals—after all, they are far too large to be bothered with that.

Some online dating sites are undoubtedly large—love is a commodity that can translate easily into global trade. For example, Lavalife is Canadian but operates in Australia, as do US sites

Match.com and Plentyoffish.[18] Not only does the need for love transcend nationality, and cultural and religious borders, it's a relatively cheap business to run in a number of markets. As there are no goods, just the potential for consumers to meet other consumers, costs to a company are low. There is no freight to ferry, no packaging, no concern about goods perishing or revenue lost through waste, and no storage costs (except that of data storage). Human resources costs are also relatively low due to the sophisticated IT systems that companies use.

Even the content of the sites (people's profiles) comes at no cost to corporations—consumers create their own content. The corporation wins in a way that's almost brazen—consumers are paying money (subscriptions) to the corporation yet doing all the work (content providing) themselves. The only true service performed by the corporation is to provide the venue—and that venue, cyberspace, is an almost no-cost proposition.

For advertisers, the appeal lies in the fact that a site like Match.com, Facebook or Australia's leading internet dating site RSVP can quantify (almost to the very user or viewer) who their audience is. Newspaper circulation or television ratings can't get anywhere near the internet's ability to track users, and advertisers are attracted to the certainty that comes with this. While old media has operated in a system of A to E marketing jargon (an A being the most desirable consumer in the market: well educated, high disposable income etc.), this old science looks wildly imprecise when compared with the information internet dating companies are able to provide to advertisers. The very nature of the product they are peddling means corporations know the deepest aspirations of their content-providers who can then be marketed to with complete precision and depth. According to Match.com: 'user profiles give us targetable information about these people's lifestyles ... In fact we know if they are pet owners, health nuts, social drinkers, or 6 feet tall. You can pinpoint the exact audience you are trying to reach with virtually no marketing waste.'[19]

In Australia, operators are also seeing an opportunity to cross-market to their audience, who may later on—after they've found love—be looking for a mortgage together or a romantic holiday. Fairfax Digital's then chief operating officer Mike Game told *BRW* in March 2006 that 'advertising that fits the goals of relationship-seeking users, including life decisions such as property purchases, could happily fit in with the website at some stage'.[20] Information consumers input with the site is also used to target them to accept 'extras' that the site may offer. Yahoo Personals, for example, 'uses all of the information at its disposal to tailor its sales pitch to the user'.[21]

Some sites store your profile information after you have left ('we'll remember who you are', says Joseph Essas, vice-president of technology at eHarmony[22]) while others delete it. With this in mind, money from subscriptions would not seem to be the main game of business. Instead by keeping the subscriptions affordable (or—in the case of some sites such as Australian-run hookmeup.com.au—free), companies can increase the number of members, therefore making the site more desirable to advertisers. *Computerworld* warns that 'sticky questions have yet to be answered over what rights such sites have to your personal information—how they use it to market other services to you, if and how they share it with advertisers, and how long they store it after you've moved on'.[23]

Carla is thirty-five and ready to get married. Only problem is she doesn't have a boyfriend. Not yet. But maybe soon. A tremor of impatience runs through everything now. The hunt has kicked up into a furious pace in the last six months, with the internet acting as her propellers. She no longer has the leisure she did in her twenties to loll around with unsuitable men. It's like lying in the park on a sunny day—yeah, sure you get to enjoy the weather but you don't really achieve anything.

Carla is typical of many post-feminist women. Raised in a meritocracy that says they can do anything, life—if it runs smoothly—is a constant propelling forward. School. Finish school. Go to university, move out of home. Travel, first job, pay rise, responsibility increases, boyfriend, more travel, break-up, new boyfriend, new flat. Live-in boyfriend, better job, mortgage, marriage, babies. That the boyfriend decided he didn't want to get married, then decided he didn't want to live with her, is causing the engine to splutter, the propeller to fail. What's she going to do now?

It's been a decade since Carla was single and in that time the rules and the modus operandi have shifted considerably—there is a churn that she's noticed that wasn't as apparent before. Venturing out alone or with work colleagues to bars and clubs she feels vulnerable and unsure. It's not just that's she single again—there's a new species of young woman to compete with; more assertive with their knowing hands, their tiny tops and skinny jeans, who not only know the rules but seem to be creating them as they go along.

Younger colleagues tell her she's wasting her time in bars. People go there to get drunk. The real place to meet people is on the internet, they say. And so she has registered and become part of a brave new world that trumpets the amount of control participants have over their love lives. But in the course of my conversations with Carla the overwhelming lack of control she feels while in 'the system' (her words for internet dating) is evident. She stresses that she never needed the internet to get a boyfriend—always did fine on her own, but it seems to be the way now. It also seems that she's ten years too late to really feel comfortable with the internet. Going online is a secretive thing, she says, something she only talks about with close friends.

Here's what happens.

She signs up to a site—registering her details and choosing a profile name (cute67 maybe or naturalblonde, or wild@heart). She then posts her profile, which includes a picture and a snappy blurb. Consumers can then click on the picture or blurb if they find it enticing, moving them further into her profile that includes the answers to questions about such things as drinking habits, religion, political views and whether she has or wants to have children. Her blurb reads: 'I'm fun but serious or should that read I'm seriously fun?' There's not much room to write more until the second page, explains Carla, a bit apologetically. (She shouldn't apologise—how can you sum up everything; the shifts, the moods, the experiences, the bits of you that are poetry, and the gristle and the toughness, your secret brilliance and all that you went through last year?) But the blurb is an exercise in branding and marketing and in this one line Carla hopes to convey the sense that she has 'two sides to my personality'. 'I like having fun, but that's not what I'm all about. I enjoy serious discussions about politics and serious movies and books, but I wouldn't describe myself as a serious person.'

If other users browsing the site like her profile they can send her a 'kiss'—an electronic flirting device. If she wants to kiss back she returns the gesture by clicking on the kiss reply button on the screen. Each kiss costs the consumer money, deducted from their account with the internet dating company. Ads for everything from building societies to banks, jewellers, health-care funds and travel providers are interspersed between the profiles. They pop up while consumers browse—interrupting romantic reveries, perhaps—with a bright purple and gold box exclaiming how you can shave years off your home loan, reminding those dreaming of love that they are in a commercial space.

After kisses have been exchanged, participants can send emails to each other at their dating site addresses—so an accountant with a failed marriage and body image issues may be emailing a woman whose boyfriend left her for another man and who now for some reason avoids mirrors. But at this stage of the courtship hothunk68 is emailing glamourpussblonde and their real, true selves are kept at bay.

If the emailing goes well, SMSing starts, and Instant Messaging, but you can't stay disembodied forever. At some point the pair must meet up for a face-to-face encounter called a 'date'. In the UK and Australia, dates were traditionally thought to be an American quirk and were viewed with suspicion. The traditional way was to go out in a big group, size each other up, get drunk, then score. A sober, clear-eyed assessment of someone would usually have to wait until the next morning. A date, with its overt tones of sizing up and choosing, never really made the cultural leap to our shores—until internet dating turned the practice mainstream. Quite quickly an enormous cultural shift has occurred in how we court and we've woken up to find a new landscape that some are more comfortable in than others.

I go to the newsagent, and the cover of *Time Out London* blares 'Date Our Cover Stars', devoting the whole issue to dating—the city's most romantic spots, a guide to gay speed dating and the chance to date *Time Out* readers who have sent in their photos and a blurb. I am amazed at and envious of their audacity—here they are on a cover of a magazine. Saying they are looking for love! It doesn't seem very *English* of them. Yet dating stories proliferate in mainstream newspapers and magazines. It is as if the media, sensing that this is the way *things are now*, have taken on the role of educating a hapless public as to *how* this dating stuff is done. *Time Out* offers helpfully: 'There's never been more ways for Londoners to find a mate. But do these modern methods work? We sent five writers to test the capital's stranger courtship rituals.'

According to Carla, the dates themselves are 'weird': inorganic, forced and rife with an agenda. When she meets a man at a café it is as if both pairs of eyes are resisting the glance that sweeps up and down. Just like Friday night at the pub, it's a meat market but it's better to pretend that it's not. Dates are invariably civilised but with an unsettling, fraught undertone. Her experiences vary wildly from the excruciating (the man who told her his ex-wife was a cunt and that he hated most of the women he worked with) to the tender (the widower whose eyes welled up with tears when he half said his wife's name, as he pushed his fork around the salad).

Sometimes she and the man will talk for a couple of hours and there is good chemistry, other times it feels forced and things end abruptly. He takes a call on his phone, picks up the bill (or often doesn't) and says he'll call. He doesn't look her in the eyes. Other times she's the one to leave with her eyes cutting to the floor. It's been six months of these dates and sometimes she feels like she needs a break—a weekend off.

She's looking for The One and wondering if he's out there and if he is, is this the best way to find him?

Canary Wharf, early on Wednesday morning, at sandwich-chain Prêt a Manger and the guy next to us wearing a suit and reading the *Times* is pretending not to listen. I wonder if it's too early in the day to talk about sex.

Brett is talking about his experiences using Gaydar—the hugely successful, global, gay, internet dating site with well over three million users.[24] Aged twenty-five, working in politics and with a body nicely toned from the monotony of lap swimming, Brett is a long way from the desperate and dateless stereotype of internet dating users ten years ago. The internet dating sites are also more sophisticated, facilitating not just romantic meetings, but sexual liaisons. The implications for the gay scene have been profound.

'If people are looking for sex you can go to a section and find out who's actually logged in and they can nominate what they want at that point in time. They can say: I am looking for sex now, I am looking for sex later, I am looking for a boyfriend, I'm looking for a chat,' he says, explaining the ways of the system. 'You can go in and say "I live in this suburb" and find all the people living in this suburb who are looking for sex now, and you get a list of all their photos and all their contact details and send out a message "I live around the corner here" and fifteen minutes later you could be in their bedroom.' Explaining the churn inherent in this method, he says, 'It allows the gay community to return to its modus operandi before the AIDS crisis because you can know so much about so many people, so quickly, it gives you more options. It allows all the sexual possibilities that an AIDS scare will back down.'

All the 'sexual possibilities' and romantic gradations are possible due to high-speed internet connections, a large membership base and well-designed search engines.

'What the whole process does is break it down to key words. It sort of brutalises you—so you become Australian or creative or intelligent—and interested in sport, scene and non-scene and you become known by that. It breaks people down by categories, so you can go into key words and type in "yoga" and find the 20 000 people who are into yoga, or you can go in and find the 60 000 people who claim they have extra large penises. You can do whatever you want and find that level of detail. Or you can do a "cupid match", where you give the system twenty things that you want and they may find you a list of people who have fifteen of those things. The computer plays match maker,' he says, talking rapidly, with the tone of someone that has been there, done that.

'The whole point of this technology is that it opens you up to people that you couldn't have met on the street. Why would you close off those options? You've got to keep those options open and hope you don't get bombarded every day.'

In creating his profile, Brett was very aware he was creating his own brand that would have to stand out from all the others on the site. 'I had the wrong idea where I could project a different new version of me—polishing off the rough edges—leaving out things that could put me at a disadvantage to my target market. It inferred I was British rather than Australian because I didn't want people to think of a stereotype when they clicked on,' he said. Other users don't necessarily use truth in advertising either. 'It's very efficient at putting you in touch with people and it's very inefficient in the quality that it provides. You can end up in an awkward situation when you actually go to meet someone and they turn out to be something that they are not. Photos are really important.'

As in life, there are winners and losers in this system: 'It's a bit like a CV. If you can't do a CV properly and market yourself—who's going to know you? Why would you get the job? There are a million people to choose from—why would you choose someone who writes a boring one-line "I'm just a geeky, honest, average guy seeking same ..." Fuck off. There's more out there—why would I choose you?

'Online I see myself as window shopping. I go, "that looks nice, he looks interesting". I wonder if I can afford to waste four hours of my time with him or I can't be bothered. It's a bad thing but it's an inevitable thing. The problem is not the concept or the technology. We lead these extremely busy lives. I often feel like I don't have the time to just hang out at the bookstore and hope some cute guy comes in. If my choice is I either find them online or I die lonely—well, I'm not going to die lonely because I don't have two hours a day to spend in a bookshop.'

Brett's met a mixture of boyfriends and casual sexual partners through Gaydar. 'I first used it when I was travelling in Croatia and I felt lonely', he says. 'I met a really nice man, but it didn't work out long term.' Following that initial encounter, internet dating for Brett became like a 'bingeing process'.

The breakfast crowd in Prêt thins out. We order a second latte that tastes of salt. Brett says, 'You log on and you can tell if you've got new messages and you can check them—you can check to see who has looked at your profile in the last twenty-four hours and see their photo and check whether you want to follow those people up. You can leave them a message marker saying, "you're nice" or "you're hot". You don't want to look too keen but you want to make sure you have an interest without going into too much detail. The point is to try and suck people into your profile in a whole variety of ways—it's all about how to get people in. You can't do that in a bar because there are too many social barriers or time issues or you can't buy twenty drinks for twenty people. What it's really about is convenience.'

It's also a great way for young gay men, particularly from country areas, to make contact with other gays. 'When I was growing up I didn't meet a gay person until I was eighteen or nineteen. I only saw any watching the Mardi Gras on television and that guy from *Are You Being Served?*, and this was in a town of 50 000 people. This was in the 1990s.'

How quickly things change. A man who has been eavesdropping catches my eye then quickly looks away. I am late for work. Brett is telling me about his new boyfriend—someone he met through friends. 'I have a good feeling about this one', he says, almost blushing. I say goodbye, but he gives me parting advice, 'You do know that internet dating is so five years ago, don't you?'

Shane, twenty-nine, is about to move in with Diane, thirty-two, and is preparing for her arrival by holding a garage sale. Out go the framed posters of Mohammed Ali in the lounge room; ditto the exercise bike in front of the television that never gets used. Shane's happy to be selling his old stuff off and buying new things. It's more than just updating his furniture; the garage sale symbolises something—he's in a relationship and it's going really well. He boils the kettle and brews coffee in a plunger. We sit on the leather lounge (not for sale) and he tells me why he met Diane the way he did.

'I thought internet dating was for losers, so I was trying to meet women the normal way—out at the pub or at a bar', he says. 'But I got to twenty-six or twenty-seven and it suddenly seemed like a really weird, juvenile way to start a relationship.' Shane would often spend a lot of money buying women drinks, which in turn would lead to both of them 'trying to get close to each other when we were totally inebriated', which then led to bad sex, or confusing sex, or no sex at all.

'I had a really bad year when I was twenty-seven', says Shane. 'I was picking up women who I barely knew and the next day it would be awkward because I'd realise we had nothing in common.' The women he felt closest to—his female friends—seemed to be off limits. 'After a certain point in the friendship, you can't make a move because everything would be ruined. But these friends were the women I wanted to spend time with. Eventually I would spend most of my time socially just with these friends, but it also meant I was stuck in this sort of adolescent pattern of hanging out with my friends and not really moving anywhere with anyone.'

But the alternative—'meaningless sex' with women he didn't really know and sometimes didn't like—was unappealing. He felt stuck between the two. Some of his friends weren't faring much better. Their relationships lasted longer, but there was a churn pattern to them as well, says Shane. 'Serial monogamy. You know, relationship lasts for two or three years tops, then breaks down, then another two or three years and another one. How many couples do I know like that? Loads.'

On the couch where Shane and I now sat, he used to recline after work, on colder nights wrapped in a blanket, dozing in front of the television. 'I'd see those ads for dating sites or those chat lines, not the sex ones, the normal ones, on late at night. I always thought they were not for me, but life was taking me in this direction with women that I didn't like. I saw no future in what I had been doing, so I thought I'd join up.'

He doesn't think too much about how he met Diane. He is happy and that's all that matters. 'My parents got introduced by their families and got married', he says. 'That doesn't happen anymore. There's no shame in saying you need a bit of help finding someone.'

I nod and look around at his things packed in boxes to make room for her things and agree with him that change—however scary—can be good.

London in July. It's a month of long sunsets and shirts sticking to your back and the crush in the pub on a Friday night, especially here, near Liverpool Street, where the bankers are enjoying the tail-end of the boom we thought would never end. The sun, still bright at 8 o'clock, gives everything in this city a rare clarity, showing up the stains on the carpets. The talk turns to love. One friend is defending internet dating. His mum, a widow in her early sixties, has met a nice man through the internet and they are now going out. 'What's she going to do?' he asks reasonably. 'Go and hang out by herself in a bar?'

Another round of drinks, the sun dipping and the men, still young, earning big money, are saying love is hard to find in this city and even harder in a bar. 'So many girls when they pick up guys in a bar can only pick up a guy they won't know and will never see again', says one young lawyer. 'They feel too vulnerable sleeping with someone they know. Sleeping with friends is too personal.'

I agree—it is, I say. And wonder how it came to that. 'That's why internet dating is good, because they are not people you know so you feel less vulnerable', he says with finality, settling our arguments about the pros and cons of the system.

But his words stay with me long after the night ends. Is that what we want? To be invulnerable?

Carla is still not comfortable with internet dating and wondering if it's for her. A good friend told her it would be a balm after her break-up, that meeting heaps of men would give her confidence. Instead she says the opposite is happening and the more she continues with internet dating the worse she feels.

She believes a reason she feels bad is because of the strong marketing aspects of internet dating. From the moment she put her profile online (a carefully selected photo, showing her right side, her good side—a photo where she looks young) to responding to emails, to choosing the venue, to that first heat-seeking glance—she feels like she is marketing herself. The website is like a supermarket. She is a product displayed on a shelf. The man is the consumer, a shopper who at each point of the transaction—from logging on, to meeting face-to-face their selected females—makes a consumer decision. This decision might take the form of—is this person good-looking enough, do they share my interests, is there chemistry?

Carla also feels like a consumer. Her eye skims over the profiles of men that are bald or have eyes that are too beady or too close together and sometimes she stops and thinks, what if they are really nice men? What if one of them is The One? But their profiles are like a mushy avocado or a bruised apple—damaged goods among shiny, bright things and not to be selected. This is the way of the system with its in-built churn, says Carla. You select a man and then you go on dates and you keep doing that with different men until the right one is found.

This constant marketing of herself has caused wear and tear on her psyche. She sees a therapist once a week and they talk about it. Carla feels she's not as confident as she once was and she looks to the outside world for validation. On dates she always feels like she has to be 'on'—firing, impressive, yet strangely disassociated, at one remove from herself. Why? If she was true to herself and they didn't like her—didn't email her again or send her an SMS or call—what would that say about who she *really* is? The therapist reckons she should cap the amount of internet dating she does to minimise the damage.

Since being single, Carla has invested a lot in herself. Her money goes on expensive, well-cut clothes that flatter her body. Her hair is always groomed—blow dried once a week at the hairdresser and colour applied every six weeks. She goes to the gym four nights a week and does yoga on weekends. She tries to read a new novel every month (borrowing heavily from the Booker Prize shortlist) and is learning Spanish at the CAE. It is exhausting, she says. Carla finds marketing yourself like a product has flow-on effects—not only is it ruinously expensive but you are always comparing yourself to other products (that is, other people) and you are always looking for ways to stand out from your competitors. Those that may not harbour narcissistic tendencies can become narcissistic in this world. They are individuals in competition with each and the game is to mould, sculpt, chisel and shape their raw materials into the best possible shape. Jennifer Aniston could be a role model—sweet girl, but no supermodel. Work hard enough at the gym and get some honeyed highlights and you too could marry Brad Pitt (for a short while anyway). This creates a churn or a whirlpool effect; if everyone is looking the best they can, except for you, then you get left behind. So you join the crowd, and with more people joining, the pull increases.

Carla works on her inner life as well: 'you can't have someone love you if you don't love yourself', she tells me. The therapist is part of that, so is the yoga and the highbrow reading list. Her guilty pleasure is splashing out on clairvoyants who give her some direction in this inexact science of internet dating, trying to conjure a husband out of all this technology. 'When will I meet him?' she asks them. 'What do you mean when I'm ready? I'm ready now.'

The inner Sydney suburb where she lives is filled with many people like her—single and professional. Rather than connected by any nationality, kin or religion, what they all have in common is that they are working on Project Self. There's the guy up the road who she sees jogging each morning, a woman in her building who is in her yoga class (they smile and murmur hello to each other in the class and at the doors of her building but nothing more), and her quasi-friendship with her colourist who she sometimes thinks knows her true self— vulnerabilities, grey hairs and all—better than any friend she's had.

In Project Self everyone is looking to meet their other half who will complete them. They crave to be de-atomised but do not realise this whole process will only further split the cells. Like Carla, they too were raised in a meritocracy where it was a given that if they worked hard enough and wanted it badly enough, they would achieve it. Is it little wonder then, that during the Long Boom, internet dating became the harbinger—the mating ritual for the material age? Internet dating combines commerce (someone, somewhere is making a profit from you, someone, somewhere is advertising to you), a free market philosophy of limitless choice and a branded experience. If you are the best product you can be, if you create the hottest brand—then you win. The endgame is to keep up with the churn and to create desire in as many other consumers that traffic through the site. And the endgame to this endgame is to find love and happiness.

For Carla, a combination of Project Self and a constant round of internet dating (hopes up for a minute then cruelly dashed by the way he didn't know how to pronounce 'pinot grigio') takes up much of her time and energy. She asks me, 'What more can I do? What more do I need to do?' Improving, marketing and promoting herself are exhausting. It tears at something fibrous in her soul and she wonders whether when she meets this future husband, if she'll have anything raw and unimproved left to give him.

But she has seen the confident hands and lithe bodies of the younger women and she has been within grasping distance of the man who could make her happy (lots of nice men who just need a bit of improving here and there) and anyway she is in 'the system' now, part of its churn and committed at heart to its cruelties and chances. She tells me many people register on several sites and alter their profiles to highlight various aspects of their personality, to stimulate interest and receive the largest possible number and range of responses. So, for example, Belinda on oneandonly.com might like sport, the beach, enjoy healthy food and barbecues at home but if you orbit around the dark side of the moon, you'll see another side of Belinda featured on Match.com. This Belinda likes nightclubbing, saunas and après ski. There is the enticing promise of bisexuality in her blurb with 'likes men who like adventurous women'. But who is she really? All of these? None of these? One of these? Maybe she is simply constructing a brand that will appeal to a certain type of consumer in two different markets.

Gary on Match.com emphasises his masculinity. He likes 'Formula One racing, the football and mountain-bike riding with friends'. 'I'm not going to lie', he writes, 'and say I like walking on the beach at sunset holding hands'. But on Plentyoffish.com he is more feminised, 'DVDs at home and cooking a special meal is my idea of a perfect night with you'.

The men Carla dates encourage her to register with more than one site. It's a numbers game, they say. It is as if Gary, Belinda, Brett and Carla are all mimicking the market itself, aiming for the widest possible reach. They imitate products looking for total penetration as that way they will have a higher take-up rate among consumers of these sites.

As with anything in this restless life, internet dating (and speed dating) works on the basis of choice and options. 'When you go on a date you may be the fourth girl from the website the guy has seen this week. And he has another three dates lined up for next week', says Carla. 'Everyone starts dating heaps of people at once then whittles it down from there.' Rejection comes easily and frequently in this world—after all, if you have a lot of options, it's easier to reject potential suitors.

With 'choice' being the paramount concern, the accepted parameters of traditional courtship are subverted; that is, when you go out with a person, you just go out with them, they are just 'heaps of people' that you then eliminate or who fall away over time. It is a convention that creepily replicates the most base reality TV shows: *The Bachelor, Joe Millionaire, The Farmer Wants a Wife*. The man starts out the program with a group of women who compete for his affections (and sometimes the chance to win a cash prize) by going on a series of dates. At the end of the show the man hands roses to the girls who he likes, while those without a rose are eliminated. And on it goes for twelve weeks, until one girl—no doubt exhausted by performing each week—is the only one left holding a rose.

Markus Frind, CEO of giant dating site Plentyoffish.com, estimates that 15 per cent of people in the USA who are active on his site are also members of other dating sites.[25] Jess McCann, an author based in the USA, has used three sites at the same time and said she was 'cutting and pasting generic responses into emails for a while'. She had two folders: one for men she wanted to meet and the other for ones who gave her 'a so-so feeling'. If one top prospect disappeared she'd bump up one from the other folder.[26] Kathleen Hanover, a business owner from Ohio, has profiles on at least five online dating services.[27] Hanover says she is time poor so she directs some potential suitors to her personal website and asks them to give her five dates' worth of details about who they are and what they want in a relationship. 'I honestly don't have time or the patience for long, drawn-out, get-to-know-you chit chat and casual dating', she writes on her homepage.[28]

In this era of choice, choice, choice and try before you buy, one wonders if this shift in the way that we now *start* relationships will creep into how we *conduct* them. Maybe once we have selected a partner like we select a pair of shoes, they become easier to discard if we discover down the track they no longer suit us. After all, there are loads of other shoes out there just waiting to be worn by you. It doesn't seem very different when it comes to potential partners. When a system validates dating 'heaps of people' at the same time— and that system becomes dominant—how we think about fidelity and how we treat others will shift towards the values of that domi-nant system. But my concerns about dating many people at once isn't concentrated on fidelity but how people in the system are commodi-fied—how much like a shopping expedition the whole experience of love and romance becomes.

Summer sun streams though the window. Carla finishes her tea and picks up her bag. She is growing weary of the hunt but has gone this far and cannot turn back. 'Anyway, it's the only way now', she says. I wish Carla luck as she joins the teeming crowds.

Marcus P, twenty-eight, and I caught a ferry from Circular Quay to Manly. The sky was dark and heaving with rain, the swell beneath the boat was building. Marcus also looked a tad turbulent. As the ferry pulled out and sailed towards the heads, he pointed at West Circular Quay. 'We went there', he said, naming a famous restaurant that I could never afford.

'How was it?' I asked.

'Terrible', he replied.

Marcus had been using the internet for four months to find a girl-friend. He was new to Sydney, new to being single and was getting tired of going to bars to meet women.

'I'm borderline alcoholic', he said. 'And the women are too!'

Marcus froze when it came to writing a profile. He just didn't know what to say about himself. Nor did he include a photo ('I'm shy') and his blurb—his brand essentially—was a bit bland. 'I said I wanted a girlfriend who I could go camping with, but would also like doing things I do—hanging out with friends, the football, the movies.'

When he found a woman he liked online or one found him, they would message each other for a bit then if that worked out, they would go on a lunch date. Marcus found the encounters nerve-wracking, not romantic and definitely not sexy. 'They don't want to waste time, so the whole thing feels like a job interview, but instead they are interviewing you to be their boyfriend. If there was something not right with you or something they didn't like, they would wrap it up really quickly. They were brisk, they'd say they'd call but you knew and they knew that they wouldn't.'

Marcus was aware of the rules of the system and its churn and knew that being commodified was part of it. But even then this knowledge was not enough to steel him for the actuality of it—for dessert not to be ordered and her, at a clip, walking out the door, not turning back, phone out already talking to her friends, dissecting him while he was still looking at her retreating. He'd imagine her saying to them, 'No, awful, truly … he's just not right. He's not The One.' Marcus senses the women he is meeting will not give him a chance unless he is 'the total package'.

Writing in the *Times* in 2008, Sathnam Sanghera says:

> It's astonishing how big internet dating has become. According to one survey, half the country's single population have dated online. And while a few years ago these people would have no more broadcast this than discussed their haemorrhoids, the stigma has gone … But online dating seems too mechanical and appears to require engagement with people determined to misinform, with 5-year-old photos, lies about their age and euphemisms such as 'drinks socially' (i.e. alcoholic), 'voluptuous' (i.e. recently had stomach stapled) and 'adventurous' (pervert).

Then there's the picnic syndrome. You know how it goes: you go out to find somewhere nice to dine al fresco and find it, but can't help walking on, looking a bit farther, just in case there's an even nicer spot around the corner and never really give it a proper shot. It's horrible.[29]

Sathnam tells me that he looked for a while on a Punjabi internet dating site, which commodified romance even further as it specified caste or gradations of skin colour. Sathnam, Marcus P and I are old school romantics in the material age of thousand dollar handbags, partners as accessories and technology supplying limitless choice. It can lead to a feeling of being out of step with the rest of your generation and feeling left behind. The restless, consumer-orientated approach to love is direct and doesn't mess around. When you go online there is no mistaking your intent. There are no glances loaded with meaning because you are looking at a computer screen. You are conducting a disembodied courtship. But disembodied is preferable to putting your physical self on the front line. Of course it is. Rejection in an age of anxiety, where we strive for a sense of control, can make our sense of control seem like an illusion, a total lie.

And so we hide behind computer screens and around text messages and the haiku-like sparseness of Twitter or Facebook status updates, and in hiding we avoid being hurt, at least for a little while. Internet dating provides the illusion of control—the mantra is choice, choice, choice—but in the milky light still seeping through the windows of The Penthouse nightclub, as I waited for a boy with a scorecard to slide into the seat next to me, I felt there was too much control. Which I guess is the point of speed dating. But is it the point of love? Wasn't that what love's about? That control is relinquished?

In some classic love stories, the tension between the protagonists involves mutual vulnerability. DH Lawrence in *Lady Chatterley's Lover* called it being 'broken open again'. Can disembodied courtship delay or prevent a feeling of vulnerability, of being 'broken open again'?

Dr Chris Chesher, a senior lecturer in media and communications at the University of Sydney, spoke to me for a *Sydney Morning Herald* article about how technology has changed courtship. 'In previous generations, you knew that you might be introduced to your future partner by your parents. But that doesn't happen any more,' he said. Technology has replaced the old way. But, I argued, at the heart of every great love story, at the core of every courtship, there lies a risk. It's the lurching heart-in-mouth type of risk, where one person declares his or her feelings to another, uncertain if love will be rejected or reciprocated.

In the churn, technology allows us to bypass some of those risks. When we send an SMS or email to the object of our affection, we can avoid eye contact. They, in turn, can avoid seeing us blush. Even courtship via telephone is fraught—a quiver in the voice or a slight stammer could give the game away, leaving the caller vulnerable and exposed. The more disembodied the technology allows us to become, the less we risk.

'Relationships are one area where people don't feel in control—so technology will give people some control in an area where there is a lot of chaos', Chesher says. 'There is a sense that if you can exert dominance on technology, you can assert dominance on relationships. You don't have to worry about face-to-face contact, plus mobiles and internet are associated with individuals rather than a householder, so you are less likely to be in contact with someone you don't want to speak to.'

In an article published in *Eureka Street*, the Melbourne-based ethicist Rufus Black raised concerns about 'the power and problems of communication in an electronic age'. 'When people don't meet physically there is an erosion of trust', he wrote.[30] When relationships are nurtured by the internet or SMS—and not by that dowager aunt or matchmaking family member—Black says there are consequences.

> What is missing when the body is absent is vulnerability. This is not to deny the psychological vulnerability that can be present in online encounters. Nonetheless, in these encounters of the mind, our physical self is never 'on the line'. Vulnerability and trust are inextricably linked, which means that a world with declining physical vulnerability is also one in which the landscape of trust is changing.[31]

Black argues that when people communicate face to face, the physical contact and placing that person in a context, such as their office or their home, lead to a greater empathy.

Chesher believes online and face-to-face contact are not separate and competing. 'They can work together, complement each other.' He cites instances of couples meeting in cyberspace, establishing a rapport, then meeting in the flesh to continue their relationship. 'Technology is strengthening social connections rather than replacing it', Chesher says. 'Our parents talk about accidental meetings that brought them together. These accidental meetings are still occurring, but in cyberspace.'

Of all the stories that we tell each other about our lives, stories about love are the most captivating. Stories about *how* we found love are more captivating still; the chance encounter, *eros*—the spark that 'ignites and connects', the way heat rises to the skin in a give-away blush. But at the core of these tales is the story we tell about the universe: how we can't control it, how it is chaotic and can be difficult but, almost as compensation, throws us occasional sweet delights. The chance meeting, the connection made and the way everything feels random and plotted all at once. Great love stories always seem to have an element of serendipity about them. The boy sits next to a girl on a plane. They start talking. By the time they touch down they've swapped emails. Co-workers are thrown together on a project. There is a growing connection. They go out for a drink and everything changes. A girl goes to a Sydney bar and meets a prince. They fall in love.

We don't trust in serendipity anymore. It could take too long to happen. And what if we are too busy to go to bars? Or we like to sleep on planes? Or we work best alone? Love makes us vulnerable. So does relying on circumstance.

Taking a 'consumer-orientated' approach to love eliminates some of the random variables of the universe. It can stop us from ending up with the stoop shouldered, cross-eyed Raelian we met on the bus, who also happens to make us laugh and is very kind. It can direct us to someone who 'looks good on paper'. If we turn the pursuit of love into a consumer activity, we can control it. We can stipulate hair colour and height and voice a preference for smoker or non-smoker, Christian or Muslim, conservative or liberal. We can nominate a star sign and a football team. We can choose.

Popular site eHarmony asks the user up to several hundred questions to create a match. Joseph Essas, vice-president of technology, says the company stores four terabytes of data on some twenty million registered users, each of whom has filled out a 400-question psychological profile.[32] The company uses 'proprietary algorithms to score that data against "29 dimensions of compatibility" such as values, personality styles, attitudes and interests—and match up customers with the best possible prospects for a long term relationship'.[33] The process requires just under one billion calculations that are processed in a giant batch operation each day.[34]

Mmmm, how romantic.

Perfect.Match.com founder and CEO Duane Dahl also takes the serendipity out of the mating game. He says, 'We wanted to take the basic concept of the Myers-Briggs indicator and apply that to relationships'. Meanwhile True.com offers 'scientific compatibility' based on how users answer 200 questions.[35]

Recently I returned to one of my favourite authors, EM Forster (his humanist mantra in *Howards End* 'only connect' looped through my inner ear as I wrote this book). In his most personal book, *Maurice*, he describes an early sexual encounter between upper-class Maurice and the gamekeeper Alec Scudder. I can't help but think if the book was written now, the unlikely pair would not have got together. Imagine if Maurice had searched on Gaydar. He would not have selected the man who climbed up a ladder into his room when he, half asleep and in some sort of turmoil, called him in.

What if Maurice had gone online and entered key words like yoga or intellectual or university educated?

It would not have been.

And what of those funny couples that one sometimes comes across in real life: she in her office suit and he in his gardening greens. His slow drawl, rollie cigarettes and deliberate ways—how his friends describe him as 'laidback' and 'easy-going' and she with her BlackBerry and her high blood pressure, her idea of relaxing being to iron and fold her underwear. But they work somehow. They're happy.

In cyberspace, with the drop-down boxes and automated match-ings they would have been ships in the night.

Trawling the blogs on the *Sydney Morning Herald* online, I find this comment from a reader, 'The best way to flirt or grab a girls attention (in Sydney of course) is to flash your overweight wallet and your exotic toys. Those of you that have nothing but dust and moths coming out of your wallets do not stand a chance. Like the infamous words of Al Pacino in *Scarface*, "first you get the money then you get the power then you get the women", that is it, all in a nutshell and so so true.'[36]

Is it the case that not just *how* we look for what we want is changing but *what* we want is changing too? Could it be that as the search has more of a consumer spin on it, so do the results?

We become more picky, more self-focused because the search engines give us a sense of limitless *choice*. The aspirational status symbol of our material age is finding The One and all that entails, including money (men) and beauty (women). But more than that, searching for The One has become some quasi-mystical quest. We have high expectations: we want the person that understands our secret selves, they are our platonic ideal and are at the core of our deepest aspirations.

When I was at university a tacky phrase crept into the vernacular of my friends and me. After a big night, when someone scored we would ask if it was a 'prestige score'. This was our shorthand for: does this person go to a good university? Are they doing the right course? Are they cool? We don't use that term anymore. It's embarrassing— but not necessarily redundant. Add the notion of 'prestige score' with a system that provides seemingly limitless choice of partners, and a society where who is on your arm is as much an accessory as what is on your feet and you'll find a lot of people unfulfilled with love in a consumer society.

The search for The One, or just someone better, is 'a sign of our aspirational culture',[37] Stephanie Donald, professor of communication and culture at the University of Technology Sydney, tells me. It is also a characteristic of the young meritocratic elite that is being pumped out by the middle classes and nurtured by high employment and prosperity. 'If you have very high expectations of yourself, you are pretty likely to have high expectations of other people and relationships. But high expectations can be very damaging,' she says. 'If you are trying to work hard, look good and save enough money for your house, it takes a lot of energy. You almost need to go home and be a failure with someone.' According to Donald, expectations are likely to be higher in 'big international cities like London, Sydney, New York, Hong Kong and Shanghai'. Why? Because 'people there are career-focused and have high aspirations. It's about wanting to get the best for yourself.'

Now we aim high, and get a computer to do all the work for us. If our flesh-and-blood match doesn't fulfil our expectations, there is a sense that it doesn't matter because of the untapped potential in the thousands, possibly even millions of better matches out there.

And so restlessness drives us ever onwards. We seem unable to stop.

So how did we get here?

In the early 2000s internet dating was still in its infancy. People knew people who knew people who did it. And if you did—you certainly didn't crow about it. But suddenly a range of factors converged to not only bring it into the mainstream but to make it *the* mainstream. Factors included a generation of tech-savvy young people reaching mating age who did not remember life without the internet.

During the boom years, the consumer, transactional character of internet dating was part of its appeal for many users. It seemed somehow of *its time* and slotted in with other trends that were emblematic of the age: the 'what's in for me?' throw-away, contract jobs, super churches that preach an easily digestible style of spirituality called the prosperity doctrine, and the proliferation of internet porn.

Longer working hours and less time to socialise are also cited as reasons for the high take-up rate of dating sites. Working hours increased in the early years of this century, which coincided with the rollout of mass home internet usage in Australia and faster broadband speed—the ingredients for the perfect cultural storm.

In 2002, in the early days of this internet dating boom, an early adopter, 23-year-old Rozelle woman Sally Smith was interviewed by the *Sydney Morning Herald* about internet dating. Deciding which messages to respond to was like browsing in the aisles of a supermarket, she said. 'Everyone's got certain tastes and you can pick and choose from the talent on offer.' Within two months she had received 300 replies. According to the article, 'The increase is being driven by the first generation of people to go through adolescence with the internet and email. They use computers at work and to shop and are comfortable and casual about starting relationships online.'[38]

By mid decade it was no longer just the young adopting the trend. In an article in London's *Telegraph* in April 2006, it was the parents of Generation Y with their ruined relationships and their fondness for reinvention who were flocking to the internet. They too had to follow the rules of the market, the modus operandi of this system with its restless tempo. 'No lengthy email correspondences, it just wastes time', was the verdict of the *Telegraph,* a paper beloved by England's conservative sixty-something set. 'Set up a handful of dates so you can see who's out there. Never agree to dinner or even a drink on your first date. Make a date for coffee instead, knowing you can be out of there in 20 minutes. And if you do like them but they don't ask you out again, just move on.'[39]

Move on, move on, move on—it's the whisper of restlessness in our ear.

'It is a clear sighted yet brutal vision of dating', wrote Sally Brampton about internet dating. 'Some see it as a great big, ageless All Bar One in cyberspace filled with dazzling possibility. For others it is the microcosm of the worst aspects of human behaviour, encouraging an intimacy that leaves people feeling lonelier than ever.'[40] Jane, a 32-year-old divorced mother, said of internet dating, 'At work we call it "seeing what's in the shopping basket". It's so indicative of modern society that you can go shopping for a boyfriend at work.'[41] As for

Brampton, she tried online dating for two weeks but 'hated it so much I never got to the actual flesh and blood dating stage. It seemed to me too sterile, too fast, too lacking on the potential pleasure of love and serendipity. I'd rather stand at a bus stop in the rain.'[42]

Before internet dating went gangbusters there was a gap in the market. Not only was romance largely uncommodified, but it was also undefined. Left cold by the pernicious 1960s mentality of casual sex—yet growing up in a world without ritualised courtship—young people were stumbling along in a world without a narrative, set rules and little clear idea of how to negotiate love and sex. Many still felt the heat in the embers of their parents' divorces, others were scared off sex by AIDS, while the PC push of the early 1990s meant that many had grown up being hyper-aware of sexual harassment. Into the mix, the gender divide seemed to be in a perpetual state of corrosion as men and women enacted all the many and varied ways of being together: roommates, best friends, fuck buddies, business partners, co-parents, soul mates, joint owners of holiday houses. It was the age of *Seinfeld*, four approaching-middle-age friends, just hanging out and having rubbish relationships.

It was the age of dancing on your own. The widespread recreational use of hug drug ecstasy among young people further added to the fluidity, the sense of ambiguity, the vibe that anything could happen and any meaning could be applied in the morning after. There seemed to be no rules. Formalised courtship mechanisms such as personal columns were for freaks and weirdos and 'dating' was Brady Bunch vernacular that had little relevance to our own lives. Love had yet to be colonised by the market and all borders were open. But this fluidity, while embraced by some, unsettled others.

In the summer of 2003 at a dingy café in Darlinghurst, Sydney, I interviewed a young writer called Anna Warwick who had compiled a selection of interviews on love in the new millennium. Through her friends, and their friends and people she met through work and at parties she asked the same questions: how do you find love in this city? And with whom? And how the hell is it done? Several surprising themes emerged, including the anxiety that many young people felt trying to find love in an age that lacked defining rituals. She found the old-fashioned stereotypes were no longer true. Women were often assertive, as likely as men to make the first move. Most courtship occurred in the pub, when both men and women were very drunk. Sometimes men turned out to be clingy and women were the ones afraid of commitment. Technology, particularly email, text messaging and online dating, was beginning to change the way we conducted relationships. 'Girls are now more likely to approach men and ask them out, while a lot of guys can actually be quite scared of girls', Warwick said. In general, she believed gender differences were nowhere near as pronounced as they used to be. Getting on with people was a matter of similar experiences and background, rather than simply sex appeal. 'There's a high level of platonic friend-ship between the sexes, and more equality. Men showed the same emotional levels as girls. They got upset if they were stood up or treated badly—same with the women,' she said.

In the vacuum of ritual, aspirational culture was not so much seep-ing into how we found love, but beginning to reconfigure it. Remember this was deep in the heart of the Howard years—McMansions, asylum-seeker panic, turbo barbecues, home renovation shows and record credit card debt. 'What's in it for me?' was practically the nation's mantra. We also aspired to, and believed we deserved, perfect relationships. How to find them? Community life wasn't as strong as it used to be—with longer working hours (to pay for all this stuff) and higher expectations, meeting people was becoming a challenge.

In the ritual vacuum, marriage rates took a dive. Figures from the Australian Bureau of Statistics showed that in 2001 marriage rates were at their lowest levels in 100 years.[43] In that year, 103 000 couples married in Australia while 55 300 divorced. Couples who did marry were five years older on average—twenty-seven for the bride, twenty-nine for the groom—than those who had married in 1981. Professor Johanna Wyn, the director of the Australian Youth Research Centre at Melbourne University, tracked 2000 people who left school in 1991 for a longitudinal study on patterns of living. When I spoke to her in 2004, they were aged thirty and had lived through the ritual vacuum. As a result their lives were very different from their parents' lives and will probably also stand in contrast to young people who have only known prosperous times and whose enthusiastic adoption of internet dating has created new rituals.

Wyn's study showed that of the 2000 people she surveyed, 36 per cent were married. Only 13 per cent had children. When they got to thirty, both men and women in her study were saying, 'I would have thought I would have had a stable partner by now but it's not happening'. In her last survey in 2002, 'they were definitely disappointed and a little puzzled [their love lives] hadn't worked out yet'.[44] According to Wyn, we shouldn't have assumed this generation was afraid of commitment because it was not marrying in great numbers. 'There's a lot of instability. It's hard to make a commitment if you can't get a house or somewhere stable to live because of high housing costs. It's deeply insulting for this group when people say they have delayed adolescence. Their lives are complex and with them we have seen a shift in the way that people live their lives. They place an enormous value on learning, experiences such as travel, the environment and their friendships.'[45]

The past and the way things were done there is gone, over.

Says Wyn, 'I sometimes think that older people seem to imagine they are going to grow up and become like we were. Those times are gone. That kind of adulthood will never exist again. This generation is forming their adulthood in the only way that they can. It's not even a matter of choice.'[46]

In the narrative of how my parents met and their friends met their partners, technology is absent—real-life community was in its place. Imagine the late 1960s in country Victoria. Communities were small, you joined clubs (tennis and netball for girls, football for men) or you were introduced by your parents or through the church or you went to the same school. Maybe your grandparents had adjoining farms and there were bits of your history knitted together. Everyone's history seemed to knit together then.

Speaking to my friend's parents about how they met, geography and community played a large part: 'I had known him all my life, but he was a bit older. His family had the farm up the road. One day he was driving past on his motorbike and asked if I wanted a lift.' Or, 'I knew his sister, she went to my school. He went to the boys' school. At the dance we started to talk. He was shy.'

My parents met when they were in their early twenties at a debating club. They got married straight after teacher's college. Then they had me (and three more like me). Most of those country town, western Victorian marriages are still going, thirty years on. They had kids and the kids became friends with each other. Some of my classmates married people from the same school, and stayed—the rhythm of their lives not starkly different from that of their parents. But for those of us that stepped outside the corporeal, organic, live community and willed on themselves this huge world of choice, choice, choice, things have played out very differently indeed.

Wyn's 'young people' are an atomised generation, rootless in a deracinated age. We often live alone, shifting between jobs, cities and countries, trying to build communities in a virtual world, but longing—maybe before dropping off to sleep at night—for some stronger connection.

At Sydney Sunday brunches (sipping strong sweet lattes, hung-over, listlessly reading our star signs to each other), reflecting on the messy nights that went before, some friends wished, with partial seriousness, for arranged marriages. Trying to create your own court-ship rituals in a vacuum leads to signals being misread, shots being fired without warning, unwanted advances, hurt and confusion. Add alcohol to the mix and it seemed like the gap between what we really wanted and what we were ending up getting was grow-ing wider and wider. This was around 2002, 2003, 2004 and in the newspapers, it seemed almost daily were stories of the plummeting fertility rate, marriages breaking up, tales of connections being missed, or things unravelling—further splits to the atom. If some-thing could fill the vacuum—provide some structure and a way that things are done, a clear outline of steps that should be taken, a path straight out of the messiness and confusion of our hearts to delineable actions and a place where we do not have to think for ourselves—what a success that would be. And so the market, flanked by technology, stepped into the breach with the proliferation of inter-net dating websites.

Back in 2003, in the too-bright Darlinghurst sun, as we each ordered a second coffee, Warwick sensed the gathering storm. 'Internet dating is becoming more and more easy and less of a stigma. But if you think that everyone you meet is a potential mate then the result is a lot of anxiety.'

If Carla were ten years younger, she might be Rachel. She told the world she met her boyfriend Paul online. It's part of *their story*, how she registered on two sites and had three really bad dates—really bad—particularly the man at the cinema with the clammy hand.

She was in two minds whether she would attend a third date at the marina. She did and met Paul. It wasn't love at first sight but 'he wasn't ugly and he had a good job and after a while I thought he was pretty funny'. They saw each other and kept seeing each other until one day they moved in together—at which point they saw each other all the time. Now they are married. It's only how they met that varies from traditional courtships, says Rachel. They are like any other couple, with their fights and passions and promises. So why would a twenty-five year old go straight to the internet—as a matter of course—if he or she wanted a partner?

'It's what everyone does', shrugs Rachel. And that is partly what's made the internet so popular for dating—if everyone's doing it, then you may as well do it too, lest you miss out. Rachel is also a pragmatist. The child of Vietnamese immigrants she had inherited their hierarchy of needs: a nice home, a good job and a lovely husband. After finishing uni she looked for the Big Three in the same way: through the internet.

'The best thing about the internet is browsing', she says. 'As long as you have an internet connection or wireless you can organise your life. The technology is there, so why not use it? Why make it hard for yourself?'

Of her disappointments using the internet, it is more likely in the job sector. 'Recruiters lie the most', she says. As for men, they lie too. But a date is a commitment of maybe an afternoon, sitting through a dull film with a dull man. If it doesn't work out you don't contact him again. Jobs are more problematic, more difficult to extract yourself from. She shrugs and says, 'Why don't you try it?' And I can't really give her a valid reason as to why not.

It's time to look online. It's London's hottest July day in 100 years and in the internet café (a tiny fan down the back, a molten keyboard).

I'm not sure if it's the weather or the browsing that's causing me to sweat a bit more and my chest to become a bit tighter. There is something quite bald, exciting, confrontational even, yet also simultaneously depressing, seeing picture after picture and page and page of all these men. They are all ages—some with their shirts off, others shy, with no picture at all. 'Picture available on request'—the square with a blank-man outline says. On these blank faces all manner of desire can be projected; he seems sensitive and warm— imagine if in real life he turns out to look like Johnny Depp! This could be where the real serendipity—the real chances, risk-taking and pay offs—reside. But one friend is far more dismissive. 'They don't put their picture on because they're too ugly', he says. As for the women, there is an apologetic tone to a lot of their blurbs—'I'm giving it a go' a lot of them say. 'I just want a nice guy, for friendship, for relationship, whatever.' It is as if the internet with its capacity for reach, for limitless exposure, can be intimidating so it's best to make yourself small and hope against hope that your modesty and your smallness is what captures a man's eye. The women with bolder profiles, bigger claims, greater ambitions and clearer photos are the products that stand out on the shelves. 'They get the most traffic, those girls', says my friend. 'It's all in how you market yourself.'

On these sites the forest has been napalmed. These men want to meet women and the women want to meet men (or on gay sites it's men wanting men and women wanting women and sometimes people wanting both—everything, the whole shelf). What they want is listed plainly in text below the pictures. The games, the confusion, the unrealistic expectations, all this may come later, but for now, at this stage of the courtship, there is no ambiguity and no subtlety.

Writer Maria Alvarez observed in an article for the *Telegraph* that internet dating is nothing short of a revolution in romantic love and noted the consumer element to this.

The internet has transformed the way we choose partners and perform rites of love. If the modern world was already heading for a supermarket ethos of choice-choice-choice in relationships, the net has accelerated it to broadband speed.

The sinister aspect of on-line choice-choice-choice and 'shopping' for love is that we reduce ourselves to objects, to consumer products, a personality-as-profile determined in sound-bites. And we begin to think too much in numbers and multiple clicks.[47]

She also observed that this u-turn into commodifying coupling has been so sudden and so profound (it is *the* way—not *a* way) that no detailed cultural analysis has appeared to decipher what it all means. There is no true body of literature reflecting our times. Our romantic narratives, Jane Austen and the Brontës, are not just an epoch of another age with only their longings and glances to guide them, but seem to be a species far removed from us.

Even the poets are despairing. Alan Jenkins, a Forward Prize–winning poet, was pessimistic: 'With online language comes online expectations, which is consumerist in the end. It's not just expression that is impoverished but human feeling itself.' He thinks fewer people will care, and sees even poetry as being unable to describe love: 'A poetry of sexual consumption maybe, but that's another thing'.[48]

It's not only the nihilist author Michel Houellebecq and the promiscuous sex and shopping girls of *Sex and the City* that reflect this disposable paper-cup style of relationship—this new, fast and almost brutal style of courtship. Maybe we have internalised consumer culture to such an extent that no analysis is necessary—this peculiar melding of romance and technology is the modus operandi of the times. And gradually there won't be any other way because that's how we'll learn to interact with each other. 'The horrific spectre is that our beings are altering under the new modes thrown up by technology', writes Alvarez gloomily.

Maybe the writers—of poems, of love songs, of books and greeting cards—know the new score but don't want to acknowledge it. To sing 'we met in a chat room. I liked your profile cos I like skateboarding too—and then we emailed for a while, then we smsed and IMed and then we met at McDonalds and girl you're so fine ...' is to savagely deny a whole range of emotions associated with blossoming love: attraction, yearning, chance and connection. And while couples who meet online tend to fall into much the same relationship patterns as those who meet in the 'real world' and will have songs and books and films that resonate with their relationship, the words of the sharp edges of beginnings—the glances and chances and the whole mating dance—do not belong in the narrative of their beginnings. Our narratives will change over time to accommodate this phenomenon. It will therefore not be uncommon to read, as I did recently, that 'Brad Thomas, from Kentucky, met his wife through Instant Messaging'.

We are already moving away from each other under the somewhat ironic guise of being connected. In the *New York Times*, 24-year-old Theodora Stites says that like many of her generation she will 'consistently trade actual human contact for the more reliable emotional high of smiles on MySpace, winks on Match.com and pokes on Facebook'.[49] She writes: 'I live for Friendster views, profile comments and the Dodgeball messages that clog my cellphone every night. I prefer, in short, a world cloaked in virtual intimacy. It may be electronic, but it is intimacy nevertheless. Besides, eye contact isn't all it's cracked up to be and facial expressions can be so hard to control.'

Each morning when she wakes up—before she brushes her teeth and has breakfast—she signs into Instant Messenger to let all her contacts know she's awake. She checks for new emails, messages, comments on her blogs or mentions she receives on her friend's blogs. Dodgeball allows her to link to her online community through her mobile phone and check which part of town her friends may be drinking or shopping in. It's like a tracking device.

For Stites, 'every profile [she places of herself on the web] is a carefully planned media campaign. I click on the Friendster "Who's Viewed Me" tab to see who has stumbled upon my profile recently, and if people I don't know have checked me out, I immediately check them back. I get an adrenaline rush when I find out that a friend of a friend I was always interested in is evidently interested in me, too. Just imagine if we could be this good in person. Online, everyone has bulletproof social armor.'[50]

Replacing the old-style communities of my childhood (where you got what you were given, including at least one cranky old neighbour, a man who stunk of bait, the supermarket gossip) are limitless online options. Writes Stites: 'I am constantly searching the Internet for new communities. Are there enough people on Plazes.com yet? Am I hip enough for Nerve? Can I be a part of Geocaching.com without having a GPS? Are the people on Fark.com my kind of people?' Real life is not as seamless and controllable as her virtual life: 'Attending these parties I found myself in awkward social situations I couldn't log out of'.

This feeling is not uncommon, with one internet dating company offering users the chance to go on dates as avatars—that is, virtual dates where you are spared the awkwardness of actually meeting. Instead a computer simulating you goes on the date. In our old communities we never got to ask if these were 'my kind of people'. There was never the chance of ducking out of an awkward encounter by sending your avatar. You took what you got and—oppressive as it was, not being able to choose—you adapted.

Technology has had a massive impact on our lives, particularly in the last fifteen years. It encourages restlessness—move on, move on, move on. It sets the speed of the churn. It works in tandem with a consumer culture that encourages choice, choice, choice. But how did we let the market in so close? And how important is this in fuelling our restlessness, moving without pause, from everything to the latest trainer to the latest model iPod, to the hippest holiday destination, to the latest hot website to the coolest new music festival?

Marketers talk about reach and penetration when it comes to brands. They ask, how far can it go? But what if we have internalised consumer culture to such an extent that the reach was not a geographical construct but something far more terrible and profound? What if the reach they are talking about went into people—to the primal matter of what it means to be human? What if the product could remove the bittersweet from life, the mistakes that we make, the chances and risks we take, the struggles and the times we fail? What if there was a product that made the difficult things easy, that promised the shortest and most painless route to fulfilling our deepest desires? That eradicated vulnerability? What if things uncolonised by marketing, things that were deeply human, like who we love, family life, spirituality, community and even our work became commodified? What sort of lives would we lead? What sort of people would we become?

In the last ten years we have seen an explosion of reach. Marketing and products have moved into new realms. Even if the goods aren't for sale, everything appears refracted through a customer service approach. Things previously outside the monetary economy have become drawn in by virtue of the language we use. When I registered for the dole after university, standing in line, trying to figure out if my life was worthwhile, I was a Centrelink client. And when I had to be wheeled into a hospital emergency room, blood flowing down my face after a mugging, I was a consumer of health services. It was as if by commercialising the relationship, it was scrubbed clean of all its dirty human muck. Customers and clients are clean, crisp words—jobless, unemployed, bashed and bloodied are not such desirable descriptors.

Commodification is a process started by the market a long time ago, with the industrial revolution. Before then many things that are now commodified used to be free, like air, water, food. Later the mind was colonised—with ideas, inventions and scientific discoveries commodified through patents, trademarks and copyright law. But it seems in the last decade the commodification of our culture has turned viral, spilling out from the borders of shop shelves, to things previously untouched by the market.

Love is found online, browsing through a selection of people who are lined up and marketed like goods in supermarkets aisles or, as one academic put it, 'somewhat like a catalogue'.[51] Or else it's nightclub hook-ups where it's not about intimacy but a quick hit of passion. And although sex has long been well and truly commodified (prostitution being one such example), the internet extends the product's reach even further. The children of the internet age have access to internet porn from childhood. Pop-up graphics are graphic. You can Google 'sex with a horse' and tens of thousands of options appear. Inescapable in cyberspace is the naked Paris Hilton talking on her mobile during sex, or the fake breasts and high arses of girls paid to look turned on in porn videos. The images soak through the consciousness of young people and things change. Adele Horin wrote in the *Sydney Morning Herald*:

> increasing numbers of men appear to be hooked on internet pornography, and the women in their lives are flailing about in unhappiness, self-doubt and self-blame. The same themes emerged repeatedly. The men spent hours online, searching for progressively harder core images … In the end they could not be bothered with real-life sex. In other cases, sex lives became porn-like, male-focused, extreme and lacking in intimacy. One interview subject reported how her boyfriend's pornography consumption affected their sex lives. The sex became impersonal and aggressive: 'It became more "porn"

style—pulling my hair, no kissing, slapping around a bit, all stuff I was initially OK with', Gracie says. 'There was no real intimacy, no thought about what I might like.'[52]

There is a new intimacy between ourselves and technology—how can we *not* walk away unaffected?

It's not just sex and love that have been absorbed into the market, their forms morphing forever from the contact. Jobs are also found online with each new advertisement promising 'hot jobs' and 'sexy positions'—but jobs too during the Long Boom became commodities lasting a couple of years until all pleasure and experience was wrung out of them. Move on, move on to the next one. Trawling search engines on job-seeking websites feels remarkably similar to the process of buying a car, finding a partner or renting a flat. The drop-down boxes: area, price. Click on options. Options pop up. Select.

And then there's religion. During the boom, the only church experiencing any real growth among young people were evangelical churches such as Hillsong.[53] Run on a successful business model that has seen the church open franchises on the Gold Coast, in Sydney's inner city and in Paris, Hillsong preaches the Prosperity Gospel, teaching their young charges how to get rich—and quick. The language of prosperity is so tightly bound up in their teachings as to be inseparable from the teachings of Jesus.

Community has also become commodified. Why live some-where for generations and accumulate the emotional capital to build community when it's accessed quite easily in chatrooms or by those with the cash to buy into gated, 'safe' communities? A sense of community can be achieved in other ways, such as by taking drugs. If you go to a dance party on Saturday night and take enough pills you will feel chemically bonded to each other. They are your community, your tribe, and that night, what once took decades to knit together, unites in an explosion of heat and white noise, love and happiness.

Should we be surprised at this process of commodification and our passivity in the face of marketers' ever-extending reach? Probably not. After all, the marketing industry has been in overdrive since the 1980s. Social researcher Hugh Mackay once said today's young were a generation marinated in marketing. The original tweens were kids targeted by advertisers who wanted to harness their pester power. The first reference to tweens that I came across was in a *Sun-Herald* article in 1988. It trilled:

> Forget about Yuppies, Dinkies, and Preppies, the new power-house in the economy are known to advertisers as the Tweens! Tweens are aged from nine to 12-the group between kids and teens. In the US, where advertisers have declared 1988 the Year of the Tween, there are 16 million Tweens whose choices can decide the fate of pop idols, TV series or the latest shade of acid washed jeans. Tweens hang out at shopping malls with their pockets full of money and their minds on the latest designer gear. 'They are an incredible force,' said an ad man. 'Who do you think put Kylie Minogue on a pedestal? Tweens.'[54]

The first tween is now hitting thirty.

It's hard to mount a challenge to marketers, and brands are a difficult enemy to fight. After all, they are everywhere and nowhere all at once. Although there seems to be no one bitching and moaning that the market has become too close to our inner lives, a decade ago, with a strong anti-globalisation movement, there was at least an indication that the brands and their relationships with us was being *monitored*. The counter-globalisation movement in the late 1990s and Naomi Klein's bestseller *No Logo* were the first signs of mass consumer protest against our society becoming over-branded and over-commodified. The movement had a lot of heat and energy with blockades, alliances between unions, green groups and human rights activists, mainstream media attention and a certain credibility that made it the cool people's protest movement of choice.

On 11 September 2000 in Melbourne, the Australian anti-globalisation movement had its bloody, violent birth. Activists linked arms along the brown banks of the Yarra, right up to the gaudy lights of Crown Casino, blocking delegates from entering the World Economic Forum conference. Twenty thousand people turned up to blockade and many of them were really, really angry. I was a young lawyer up from the country for a client conference with a barrister. The conference finished early and I rushed down to Crown Casino, as close as I could get in a cab, before walking over the bridge toward the police horses and the protesters in their human chain. I hung at the edges, watching, envious even, at the tribes in their costumes and with their placards. I admired their passion, and their anger. But from my outsider's position they also seemed too kinetic to really connect with anything, too diffuse and disorganised.

I spoke to a *Sydney Morning Herald* photographer who was at the demo with his cameras only to be confronted by a mob turned ugly. 'They said we were corporate media scum, the enemy. They tried to smash my camera.' He remembers a 'weird vibe', large pockets of hostility and a general confusion. 'There were all these different tribes there. People had their own video recorders, saying they were the independent media. They were going around filming everyone. It was like a dance party. There were ravers, fire twirlers and hippies, and then there's guys in overalls from the CFMEU and I thought, "Shit, what's going to happen now?"'

What happened was the cops came in. The cops were organised—more organised than the protesters. They had capsicum spray, dogs, riot shields and batons. During the clash the photographer was thrown to the ground by police who used swift, brutal tactics to disable him; they put their knees into his back, forcing him onto his front with his jaw pushed up, their fingers in his mouth. 'I said I was from the *Age* but they weren't distinguishing between different types of media', he said. When it came to two tribes going to war, the police were the stronger tribe on the day. 'They had all trained together. They knew each other and had a common purpose,' he said. The protesters, by comparison, were strangers to each other, still trying to find a common language and reach a shared understanding of what globalisation meant for them.

In protest movements throughout history, if you introduce batons and blood, and give people a little pain to connect them, then the momentum only becomes stronger. The resistance only gets fuelled. Why hasn't this been the case with the anti-globalisation movement? Why did it burn out so quickly? A few reasons. Activists got distracted. For a start there was the intractable war in Iraq that sucked a lot of resources and energy away from other social causes. The refugee issue dominated the Howard years, which many activists viewed with a sense of urgency. With children in detention, refugees sewing together their lips and attempting suicide, it was hard to concentrate on Nike's latest marketing campaign. And so brands went quietly about their business, moving closer to us, as the spotlight has shifted to the more menacing moving targets.

Dr James Arvanitakis met me under the looming tower building at the University of Technology Sydney (UTS), where he lectures in humanities. His long hair was pulled back in a knot and he wore a t-shirt bearing the legend 'Laneway Lovin''. In a previous life he was an economic forecaster earning a lot of money. Seeing firsthand the working conditions in the Third World shocked, then politicised him. The metals that had gone into making his beloved German sports car were killing 14-year-old mine workers in Peru. For Arvanitakis, knowledge of the global supply chain and its consequences was knowledge he could not turn his back on. He left banking and became an activist with a specific focus on counter-globalisation and trade. Arvanitakis has seen the anti-globalisation movement spark up like a flare before burning out just as quickly. He believes the *No Logo* generation had partly been defeated by dealing with a beast as amorphous as the market, making it hard to win any battles—or even engage in battles in the first place. In a way the restlessness of both the market and young people made opposition to the market difficult: we had trouble *staying focused* and the market refused to stay *in focus*.

Drinking a coffee in the drab and functional UTS cafeteria he told me, 'The market has the ability to change form. It is the ultimate chameleon. The market can always change its shape to suit the times, so when there's concern about corporate behaviour you get codes of conduct to appease the public, but ultimately the codes are unenforceable. What the market is good at is enclosing that innovation. So you've got a *No Logo* generation established as a social movement, and they identify this whole human rights thing and people having a global responsibility and people connecting across cultures, and all of a sudden you get marketing campaigns reflecting this such as IBM, Apple and Nokia with their "connecting people" ad campaigns. They feedback to consumers this endless loop. The greatest irony is those campaigns against the market often give the market their best ideas. It's an interesting battle.'

So the anti-globalisation movement burnt itself out, the market cannibalised its critics and all the activists are busy doing other things, but that still doesn't explain how we have had such a dramatic culture shift during the Long Boom. How did we get from brand bashing and anti-globalisation to hyper consumption?

I know who to ask.

Adam Ferrier is managing director of one of those companies that everyone secretly wants to work for. Naked Communications is located in the garment district of Surry Hills, in a building that from the outside looks like it could be either a crack house or performance artist collective studio space. I wait for Ferrier in the foyer, where books by Noam Chomsky and the Dalai Lama are provided to pass the time instead of glossy mags. The office is open plan. The girls are barefoot and wear cute little rah-rah skirts and the boys wear t-shirts bearing obscure, faintly aggressive slogans. Ferrier, in his early thirties, has longish dark hair and sleepy eyes.

Young people today are living in a totally branded world, he says. 'I don't think they've ever experienced an environment that isn't ever completely saturated by marketing. It's like a cat brought up in an apartment—no matter how nice and shiny the apartment is they can't decide whether it's good or bad or if they like it or not, because they know no other way. They internalise the culture.'

In this environment things have moved very rapidly for brands. Growing up in the 1970s and 1980s Ferrier noticed 'brands used to belong on the TV set, on a few outdoor billboards and on the supermarket shelf—that was my experience of brands—everything else was free from a brand world. You compare today and what they go through and everything is a branded culture. People under twenty-five know that everything they do online is going to be influenced by brands. They are listening to iPods all the time or going to events that have a heavy brand sponsorship so they are constantly, totally involved in brands, and therefore brands give those experiences and brands are totally okay in their world.'

As for *No Logo*, well, that's just so Gen X. Move on, it's over. 'Gen X saw brands kinda evolve and grow off the TV set and then there was the Naomi Klein *No Logo* era and we were very sceptical and cynical and thought brands were invading our personal space, but that came from a theoretical or philosophical point of view, a cerebral perspective rather than practical perspective.' Ferrier reckons the days of brands being all good or all bad are over. 'You can't just win people over with a good ad campaign—there has to be trust built in other ways, such as providing good working conditions or a positive experience for the consumer.'

We are now in phase two of a branded world, where brands and people work together to build a better world. Witness talks in 2009 between Coca-Cola and the city of Venice. Venice Mayor Massimo Cacciari insisted the city could not survive 'by philanthropy alone'. The deal proposed vending machines be dotted around Venice selling Coca-Cola products. According to the city council, funds from the deal would go towards restoration and future flood prevention.[55]

Ferrier believes consumers act as watchdogs for dodgy brands and in response brands strive to increase pleasure in our lives and act with a modicum of social responsibility. It's meant to be a win–win situation. But I'm not so sure. Are we really so easily bought? I think about coffee chains such as Starbucks or Gloria Jeans. How for a while in Sydney they seemed like the only cafés in the CBD that were open on weekends. How they provided newspapers and comfy couches and soft folk music being piped (not too loud, not too quiet, just the right tempo for sipping coffee) from speakers hidden somewhere in the wood panelling. How I didn't really want to go in there, but when I did, it was rather good. Was that a form of seduction? Is this why brands are winning, because they know the winning formula? They know how to turn us on?

Ferrier was doing a good job of convincing me that brands have become more responsive—after all, if we were totally cynical about initiatives they used to keep us happy, nothing would be done. 'I remember hearing [the late] Anita Roddick [founder of The Body

Shop] speak. Nike had just released an organic shoe and I asked a question: "The market has released an environmentally friendly shoe. What's my take as a consumer? Should I buy it or are they just trying to pull the wool over my eyes?" and she said, "Embrace it—buy the shoe, change the corporation's behaviour". Harm minimisation, if you like, or positive reinforcement. Brands are really responding to that. You have more and more movies such as *OutFoxed* and *Supersize Me*, so there's a backlash. Naomi Klein—that's maybe where the conversation began.'

Where the conversation began was with the alarm that parts of life previously untouched by marketing or colonised by brands were being discarded in favour of the hotter agendas: the anti-war movement, civil rights for terror suspects and climate change. But did we give up the fight too easily? The terms of surrender were nothing less than giving brands access to colonise not only our public spaces but also our inner lives. Says Ferrier, 'The purist view of a life without brands and a freewill that entails and the free public space that that entails is no longer on the cards anymore. That's gone forever. Now we have to work with brands to shape the culture. Within that there is the understanding that we won't be able to have a culture free of brands ever again.'

The path we are on takes us to a future that is chilling. A branded future. 'I see a future where you have a new housing estate and it will be called the McDonalds housing estate—you will sign a contract with Starbucks to only drink coffee from there for the rest of your life. In return for that they'll give you a free car. Another company will have their brand in your living room and you'll wake up and see that brand. Our world will be much, much more branded,' says Ferrier, as I look for a hint of alarm behind his sleepy eyes.

Have we opened the door too widely for brands to step through? Have us cats been locked in the apartment for too long? I reckon when it comes to certain things, such as falling in love, brands have no business being there. Adam Ferrier disagrees with me about internet dating. The pub, he says, really provides the same service but it's more hit and miss. Sathnam Sanghera admits he's never pulled at a pub, and for many people it's the last place where they would feel comfortable looking for a partner.

I think about certain nights at the pub. Sometimes there was a sense of being both hunter and hunted, in a really dark forest where nothing was clear. Signals easily misread, ambiguity as thick as cigarette smoke in the gaming rooms, and alcohol further adding to the confusion. It's almost like internet dating has left us exposed—saying, 'There you go, the person you may be looking for is there, no need to play hide and seek anymore'.

Is it a good or a bad thing that the market is facilitating romance for profit? Commodification is value neutral—as long as they can market it—how it shifts the culture is immaterial to them (whoever *they* may be). If we really find it offensive or intrusive we can choose not to use the product. The market will then react by withdrawing the product or adapting it. Accept the product (as we have done with internet dating) and the door opens a little wider for the market to creep a bit further into our inner lives.

Marketing has been creeping around love for decades. The way it sells things with the aim of making us feel sexy or attractive or youthful or cool. Boil it down and it's our desire to be loved that drives the purchase of so many products—be that eye cream or skinny jeans or Coke Zero. Says Ferrier, 'I think marketing's goal is to touch everything and to find more and more clever ways to engage people and brands. Wherever there's a desired emotion you will find a brand pretty close behind that emotion. So people want to feel optimistic—you can buy optimism in a bottle. When people want romance, there will be brands that facilitate that experience. Commodification is here, there and everywhere.'

It was 2008 and it seemed that romance had definitely been packaged up and commodified in online dating sites. I knew because I was surfing them nightly. This time it was not for research or for this book, or as a social experiment but, well, because I was feeling quite despairing and wondering if I'd *ever* meet anybody. I was moving towards my mid-thirties; the end of the start and the beginning of the middle. Thoughts of isolation and dread haunted me more than ever before. I also felt like I had been left behind while everyone else was off on some great adventure. Not only had I attended the weddings of many of my friends, but I'd also lived through their divorces and *second* weddings. Would it ever happen for me?

The isolation I felt was not just emotional in origin, it was also geographical. You see, I was living in Belgium. I had moved to Brussels on a whim (broke, the offer of a house-sit, a book to write) and knew absolutely nobody there. I would be living alone and working on a novel, meaning it was unlikely that I would meet anyone. Brussels was the place at the end of the spiral (where had I been living that year? I could scarcely remember, except that I had moved around a lot: London, Sydney, Melbourne, London, Berlin, London, Milan, Riga, Paris, Prague, moving on, moving on in a vaguely restless, unsatisfied way).

I took a day train from Berlin, my home for four months, to Brussels. We stopped in Cologne and I, nostalgically—already!—bought a Bratwurst. By nightfall the train had pulled into Brussels and I realised I didn't even know what language they spoke here: French? Flemish? Dutch? English as the lingua franca? It was the evening of the US election and as I taxied up to Ixelles, I looked out the moving window for festive, lit-up balconies or the overspill from a hotel perhaps, people celebrating what could be the election of the first African-American President. But all was dark.

That first night was a portent. The feeling of aloneness, of being separate, never lifted, and I was haunted by the knowledge that I was unknown in this country in the most fundamental sense: no one here *knew* me, and I did not know anyone. No colleagues, friends, lovers, family, acquaintances. There was no past here. There would be no future. In my wandering around Brussels this knowledge made me feel like a ghost: intangible, slight, vulnerable, off the grid. I was alone (alone, alone) all day and night. I grew sick of myself and restless. A sort of toxic energy swirled within me and around me that couldn't be channelled into the book. To shake it I would take my daily walks around the magnificent square trying to lock onto faces in a crowd whose imagined lives would take me away from my own. Maybe it was just my state of mind but no one smiled at me—there was no *acknowledgement,* even of the most fleeting kind. Fridays, and by a sad urban canal I would sip fish broth from a stall, standing up and looking at nothing in particular. Nothing in particular looked back at me. In the stores of Sainte Catherine I touched the fabric of jersey dresses, stroked fur collars; the lull of the tactile. I blushed when the shop assistants addressed me in rapid French. I couldn't understand so I'd hurry out, back onto the street, returned abruptly to my own company.

I took day trips out to the countryside: Antwerp, Ghent, Bruge, Leuven. I ate solitary meals. What else? A lot of scribbling in my journal. A nice mussel chowder. A guilty plate of chips. A rowdy EU pub and the novelty of smoking inside. Under scaffolding, a beautiful old bar the guidebook described as 'fin de siècle'. A travel piece for a newspaper about Belgian beer where I got unhappily drunk on my own and wrote descriptions in my notebook: 'blond? gareth evans here? pear? toosour? Bubbles—enough, quite storng'.

Some nights lying in bed I would pick up a wireless signal—and that horrible lonely feeling that had been haunting me all day would immediately lift. Gmail! And IM! And Facebook! I was BACK!! I felt cheered and revived. Online I was flying—I could be in London, I could be in Warrnambool, or back in dear old Deutschland. Well, in my mind I was there. I could gather my people around me and never let them go. In Brussels should I be hit by a tram, not one single person in the country could identify my body—but in cyberspace I was *known*. I had three hundred friends on Facebook, but not a single friend in the country where I was living.

Weeks passed. Winter came. Snow swirled and built up in banks against the buildings. Out on the balcony (glowing beneath me the lights of the all-night convenience store, the White Knight), I would stand transfixed. The snow was swirling like in a dream and back-lit in gold from the street lamps. On Wednesdays at the market in the square, cheery groups of friends met after work in their heavy over-coats and wool suits, buying cheese, drinking mulled wine, eating standing up at the Thai stall—all about my age, just like me but Flemish. Oh, I missed my friends. I tried to replicate the feeling I got when with them by going online. I contorted my body and my compu-ter to get a signal. Sometimes it worked and the hours would fly.

Facilitated by Facebook, I eventually made two new real-life friends, Simon and Raine, a married couple who dressed the same (pink sweaters and green Lacoste polo shirts) and were kind and gen-erous to me. I studied them over candles, red wine and venison with juniper berries, one rainy night at a restaurant. As a couple, they didn't wear masks. They had their stories and their terms of affection, their sudden fights and mysterious silences that indicated deep geological layers. They told me how they met and about chance and all the coin-cidences that led to them being together, and Raine would squeeze Simon's hand and some palpable tenderness would flow between them. I knew then, if I didn't know it already, that I didn't want to be the person with a face pressed to the window (watchful at the balcony, seeing the meetings and the greetings on the square below, being that ghost) and so later that night I went online to find a boyfriend.

I picked a smaller site, with only a couple of hundred thousand people to choose from, rather than millions. It was a brand I liked and trusted (Guardian Soulmates). The computer guided me through the steps of putting together a profile. I had to select a photo, write something about myself and tick boxes about what sort of man I would like to meet. This forced me to think clearly about things I usually didn't address—like how young is too young? What if he's got kids? Could I still love him if he works in finance? (Twenty-two, that's okay, yes.)

Then suddenly, I was on the site, telling the world I was looking for love. I felt nervous and excited all of a sudden, yet also exposed. Who knows who I could meet? I emphasised travelling on my profile, maybe hoping to meet someone as footsore and world weary as myself, someone ready to *stop*. I also mentioned I liked to read and write. Yet after I logged off I fretted about what I had written. How boring I had sounded! And my photo too; not terrible, but not particularly sexy either. I was wearing a woollen scarf.

Yet the next day I had been contacted by three men who the computer declared were my 'fans'. The rush was immediate. I had also been checked out by several others, but they had not gone so far as to 'fan' me. In order to make contact with the men that had contacted me, I needed to become a subscriber (at a cost of £53.85 for three months), which I did without hesitation. Aha! Here was the commerce. Here was the transaction, this is the portal we go through where all that once was free becomes commodified. But this was the way for me now, and I too would be committed to its cruelties and chances. The week continued. I spent most nights on the site. My most ardent fan 'Holland' was not my type, but I became his fan so he wouldn't feel rejected. Some men I checked out, checked me out, but didn't become my fans. I became fans of some men that did not reciprocate the gesture. They had clicked on my profile and had not been interested. They were not even being polite. After a week it was only the dreaded 'Holland' who was pursuing me. But it was a strange pursuit: he was yet to send me as much as an email. He just visited my profile every day, like I imagined someone would to a shrine or a particular item of clothing they liked that was in a shop window.

I needed more fans so changed my profile picture to something a bit more fleshy. I rewrote my blurb to delete references to 'enjoys reading'. A few more men visited me but none were as consistent as 'Holland'. The whole exercise was beginning to fill me with anxiety. When I logged on, would I have a message or an empty inbox?

I could get more 'traffic' one friend suggested, if I agreed to be a 'featured single'. My profile would then be advertised more prominently on the site, even on the front-page of the *Guardian* news website (with its millions of hits a day). As with property, it's all about position, position, position. But I shirked at that as it seemed even more like advertising and commodification than it already was, plus all my friends read the *Guardian* and I did not want them seeing me up there, advertising myself. And so I stayed on the online equivalent of Old Kent Road.

Yet still, the anxiety ... Logging off at night I felt I'd left a part of myself (my virtual self) alone, unguarded in a large, dark nightclub. Friendless, and yes, even *vulnerable*, that thing we were all trying to avoid out there in the real world. In the shadows on the dance-floor I saw 'Holland', looking but not talking. Watchful, unsure maybe, or was he a more malevolent figure? Hard to know. I logged onto Soulmates in the morning and saw that he had visited me again in the night, but not left a message.

Days became shorter in Brussels, the weather foul. Simon, Raine and I drank Belgian beer in bars that smelt of wet wool and reminded me of Melbourne. Restlessness was rousing in me again. Move on, move on, move on, it whispered. So I moved back to England before November ended. A ticket on the Eurostar to Kings Cross St Pancras one Saturday night, everything I owned in a case at my feet.

I disabled my profile the night I packed my bags. Led myself by the hand off the virtual dance floor and back out into the world.

The media is all over internet dating. They love a trend, no more so than when it involves young people, sex and technology. Back in London at a picnic in Hyde Park a young picnicker asks about my weekend then rolls her eyes and says with genuine cynicism, 'Oh, so you're going speed dating for a story—that's what they all say'. Maybe they do. But it seems all the articles, all the profiles, all the excitement, all the success stories and photos of couples in neatly pressed shirts in soft colours are missing the point. What if something that is meant to bring us closer together—something that connects us—in fact does the opposite? It atomises us. Pits us further apart from each other. And the thing that has been our binding for an age—romantic love—is fraying at a rapid rate under this system. What if the system and the technology that enables it have a rhythm that drives our restlessness and if we keep moving we'll never be sated and never feel happy? That this system embodies consumer culture so are we willingly commodifying each other and ourselves? Despite the early promise of the anti-globalisation movement we have been distracted and unable to keep tabs on the market as it has moved ever closer into our inner lives.

In the months when I started writing this, in mid 2006, I was propelled by my own brand of restlessness, which, left unchecked, developed years later into a kind of terminal turbulence. Back then, I quit my job. I threw out my furniture. I got the limit on my credit card extended and packed away my clothes. Although I wasn't to know it then, it marked the start of a long period in the wilderness. Of risk-taking and failures, some success, great highs and low lows. The Sydney that I left behind was glittering and hard, all surface, it seemed. I craved some sort of deeper experience and thought the root of this urge was geographical in origin. I needed to get away. So I travelled a lot, met a lot of people, went to new cities—the questions that dominate this book, dominating my mind. Have we allowed the market in too close? Is internet dating an embodiment of some sort of invasion of the marketplace into our inner lives? What happened to the *No Logo* generation? Have they given up on their challenge to brands?

Walking through Central Park in New York I had an argument with a former colleague from Sydney, who said that as long as the market is facilitating love, and not something like childhood obesity or drug addiction, then we couldn't worry about it. Driving along a motorway in Bologna with an Italian man seemed to be the only time I found someone that agreed with me. His rationale was simple— romance and love, the old-fashioned way, is where all the beauty, the magic and the mystery lie. To mess with that is to harm something very special and very fragile, in a universe where special and fragile things are disappearing. That weekend we had long talks about love in too-sunny piazzas and restaurants, driving along back roads (the smell of maize in the air, a bright corridor of sun, a traffic accident on the motorways—fires lit around the wreckage). Everything deserted as it was high summer. He had a freshly damaged heart and I had questions and instincts but not answers. 'Is there such as thing as The One?' 'What if you never meet the person?' 'Why does love often feel as bad as it does good?' we would ask each other. And when it got too hot we would leave the piazzas, questions still unanswered.

At pubs in London, at a friend's barbecue in Warrnambool, at a restaurant in Melbourne, in a health food shop in Bondi. Everyone knew people who had done it and found love. Everyone was time poor. Everyone was busy. I felt mean. Who is to argue with love? Who is to argue with the market? an economist friend reasonably asked as he dragged on a cigarette on a park bench in Holborn.

A week later in the backblocks of Italy, I was lying on a couch, hiding from the sun so I could keep reading the short stories of F Scott Fitzgerald. In one clean, dazzling burst, he wrote of young men not wanting to do the fox-trot with just the one girl. Ahhh yes, nothing changes. Technology changes but we are the same—trapped by our desires, seduced by choice, restless, adrift, yearning. But still, still ... We are giving away too much here and without any protest. We don't know how we will change. We never think about the consequences. How this could calcify our hearts. We are so busy acquiring—people this time, as well as stuff—clothes and houses and cars and iPods, *stuff*. Hundreds of thousands—no, millions really—of people to choose from on the internet and we are pulling them off the shelves in huge bundles. We are bingeing on choice. But what happens after the shopping's done?

It was 2006 and I had been living in London for a month and yet felt like I had not really left Sydney. Email and a high-speed internet connection at home change everything. I used to speak to my mother only once a week when I lived in Sydney, now we email most days. But with the constant contact there is a constant craving for more. Technology was both powering and feeding this need, this restlessness, this churn. In August 2006, *The Times* and the *Guardian* lead with hysterical features of young professionals addicted to their BlackBerrys. 'How To Spot a CrackBerry' an article advised, saying that addicts check their screens for new messages every eight seconds.

I check my emails before I've changed out of pyjamas. The first, sharp hours of the day are for correspondence—opening emails, responding to emails—checking websites, reading the news online, surfing the net. To start my day without checking my emails feels akin to leaving my wallet and phone at home. It's hard to function without doing it. I'm not alone in my habits and addictions. One in four British internet users keep a blog, while social networking sites such as MySpace and Bebo are visited by sixty-nine million people worldwide.[56]

I started doing something else too—something to be vaguely ashamed of. I would get up in the middle of the night and check my emails because that's when it's daytime in Australia. My friends and family would be at work, in front of their computers, and I want to be in front of mine as well. The more I connect through the computer and texting, the more connection I want, even when I should be asleep. But I am never sated and I think sometimes I never will be.

I find the reality of London a strange contrast to this constant contact. There's a rawness to staring at people in the street, something indecent about pressing up against them in the crowded Tube. Across a busy road, locking eyes with a stranger for more than a second sometimes feels loaded with a weird poignancy. At my darkest moments I think we only kid ourselves that we are so connected, instead we are dropping further and further out of view from each other. When we click into the mentality of viewing people in a transactional light, when we are dating eight people at once so we can then pick one of them. When we spend twenty times three minutes with each person in a mating round-robin. When we become consumers in all we do and when other people are the products we are only further atomising and alienating ourselves. There is perversely this distance between us when all we are doing is striving to become closer.

In our restlessness, fuelled by the market and technology, by the seemingly limitless choices they both offer, we are losing the art of being alone. British pediatrician and psychoanalyst Donald Winnicott popularised the phrase 'capacity to be alone' in the 1950s to describe a pivotal stage of emotional development. In the *Boston Globe*, writer Neil Swidey explored how this capacity is dwindling; he believed with technology we need never be alone.[57] He spoke to Amherst political science professor Thomas Dumm who suggests that people today still have to deal with loneliness but they are less equipped to do so. Dumm says that 'Rather than going deeper they try to push it aside'.[58] For Dalton Conley, a sociology professor at NYU, the dwindling capacity to be alone is reflected in the changed American ethic. He describes how once the American ethic was 'the lone guy on horseback', now it's people 'managing multiple data streams' who find it hard 'to unplug and be alone'.[59]

The changes arising from multi-streaming are profound, not just in our behaviours and a move away from unplugged 'alone time' but the configuration of our neural pathways. Just as the thumbs of a generation who communicate through texting are more ambidextrous than the thumbs of those in the pre-mobile era, so too will the brains of those accustomed to dealing with multiple and simultaneous streams of information change and adapt. James Harkin, author of *Cyburbia*, says, 'This new kind of involvement that we have with our electronic media is more intense and more pressing ... The delivery of a continuous stream of messages might well be slowly stretching our brains, turning us into creatures who are better at doing many different things at once.'[60]

Harkin describes a never-ending information loop of 'electronic messages sent back and forth between us at breakneck speed'.[61] This information loop might go something like this: you log on, you check Facebook and see what your 350 friends are doing; you flick through their photos, making comments on the ones you like, tagging people that you know in the little red boxes (which then sets off a chain, where the tagged photo is sent to them, and they can then comment on it, etc. ad infinitum), before moving onto the news feed section—seeing what all your friends are doing, and commenting on what they're doing (writing something pithy in a drop-down box with your picture attached, or else just clicking on a 'thumbs-up' button to indicate that you've seen and you like their status update), before doing your own status update, which then causes the whole feedback loop to repeat, so people who you are friends with can comment on you and then you can comment on their comments.

After Facebook you may update your Twitter feed (in 140 characters or less 'tell us what you are doing'), plus read all the updates of the people you are following (Stephen Fry is 'swimming with the most divine sea turtles in Indonesia' and Lily Allen is 'in Terminal Four') or, if you are one of the millions of people who have a blog, you can update your blog, check for comments and post comments on other people's blogs, on articles or on news websites.

All this and you haven't even checked your email yet, or Skype or IMed. If you are on a dating site, as I was briefly, you also check to see if anyone's contacted you, become your fan or checked out your profile picture. You have to cruise as well, and check out other profiles, and respond to those profiles; you have to flirt with people you have never seen.

Phew! That's a lot of work.

This rapid-fire information loop encourages our restlessness, our skating across the surface of life by speeding up our communication. So what's fuelling all this online activity, this restless roaming from one site to the next? Dalton Conley says it's 'anxiety borne out of a deep-seated fear that we're being left out of something, somewhere, and that we may lose out on advancement in our work, social or family lives if we truly check out'.[62] Or maybe it's just the rush of getting a message—interacting with our neural pathways like a small hit of a powerful drug. One blogger on the *Daily Beast* said, 'Online communication has become the coke of the 00s'.[63]

Joel Stein, a columnist at the *LA Times,* calls it 'hyperinteractivity', where our heads are in a very different space than where they are when, say, reading a book or knitting a sock. Hyperinteractivity is fuelled by the phenomenon of feedback. Giving feedback, receiving it and reviewing or rating everything: the hotel room you stayed in (TripAdvisor), the meal you had at the restaurant last night (Eatability), the movie you saw (yourmovies.com), the service at the day spa (totaltravel.com), the book you read last week (Amazon), the album you downloaded, the concert that you saw, the article that you read (any news website), the music video you saw (YouTube), the dates you go on, the sites you visit, even the sex you have. It seems any experience now, good or bad, must be rated, assessed, commented on and published, and then those comments can be commented on. You can even comment on other people's secrets at secrettweet.com, which encourages people to post their innermost secrets online anonymously. You can leave feedback on the fact that someone's husband is not the father of their child, or that they eat their toenail clippings.

One of the more depressing jobs I've had in the media was working in the feedback area of an English national newspaper, moderating blog comments. I'd sometimes start at 6 a.m., and pick up an article written by, say, Boris Johnson or Melanie Phillips and steel myself for the diatribe, the literal torrents of hate (and occasional agreement) that I would have to wade through for eight hours each day. On rolling shifts that started at 6 a.m. and finished around 8 p.m., a team of four or more of us were charged with reading, moderating and posting comments connected to the day's blogs, news and opinion stories. Moderating comments was like tackling a massive basket of ironing that never seemed to get any smaller. Each new day the email folder would be full again of rants, raves, opinions and observations. Suddenly the world seemed to be having an amphetamine-fuelled conversation with itself, but the words were coming so fast I doubted anyone was listening (although Sathnam put it this way about Twitter: 'the banal thoughts of strangers are surprisingly comforting and compelling: it's like following mini-soap operas'.[64])

Regardless of whether you listen or not, the levee has been broken wide open. Hate, love, affirmation, friendship, desire: our inner lives, the shameful things, and the beautiful things—but *private* things—have flooded into the public realm. Could this be connected with the normalisation of internet dating sites, where the public conducts debates, conversations and courtship? Where the virtual has replaced the actual communities of politics in the pubs, Town Hall debates, Speakers corners and nightclub hook-ups? Lady Susan Greenfield says she finds it strange we are 'enthusiastically embracing' the possible erosion of our identity through social networking sites, since those who use such sites can lose a sense of where they themselves 'finish and the outside world begins'. She claims that sense of identity can be eroded by 'fast-paced, instant screen reactions, perhaps the next generation will define themselves by the responses of others'.[65]

Could it be that online emotions are preferable to the more fraught dealings in the real world? Social networking sites can provide a 'constant reassurance—that you are listened to, recognised, and important', Greenfield continues. This is coupled with a distancing from the stress of face-to-face, real-life conversations, which are 'far more perilous … occur in real time, with no opportunity to think up clever or witty responses' and 'require a sensitivity to voice tone, body language and perhaps even to pheromones, those sneaky molecules that we release and which others smell subconsciously'.[66] She says she fears 'real conversation in real time may eventually give way to these sanitised and easier screen dialogues, in much the same way as killing, skinning and butchering an animal to eat has been replaced by the convenience of packages of meat on the supermarket shelf. Perhaps future generations will recoil with similar horror at the messiness, unpredictability and immediate personal involvement of a three-dimensional, real-time interaction.'[67]

Blogging on the *Daily Beast*, one eighteen year old spoke of a similar sense of being disconnected from the real world: 'My generation is fully immersed in the demise of meaningful communication. We are the kings of instant communication, but get most of us into a real-life, face-to-face conversation about something real and be prepared for awkward silences galore. We just don't know how to have legitimate, lengthy conversation, instead we drag the same exchange over weeks of back and forth comments or posts on Facebook or MySpace. Something that could've taken only a few minutes to an hour and benefited both parties now takes days or weeks and is reduced to antiseptic little blurbs on the computer screen.'[68]

Remember Theodora Stites, who of attending parties said 'I found myself in awkward social situations I couldn't log out of'.[69] Could this be the same for finding love in real life; the awkwardness, the chances we take, the rejection that may occur when we're face to face? Remember Rufus Black writing 'in these encounters of the mind, our physical self is never "on the line". Vulnerability and trust are inextricably linked, which means that a world with declining physical vulnerability is also one in which the landscape of trust is changing.' This technology fuels our restlessness, takes us away from the stillness we feel when truly alone—it quickens the churn.

Many people are questioning the impact that technology has had on their lives. Mark McKinnon, former Republican adviser, writes in the *Daily Beast*, 'Somewhere along the internet highway we fell under the spell that more communication is better communication. Sometimes more communication is just noise ... the more I have tried to maintain links to the ever-expanding universe of acquaintances in my orbit through the ever-increasing number of tools to connect with them, the less I am spending real quality time on people who really matter to me.'[70] Lee Woodruff, also in the *Daily Beast*, writes: 'as we spend ever increasing amounts of time as a society online, isolated in front of some sort of screen, a sea shift begins to occur. We raise a generation unable to concentrate on anything long and involved, on Homer's *Odyssey*, Harper Lee's classic or even a live performance of *The Nutcracker* ... We lose the art of crafting thank-you notes, or the impact of a well-written sympathy card after a loved one dies. Remember letters? When was the last time you sent one? ... Our communication is now ephemeral.'[71]

If our communication is ephemeral, are the things that accompany it ephemeral as well? What about our relationships, passions, hobbies, causes, feelings? Does the message become the medium? Is everything fast and coarse and destined to slip from consciousness as soon as it is read from the screen? Lately I have found myself sending condolences via Facebook to friends who've suffered bereavement, such as the death of a parent. 'Sorry for your loss, thinking of you, sending good vibes your way', I'll type. Later I'll check that person's status update in those days after the funeral and it reads: '[Insert name] would like to thank all their friends for their support in this difficult time'. Meanwhile I've noticed when a friend dies, their Facebook wall acts as a sort of condolence book. Is that good or bad? We are in touch at least, but can these electronic messages provide true *condolence*? By that I mean do they provide comfort, sustenance, support in the way a card or letter (or even better a hug, a casserole brought to the house) once did?

Remember the original question I asked myself: is it better to live broadly or deeply? We are living more and more broadly but not more deeply.

To counter these new rituals based on technology, to slow the churn, to go deeper, there are some inventive rituals emerging. One English trend spotter reckons that 'no email Mondays' will replace casual Fridays as people try to stop the tide of emails that they are finding increasingly difficult to contain. Several people I know have recently been talking of 'culling friends' on Facebook—deleting people from their site who are no longer in their life in a meaningful way and instead spending more 'face-time' with people in their immediate circle.

Could we even be trying to consider ways of being alone, relearning the art of being unconnected? For a long time my friends and I called this unconnected, unplugged state 'the cave'. The cave, where you may be for a night or up to a month, is an introspective but necessary place. It's where you go after a break-up, major disappointment or burn-out. Things are quiet in there, almost like they are muted. Friends do different things in their different caves: some have loads of early nights, or a week at home tackling a difficult but satisfying novel. Others listen to loads of classical or mellow music, go swimming in the sea and turn off their phones, or stay away from toxic or abrasive people. The cave is a chance to step away from the feedback loop, the constant communication and intrusions of modern life. After being in the cave, the aim is to step out refreshed, renewed and ready to connect again.

Meditation helps us step from the default speed of living broadly—to go deeper.

On a Wednesday night just after Christmas 2008, the meditation room at the London Buddhist Centre in Bethnal Green was at capacity, the crowd mostly young Londoners who didn't seem to share the stereotypical appearance of meditators: beards, clothes made of hemp emanating the smell of patchouli oil. All of us were learning or relearning how to meditate—how to go deeper into our heads, unplug, be still.

A year earlier I had done an urban retreat at the centre for a CNN story and interviewed Maitreyabandhu, who lives and works in the community at the London Buddhist Centre. He explained the growing popularity of meditation, particularly among young people: 'Modern life is incredibly complicated and fast. That has a very stressful effect on the mind and body and people's quality of life diminishes. We are obsessed with choice. People often choose things that are not to their long-term benefit. You can easily feel you've taken the wrong path. People are really busy—they might be well off but they are unhappy.'

The people who come to the meditation centre often work in stressful jobs and do their unwinding at the pub, or on the internet at home after work. The unwinding we do in front of our laptop at night doesn't allow for true peace, says Maitreyabandhu—rather it acts as a distancing or distracting mechanism that keeps us stimulated but does not allow us to penetrate any depths. 'People feel there's a definite meaning vacuum. Materialism is not helping us. People are increasingly realising materialism is not working, choice is not working. The basic assumption is the more choice you have the happier you'll be. People need to get a sense that their lives matter. They get it from people, and also from meditation. You enter another world.'

As a result of our rushed lives we can lose touch with ourselves. Meditation then becomes a way of 'checking-in' and assessing how things are going. Says Maitreyabandhu, 'We can become alienated from our more subtle emotions. We are alienated from our bodies. There is a real need to get in contact with something alive. We easily get stuck on the surfaces of ourselves. In the West we forget the mind has depths. There are depths of the mind that are really satisfying and profound.'[72]

The East Village, New York. It's summer and I am eating pasta with a native. Brendan and I are having a rushed dinner before he goes off to work at a club nearby. The club is holding an underpants party, he explains. Men turn up and leave their clothes at the door and drink with and talk to other men just wearing their underpants. It's not seedy, explains Brendan, it's sort of quirky and fun. The lighting is low but it's not blacked out like a sex-on-premises venue and you can check out if he has Confederate flags imprinted on his boxers or a leather g-string and the conversation and all else can roll on from there. I am intrigued. I have sharp recollections of parties of my teenage years when on the hottest nights of summer after we'd been dancing all night, we would all move to the sea, throw off our clothes and plunge in the water. The water would always be icy and rough and would at first feel strange against the slime and sweat a night of dancing would produce on our skin. It always felt good. The nights were never overtly sexual, just playful and alive. Dark shapes of our bodies in the dark sea. Boys would submerge only to grab your ankles and pull you under as you gasped for breath amid the turbulence.

I followed Brendan to the underpants party. Just a peek, just one, I promised. So behind the red curtain beneath a Chinese restaurant on a hot night in New York, I spied not some libertine paradise but men, mostly with nice bodies and tight underwear, standing around a bar drinking beer, swaying slightly to the beat (Stone Roses mashed up with Beyoncé) and nodding at each other but not touching. And I walked away and I thought about it for a long time after that summer had passed.

It's a sunny day: Fitzroy, 2009, my thoughts turn again to love. Lovely, lovely love. What the hell are we doing running it through the meat-mincer of technology? Feeding it into the crack pipe of the internet and smoking it? What will become of it now? More importantly, what will become of us?

I fear the end of people looking for love or at least some sort of connection in real life. They instead outsource the task to the virtual world—their avatars go on dates, their online profiles sell and market themselves, their social networking sites 'meet' new people.

Could it be that commodification of love through technology gets taken to its logical extreme where we can no longer be bothered with the often unglamorous, difficult slog of having a partner, instead living apart, indulging our sexual needs through services provided by the market: prostitution and sex tourism. Sometimes I think we are already there. We don't know each other and we don't want to know each other or be vulnerable. We resist, unlike DH Lawrence's characters, being 'broken open again'. Instead our most primal needs, sex and love, will be outsourced to various service providers.

In June 2006 I came across a particularly chilling article on female sex tourism in the *Observer*.

> But Negril is not as dreamlike as it looks. It is no longer visited primarily for sun, sea and sand. Instead it is the destination of choice for an increasing number of British female sex tourists. An estimated 80,000 single women, from teenagers to grandmothers, flock to the island every year and use the services of around 200 men known as 'rent a dreads', 'rastitutes' or 'the Foreign Service' who make this resort their headquarters. The gigolos working on Negril beach offer a simple explanation for their role in what is commonly, though euphemistically, called 'romance tourism'.
>
> 'For us it's a fun and easy way to make money,' says Leroy. 'For her, she gets some real good lovin'. All the English ladies who come here complain about the men back home. They say they are cold and selfish, mechanical and uncomplimentary. We know how to make a lady feel good.'[73]

On Saturday morning in our back garden over croissants and coffee I read the story out to Harvey, my straight-talking housemate. He makes the point that all the men seeing prostitutes and now all the women seeing prostitutes should 'just meet down at the pub, get together and save themselves some money'.

This new way of doing things is bleak. The article goes on:

> A lot of the women talked about how big the men are and how they can go all night. I was shocked at the way they objectified the black male body. But what I found most depressing was that the whole thing is not real. So many of the women think they have found real love. It's all very delusional. At first I thought it was all about white women exploiting black men.

But it's not. It's very mutual. The guys are just as exploitative and you come away thinking this is such a sad, sick world that we live in.[74]

This vision of the future of men and women so estranged from each other that they can't help but commodify others for sex (as long as they are not of your class, they are not one of you, then it's okay, then it works, because that's how commodification has always been built up, through power structures) is a Houellebecqian nightmare. It's a world where relationships between men and women are so damaged that a chasm has appeared. A gap in the market. And so the market enters, as the market is wont to do, offering services to rescue us (however briefly) from our loneliness. A prostitute to fuck so that we can feel close to someone for a bit. Sex tourism so we can pretend we are having a holiday romance. The market is kind enough to take the 'muck' out of the product. When sex is transactional you are less likely to fall in love or feel obligation, you just squeeze the pleasure out and feel none of the pain. The market is value neutral and moves in when it sees a gap. And in this 'sad, sick world that we live in' the gap is filled by transactional sex. Fucking without involvement. Or disembodied courtship through technology. Or internet dating where it's easier to discard people because of the sheer amount of choice. Or speed dating because after three minutes, if they're not right, you can move on. Anything, it seems, to avoid feeling vulnerable.

Houellebecq writes in *Platform*:

As women attach more importance to their professional lives and personal projects, they'll find it easier to pay for sex too; and they'll turn to sex tourism.[76]

His type of intense commodification of coupling is still at the extreme end, although it is becoming mainstream, just as internet dating is 'so five years ago'.

I think of the underpants parties and those long ago nights at the beach. I see them as experiences separated by time and space. Hidden like the beach itself by the dark, hidden like the parties under the Chinese restaurant, without a licence, no advertising, just word of mouth.

I think about what's mainstream now. Our restlessness made manifest. Churn love. Serial monogamy. Never being happy enough with what you've got. Looking for The One. Going online, creating your brand, checking your emails, surfing other profiles, selecting, discarding, dating 'heaps of people' at once. Eliminating them. Watching your reality be the reality on reality TV and the whole stupid loop endlessly feeding this shit back to us, but interspersed with ads (if we didn't know we were in a commercialised space, we certainly can't hide from that knowledge with the pop-up ads, graphics and banner advertising) so we can think about our home loan while oscillating between desire and suspicion, thinking about how his legs would feel wrapped around yours, thinking about the weight of him moving across you, wondering if she's lying about her age or he's lying about his income. It's just like shopping—desire for what we can own, suspicion about their promises. The truth we accept a little benignly, all products lie a little. We have let the market in (so close, too close) and now it's here to stay.

I like to think that while this becomes the dominant system, there are still dark rooms and dark beaches where people shed things or at least are together in a corporeal sense. That there is some truth going on or at least some space that is ours alone. Places uncolonised by the market.

Somewhere between the final whistle at speed dating and those hazy moments in bed on Sunday morning listening to the Psychedelic Furs, I reverted back to the ways of the past. The way it was before there was a ritual vacuum and we were led only by instinct.

Maybe it was a reaction to the weirdness of speed dating—the baldness of it, the depressing banter and rushed conversations, the pens and the clipboards and the scorecards. The hesitant passion for plankton, murmured to me by a stranger across the table. Maybe it was a drunken grasp to some wilder time. Maybe it was because he was built like a rower and had great eyes.

After the pens and paper had been packed away I went to a night-club and picked up a guy the old-fashioned way—standing at the bar, talking over the music, moving off the dance floor, pashing on the couches when a Beyoncé song came on, moving outside, kissing him on the street as drunks threw up nearby and a Moroccan tried to sell us a rose in a plastic cylinder. We kissed and talked on the street for a couple of hours. It was funny and tender, sordid and strange. Grinning, with chapped lips, I walked away from him at 4 a.m. and threw the speed-dating scorecard in the bin.

WORK

Welcome to Warrnambool, where the signs into town warn you about the 35 000 'friendly people' and smaller signs tell you it was twice awarded Tidy Town. I am taking you on a stroll around the town's wide, handsome streets. The wind has dropped and the sun is out and instead of taking you to popular tourist attractions such as Lake Pertobe or to Flagstaff Hill, I'm going to show you where I used to work.

Here is the site of my first job, a newsagent where I worked for six weeks on the tills. I probably wasn't mature enough for the workforce as I was barely fourteen. They never did ask me back after the trial—I was slow and easily distracted, often late for work, and too frequently passing a greasy thumb through the pages of glossy magazines. Twenty years later I go there occasionally to buy a newspaper and get startled when I see the same people working there—greyer, but more or less unchanged—still holed up in their fiefdoms of the Tattslotto counter, or among the Parker pens.

Around the corner was the grocer where I worked in the meat section on a Saturday morning, wrapping cuts in plastic, folding sausages onto Styrofoam trays, the chill of it, the congealed blood, cold hands, the almost metallic smell of the meat, feeling shy around the butchers. I didn't last long there either.

I didn't hit my stride until chicken outlet Ollies Trolley hired me. They were independent. They were proudly regional. They were a 'family restaurant'. They were taken over by KFC. I worked at KFC for almost four years and later, mimicking the machinations of the corporate world, I was granted a transfer to the Swanston Street branch in Melbourne. I, as corporate speak would have it, 'grew with the company'. Apart from five years at the *Sydney Morning Herald*, it's the longest I have worked for one organisation.

I started as many others started before me: in an ill-fitting, unattractive uniform, with a badge that read TRAINING pinned to my chest. There was a narrative in this job that in retrospect seems perversely satisfying. When I was TRAINING, I learnt stuff. I got better at things. Using the till became easier. I learnt to recognise the different parts of a chicken (leg, wing, thigh, rib, breast) and how to place them snugly together in a five-piece box. I learnt how to cook chips, the correct way to stack a drinks fridge (labels facing the customer) and selling techniques such as the 'up-sell' or super size.

Socially, you are in Siberia when you are TRAINING, except of course with other people who are training. You help each other out, you give them your nuggets when they can't complete a six-pack or construct their burger if they're busy. My other colleagues were older, cooler, they smoked out the back with the surfie boys who cooked the chicken—boys who were the objects of such longing, such intense crushes that even prolonged exposure to the cool-room didn't chill my blushes.

But gradually things changed as they did with everyone. You get a bit more responsibility. You get rostered on drive-through. You mop the floor and clean the toilets without complaint. Suddenly you are not perceived as 'up yourself' or 'thinks she's too good'. You humble yourself to the job, or else the job humbles you. The tough older girls soften, then make a bit of room in their circle. They offer you a cigarette in the carpark and, when you accept one, you're in. The boys in the kitchen start to talk to you—ask your opinion on the new Zinger range—and later invite you to their parties.

You get older. You are now a smoker. You steal food—for yourself and others. You become quick with the tongs. With stacking the drinks fridge. With making a Works Burger. You realise thirty-two nuggets can be crushed into a six-nugget box. You start to train other people. You treat the new people badly—well, if not badly then with a measure of aloofness that says 'bide your time baby, once you get a few more fryer burns, we might talk'. You suddenly have more confidence to turn down the Saturday night close shift. You also develop some social confidence, the kind worn so casually by the older girls when you first started. You have arrived and are now as brazen as them. When it's quiet and the manager is down the back making batches of potato and gravy, you unwrap a bacon and cheeseburger and eat it out the front without even bothering to hide—not caring who sees.

The point is—while I frequently complained about KFC, while the people that made a career there as managers were the objects of pity and scorn (anyone aged over twenty-four who worked there was assumed to be phenomenally stupid), it provided a narrative, career certainty and character development that I haven't really encountered in any other workplace. There was (to quote sociologist Richard Sennett) 'a clear story—in which experience accumulated materially and psychically; … life thus made sense as a linear narrative'.[1]

In a restless economy, work becomes bits and pieces—we chop and change from one employer to another, from one project to the next, leapfrogging between teams, offices and colleagues. We may be continuously learning (or as big companies like to say in their brochures and on their websites—'we support life-long learning') but how many jobs offer the sort of clarity I experienced at KFC? Where you know you're learning, where 'experience accumulated materially and psychically' and when you've learnt what you need to know you can take off the training badge and get an extra dollar an hour? KFC was not a workplace where you dwelled in ambiguity or uncertainty. A program called the Star System tracked training and achievement.

The chart hung in the manager's office and you would get a sticky gold star next to your name when you learnt new skills. Additional responsibility, increased social status (among the other workers) and increased pay were all satisfying by-products of time put in at KFC. In the pecking order you knew where you stood, where you were going, and where you wanted to be.

Nothing has been as clear since.

Casual work seldom felt as streamlined or as incrementally satisfying. Aged eighteen, I moved to Melbourne where I lived for the next six years and worked in literally hundreds of jobs. Sometimes I worked three jobs at once, other times the jobs would only last for a week or so. Some, such as selling beer at the Grand Prix or ice creams at Moomba, were three-day contracts. It never mattered. These were junk jobs, easy come, easy go. Some generated an annoying amount of paperwork for such fleeting encounters (a super account with a $1.87 employer contribution sits somewhere a decade later), some were cash in hand. Mostly there was no training, never any sign of a union and poor health and safety. Sometimes people didn't get paid. The restaurant shut down overnight, bills and wages left owing, owners did a runner, and everyone else moved on, dispersed. You had to cut your losses. Some jobs were dangerous, people got bad burns, or hurt their backs or fell off ladders, or slipped on floors. Casual workers were a curiously clumsy lot. In other jobs sexual harassment was the norm; from the boss, from the customers—but rarely from other workers—who often offered the only solidarity they could, the solidarity of treating you like a human being.

Turn up to other jobs and you would immediately be startled by their murky internal weather system: the seething hate for the employer was so strong that employees openly stole cash, drinks, food—as much to even the score as from genuine hunger and economic need. There was bullying. There was public humiliation—of being yelled at or put down in front of staff and customers. Of being called 'stupid' and a 'fuckwit' by someone older and more powerful than you. In the churn there were the occasional acts of kindness, people who would cover for your shift when you had a twenty-first or were patient when showing you how to work the coffee machine. But ultimately it was a world without loyalty—at either end. People would turn up to work on Tuesday but not on Wednesday. Gone—just like that, and the employer would say something like 'she could have at least returned her apron' but that would be it. The sign would go up on the window for more workers, and by the next week the erasure would be complete. People would not even remember *wotshername*. There were so many people passing through these jobs, so many *wotshernames*, so many new faces that name badges were actually a useful tool, rather than merely a means of infantalising the workers.

Churn jobs, the lot of them and, although they felt disposable, it also felt like myself and fellow members of the restless workforce were in some sort of engine room, heaping coal on the great furnace of the economy, keeping things moving. And we were: someone had to heat up the pies at the MCG, someone had to scrub the burnt cheese from the commercial-sized lasagna tray at the seminary, some-one had to make the sandwiches and coffees for the office workers of St Kilda Road, someone had to wipe the tables and refill the salt and pepper shakers in the hotel breakfast room, someone had to stack the bread rolls in the bakery window and polish the windows, someone had to paginate the documents for the commercial law trial, someone had to unstaple the thousands of cheques from the letters when Telstra made its IPO, someone had to open the doors at the auditorium when the Australian Chamber Orchestra had taken their final bows. That someone was me—and many more like me.

Despite the fact that we need people to do these jobs, there's no dressing up that they were mostly junk jobs, basic and utilitar-ian, a world of loose bonds and loyalties, where people came and went, often unmourned, quickly forgotten. They shared a sort of Hobbesian flavour of being 'nasty, brutish, and short'. As we were all 'just passing through', there was often no stake built into the work itself—employees didn't care about employers and vice versa—and nothing was vested in each other, other than the most basic covenant that you turn up to work on time, do your job and in return you get paid an hourly rate. The add-ons like sick pay, holiday pay and long-service leave were not part of the transaction.

I didn't get too upset about these churn jobs. I had other things on my mind during those years. I was studying for a law degree, which I found so arduous and dull that the hours sweeping the floor or pulling the beers or unstapling the cheques actually felt like a relief. But it meant that I didn't dwell on one of the worst aspects of churn jobs—what Joan Didion once called the 'dread of the meaningless which is man's fate'[2]—that existential aspect haunting even the most exhausted worker as they climbed into bed and set the alarm to start it all again the next day.

Dread seemed to be more pronounced in those restless jobs where not only was the work undervalued, but the employer had divested all sense of purpose and energy in the development of the employees. The work was literally 'casual', where the idea of personal progress was something to be pursued *outside* the workplace. There was no long term and sense of linear progression where the worker could take pride in incremental improvements and small gains, and be *recognised* for making progress or an achievement, no matter how modest. In churn jobs there were no narratives of achievement and progress and there was little or no recognition. The 'dread of mean-inglessness' ghosted around the quiet moments in the casual shift.

These junk jobs were a way-station on the way to somewhere better. Well, that's what I thought. But lately I think the way-station, or at least features of it, have become the *way*, how we work infected by our profound restlessness and the dynamic, restless economy. In all our rushing around, though, we can still be surprised by temporal drifts and unsettling glimpses of meaninglessness.

Is context important? Maybe. This was the 1990s in Melbourne. The Kennett years. In the time preceding there was not just a drift but a desolate exodus of the state's citizens to Queensland. This was a time just after the Pyramid suicides and foreclosures and businesses shutting down, a time of unmanageable interest rates, double-digit unemployment and broken dreams. Homes being half-built then abandoned. Industry rusting, investment scampering off up north. A time of the collective blues. A time when one of the places that offered me the most work was as a filing clerk in an accounting firm that specialised in insolvency. It was a time of mass sacking in the public service, the closing of schools and hospitals. It was the era of Elliot Perlman's *Three Dollars* where his ordinary middle-class characters realised that the difference between them and the homeless men in the Flagstaff Gardens was only a couple of pay packets away. This was a time when the social contract seemed not only forgotten but was violently torn up and its pieces set on fire. The people tearing up the contract were the state government.

How could business, small and large, not follow the cue? How could all of us not follow the cue, internalise something of the spirit of the times and carry it with us, nursing it through recovery and then prosperity? It was a time for strong leaders, unpopular decisions, receiving a bit of pain as, pants down, you bent over, gripping the desk. Of the murmurs of fascism and of the brutal form of architecture that followed, of years that felt like endless winter. Bleak city, they called Melbourne in Sydney, and they were right. The Nylex sign on Punt Road always seemed to read seven degrees, my toes were always cold, and I was always somewhere—everywhere—waiting for a tram. I used to write poetry waiting at tram stops, and reading over it now there are recurring themes: rain, waiting for some form of public transport under 'threatening' skies, elderly people looking lonely in North Melbourne laundromats. The relief at the sound of the No. 8 tram as it turned at the Domain Interchange. The bare branches of the trees along St Kilda Road, draped in blue lights and described in one stanza as 'hysterical'. I don't think I meant it in the 'funny' sense.

It was the time of the heroin epidemic, of overdoses in the lanes behind Russell Street amusement parlours, where beggars would ask you for $7 because that's how much a cap of smack cost, where the most popular dance craze was moshing—less a dance than annihilation. Getting as close as you could get to strangers without fucking—glued together with sweat and beer—then jumping, hurting, hurling yourself into them and away.

Towards the end of this endless winter my friends and I used to meet in the bars that had started up in the laneways at the top of the city: Meyers Place, Spleen, Up-Top Bar. We'd meet at 10 or 11 or 12 that night when we'd finished working in our junk jobs. We'd buy expensive drinks such as gin and tonic and say, 'Oh, I've really earned this'. And we had.

Some of us started meeting for breakfast before classes at the newly opened Il Bacaro in Little Collins Street. We'd order flat whites and figs with honey, prosciutto and feta, trying on sophistication, an urbanity that didn't yet fit. We didn't know it then but we were rehearsing for the next decade, where we'd work hard and spend hard and then spend some more. We would complain about our jobs, and the government (although this talk was quite abstract, we were too young and too middle class to really suffer) but there was a smug sense that all this was temporary, that we were slumming until we got into our 'real jobs'—jobs in law firms, banks, management consultancies and newspapers. Jobs that had a narrative, promising progress, a sort of well-paid intellectual's version of KFC where there was a ladder that you could see and that you could climb.

We'd sit in a booth at Il Bacaro looking out onto the street, order another coffee and talk about the graduate programs we would be applying for and the travel we would do before we would start our jobs—our lives, really. We were twenty-two, twenty-three, twenty-four—young. We wouldn't mourn the casual work, we wouldn't miss its restless rhythm, rushing from one shift to the next, uniforms stuffed in our backpacks. We didn't realise, of course (and this is the arrogance of youth); that these future jobs too would have a churn, in fact, every job seemed to come with a churn. Although the jobs themselves would change, the way we had been working would become the way, not the way-station.

So what is restless economy work?

It caught on in the mid to late 1990s. It is contract, sub-contract and casual labour. It's part-time, sessional, seasonal, project, free-lance and temporary work. It's no commitments, no unions and keeping it loose. It's work that like buses either comes all at once or doesn't come at all. It's having your week set out in a roster that has peaks and troughs measured out by the hour. It's work where its frequency and rhythms are subject to the vagaries of the economy and those vagaries are now plotted with the short term in mind: weeks and months, not years.

It's living by the maxim 'no long term' and, as such, it's work that requires a high degree of 'living by your wits'. It's hundreds of colleagues coming and going all at different times, and in different shifts, caught in their own churn. It is work that stops and starts. It is work where you have difficulty controlling the flow: the hours, the length of your assignments or the pressure to get things done quickly.

It's forty or more jobs in your lifetime and a least three major changes of career. It's work in the age of mergers and acquisitions, where form is constantly mutating and the question 'Who do I work for again?' is no longer strange. It is feeling powerless and uncertain as a matter of course. It's work in an age of the publicly listed company, where shareholders' interests are more valued than those of the workers. It's staying with the one company then that company getting sold and broken up into little bits and pieces. It's work in a dynamic market where, as economist Bennett Harrison believes, the source of 'hunger for change' is 'impatient capital'—a desire for rapid return.[3]

It's work that comes in bits and pieces. It's feast and famine. It's having too much work that you wonder if life is passing you by. It's sometimes not being able to sleep because you don't know if you'll have enough work to pay the bills. It's freedom and fearfulness, exhilaration and dread: opposite emotions that roll around in your gut at the same time. It's wondering if you've fucked things up somewhere along the way. It's new economy work—the work of flexible capitalism where, according to Sennett, 'workers are asked to behave nimbly, to be open to change on short notice, to take risks continually, to become ever the less dependent on regulations and formal procedures'.[4] This is restless work, of 'no long term', of 'loose bonds and loyalties' and more of us are doing it than ever before.

It was during the early years of this new century that the old ways of working were being enthusiastically dismantled, like some sort of machinery that not only looked all wrong, but was no longer fit for purpose. The old way was dead, like systems set up by a socialist state rendered defunct by unleashing the roaming, ever-hungry beast of the free market.

Workers were becoming untethered by the old bonds of a job for life and instead there emerged new ways of working and new names for it: slash workers, enterprise workers, portfolio workers, shamrock organisations, free-agent nation. It was like being in a restaurant and handed a menu where previously there was none. Management gurus stressed choice in all of this, the opportunity to fully self-actualise, and to pick a way of working that fully matched your lifestyle, that matched *you*. Anyone who didn't was a mug. The message was 'be yourself' and also 'look after yourself'. No man is an island, apparently, yet this style of work encouraged you to develop an island mentality.

In free-agent nation (a term used to describe independent contractors) you and others like you formed an archipelago of services that connected with the mainland of the employer, yet you stood distinct, separate. Former Al Gore staffer Dan Pink promoted the concept of free-agent nation where workers are free agents who 'can achieve a beautiful synchronicity between who you are and what you do'.[5] In *Fast Company* magazine Joanna Baker talked about how being a free agent enabled her to practise yoga while those working the 'old way' were stuck in traffic: 'I didn't want to give up Joanna Baker to be a cog in their machine', she said, referring to herself in the third person. 'I get to do yoga every day in my house. Other people are commuting while I'm doing yoga.'[6]

This was work for a consumer age, ego work, *restless* work, where you got to pick and choose the terms and conditions. You selected bits and pieces the way you would when standing before the fluoro-attired workers at Boost Juice: 'I'll have orange, carrot and pineapple. Not too much, just a chunk. I'll also have a Ginseng extra, thanks.'

The former Howard government developed policies around this new way—WorkChoices—with an emphasis on individualism and small business. The conditions of work (theoretically) became open for us to order and negotiate; we were cut free from the collective, of someone deciding what was best for us.

Jobs resembled products to be consumed. We moved from one to the next with greater ease than ever before. When a job was no longer useful for us, or we were not getting maximum benefits from it, we moved on to the next one with scarcely a backward look. Employers started saying with a shrug that many young workers only stay for a maximum of two years before restlessness kicks in. Likewise, employers were more likely to see workers as products, brought in as a casual or contractor when the work needs to be done, released when it's quiet.[7]

All but the most essential workers were often stripped away and held at arm's length through temp agencies. A floating population of temps took the place of permanent staff. To be an employer—with all the liabilities it entails—became unfashionable. Instead, employers were encouraged to embrace a 'cocktail concept' of workplace organisation: that is, equal measures of permanent, contract and temporary employees that 'can create better flexibility for the business to meet both the peaks and troughs'.[8]

Sennett believes the 'stable past'—of a long-term workforce—is over. Instead, restlessness rules. He argues that companies have become more flexible organisations that structure the workforce with 'short-term, contract, or episodic labor'.[9] A workforce that consists solely of permanent staff has come to be regarded as 'unsustainable' for business because when there is a downturn the business is then saddled with a 'high fixed cost of labour model', i.e. wages. In a study of the collapse of Ansett Airlines, *Human Capital Magazine* blamed the company's permanent full-time staff as 'a major reason for its fall. No social or equitable purpose was fulfilled by Ansett's high proportion of permanent employees because when the company collapsed, all employees lost—even those who were living under the delusion that they had permanent jobs.'[10]

It is far better, according to this reasoning, that workers not labour under 'delusions' of mutual commitment and loyalty. Instead, under this new model, the commitment flowed one way: the employer gives you work when the economy is good, but in a downturn you're on your own. It's mysterious how individuals can think they are a winner under this arrangement, but companies have done a great job of making it sound as if anyone still boneheaded enough to be working for one employer was bound for the scrap heap.

In this shift in thinking, in this breach of mutual commitment, long-serving senior employees are also regarded as deadwood. One employer told me that if she saw the résumé of someone who had been employed with the same company for fifteen years she would 'think there was something wrong with him'.

Throughout the 1990s, the restless work-style gathered steam as we transitioned from an old-style stable, collective way of working into a casual labour economy. Job creation surged in part-time and casual employees, doubling between the early 1980s and the mid 1990s. Almost one in five workers in Australia now regard themselves as casuals. In fact, Australia has the second highest rate of casual labour in the world, just trailing Spain.[11]

For the past twenty-five years, the growth in casual employment has outstripped the growth in permanent jobs, with women and younger people more likely to be in casual employment. This change happened in a generation. My father calculated that aged sixty he has had fifty jobs, including summer holiday jobs. His longest stint was thirty years with the same employer. At thirty-three, I had worked in 144 jobs—the shortest stint lasting only a matter of hours, the longest lasting five years. So why the big difference in numbers? Am I really that much more flighty than my father? Maybe, but not almost ten times more. There's something more universal responsible for the shift, something that everyone's going through: some deep structural change.[12] The experts think so.

The move from a job for life to more temporary forms of work is nothing short of a 'revolution' for some and it's 'not just a matter of a few bloated corporations trimming jobs. It is a new way of doing business and organising work that spells the end of secure, long-term employment for practically everybody. An unwritten covenant between employers and employees is being annulled.'[13] Some argue full-time secure employment is a relic of the early industrial revolution. According to *Human Capital Magazine*:

> Workers had to be concentrated in factories in order to suit the production methods of the time. As part of this model, employers needed to 'own' their employees as far as possible and so the employment model became one of full-time work with a definite place to work, set start and finish times and set remuneration scales.[14]

In today's business model, 'employers are now reluctant to commit themselves to full-time, full-year "permanent" employees and prefer to get workers—from clerical staff to sophisticated consultants—on a project-by-project basis'.[15] This business model can apply across industries from manufacturing to service-providers such as event management. Why the 'reluctance' on the part of employers to have a stable, fixed workforce? Why encourage such restlessness? The rationale is efficiency and flexibility: 'Without the long-term commitment and salary burden of an extensive full-time work force, companies are more agile because part-time workers' hours of work can be easily changed and "temps" work just as long as required'.[16]

In a dynamic economy, an *agile* company needs an agile workforce. The company can be more efficient if they use 'just-in-time production'—a method that keeps a tight pace with the pace of consumption. For example, if one hundred office workers want sandwiches between 1 p.m. and 2 p.m., then sandwich bars employ workers for a two-hour shift in the middle of the day, releasing them when the peak is over. One employment website advises, 'if a company starts making a new product, all aspects of the launch—such as sales, marketing and telemarketing—can be handled by a temporary workforce. If a cross-country road show is planned, a temporary staff can be assembled in each city.'[17]

The disappearance of entire industries including the decline of the manufacturing sector in Australia has also meant a shift in work patterns.[18] In 1965, manufacturing employed one-quarter of Australians in the workforce but forty years later it had fallen to barely one in ten. The pattern has been repeated in the USA, Europe and the UK as jobs have moved to Asia.[19] In its place was not the old model of a job for life—secure, highly unionised work—but its opposite: casual labour.

A change from doing everything in-house to outsourcing anything that wasn't a key function (i.e. a temporary workforce putting together the 'cross-country roadshow') is part of the change in how we work. According to job search giant Seek: 'Some organisations are setting adrift whole departments and concentrating on "core purpose"—outsourcing such areas as accounting, legal, marketing and human resources. This is how they hope to stay in the game.'[20] When whole departments are 'set adrift' so are the workers that once staffed those departments. It's not uncommon for workers that were once employees to work outside the organisation but to sell their skills back to that organisation as a freelancer or casual worker. So you may have someone who was part of the in-house events team get retrenched, who then sets up her own small business with her former workplace as a major client. This is Pink's free-agent nation in action. However, with the downturn, should the company have a spending freeze on events, the 'free agent' doesn't get any work, and there is no safety net protecting her. The company owes her nothing. She is powerless before the economy.

Naomi Klein describes how 'enforced casualisation' of the workforce has a destabilising effect where 'in every industry temporary contracts are replacing full, secure employment'.[21] So pervasive is the feeling of insecurity in new economy jobs that William Bridges states in his book *Job Shift: How To Prosper in a Workplace Without Jobs* that the lack of job security in today's workplace means that 'all jobs in today's economy are temporary'.[22] Management guru Charles Handy agrees, saying that being employed by a corporation is 'not a guarantee anymore' and when they are made redundant they need to recognise that 'nobody is going to look after them in the way they used to'.[23] Further, he declares that 'in that sense we are all independent agents'.[24]

Even if your pay-slip and employment status indicate that you may be permanent, don't labour, like the Ansett staff, under the 'delusion' that you have a permanent job. Rob Lieber in *Details* magazine says, 'The time of considering yourself an employee has passed. Now it's time to start thinking of yourself as a service provider, hiring out your skills and services to the highest, most interesting, bidder.'[25] According to former Apple executive John Sculley, 'The new corporate contract is that we'll offer you an opportunity to express yourself and grow if you promise to leash yourself to our dream, at least for a while'.[26] The leash, it was implied, could easily be slipped off.

The message from all of this? You should not rely on your employer. You can only rely on yourself. To survive in this self-actualising, individualistic world, workers must develop their 'soft' skills, such as communication skills, adaptability and, most importantly, the ability to market themselves.

Although it undermines traditional collegiality, management gurus are encouraging workers to mimic the market and turn themselves into products—branding themselves like a product would and putting themselves in the marketplace or even their own workplace with the hope of gaining attention and distinguishing themselves from their colleagues/competitors. Tom Peters, a management writer who devised the concept of A Brand Called You (where readers are instructed how to market themselves like a product), says:

> Everyone has a chance to be a brand worthy of remark ...
> Regardless of age, regardless of position, regardless of the
> business we happen to be in, all of us need to understand

the importance of branding. We are CEOs of our own companies: Me Inc. To be in business today, our most important job is to be head marketer for the brand called You.[27]

He also encourages us to 'establish your own micro equivalent of the Nike swoosh'.[28]

The *Sydney Morning Herald*'s Money section prepped workers on how to adapt to this more individualistic world in its cover story 'Me Inc.' [29] The implication of the story was that no one else is going to look after you in this new Darwinist world of work, so you better learn how to do it yourself. Once you've established yourself as a brand, the onus is on you to get out there and sell yourself, either within your own workforce or as a free agent. In a branded world, you don't socialise, you network, you don't have friends, you have contacts, and your currency is your reputation.

In 2005 I spoke to Elliot Perlman, author of *Three Dollars* and *Seven Types of Ambiguity*, about this trend. He said: 'You turn your address book into a resource so that your friends become clients, and that's appalling. It's heading towards a situation where the only conclusion is you are only as good as your commercial value—and your friends are sources of commercial value—so if you can't advance someone else's career you are not worth much and vice versa.'[30]

It's a month before Christmas 2007 and I have gathered with some of my fellow citizens of the globalised, casualised workforce on the top floor of a pub in Soho, London. A free-agent nation gathering. We work for ourselves, move about, going where the work is. Outside there is a frost and an early darkness, too many *Big Issue* vendors and the hordes that squeeze and push down the wet steps of the Oxford Circus tube station. It's Christmas party season for some (accounting for the high volume of early drunks), and for us, residents of the free-agent nation, the end of this particular batch of work.

Having been working together for most of that year, we are limping off at different times to other projects—some are staying to work a couple of days a week, others are taking a break to return the following summer. There are no real goodbye drinks, since there are no real clean breaks, just drinks like these where we touch base and see who's going where and when. Charlie is going to South America to write a guide-book, Dean has been offered a full-time job with the company and is moving to their newsroom in Hong Kong, Paul is trying his luck in New York and Matt is going to stay in London. We are less like colleagues than journeymen who meet each other occasionally on the road. We talk about meeting again, maybe in the English summer when the work picks up. In our talk we sound like fruit pickers or itinerant labourers.

The fact that we are journalists yet our working lives sound more akin to fruit pickers is not mentioned. Nor is the fact that long-term planning or a mortgage is impossible in this type of working life—it's simply the way it is. We are foot soldiers in a new type of world—casual contracts, work spread across the globe, no superannuation or holiday pay but a glorious type of freedom that allows us to attach ourselves to news organisations for a bit, then leave for a better climate or another job. This new way allows us to keep it loose.

This new way of working is also in step with globalisation. It's work without borders, with 'dynamic' conditions that can be changed at a whim to suit the 'peaks and troughs' of the market, and as such we are on a variety of short-term contracts, or not even contracts—a day rate where work is boiled down to the barest transaction, of your day in return for some pay. This allows the company to have an agile workforce that can grow or shrink according to either the news cycle or economic conditions, almost without a lag, and therefore additional liabilities for the company. It scarcely needs to be added that none of us are wide-eyed and labouring under the 'delusions' of permanency.

It is restless work where no one sticks around long enough to develop strong ties, a solid reputation within the company or anything more than the most basic skills. It is a world where there is no such thing as promotion because of short-term contracts: workers are brought in to do a specific job and when that job is over they move on. In this new way of working—keep it loose, keep expectations low, have ties that are slack—there is no acknowledgment of the accumulation of experience, which appears discontinuous and meaningless to anyone other than the carrier of that experience.

I returned to Australia in January 2008 and found, unexpectedly, that I longed to buy a house, to own something solid—anything—but I had no steady income and did not know where the next job was going to take me. I dreamt of houses the way other girls dream of weddings. I was desiring of the thing itself, but also what it represented—security, permanence, certainty, a place to shelter when the world feels a bit rough, a shield to ward off vulnerability. I would press my face to the windows of real estate agents and dream.

Meanwhile, emails—dispatches from free-agent nation—bounced in at all hours from different time zones. They were writing books, researching travel guides in Columbia, doing freelance travel articles and hustling for work. Always hustling. I did not tell them I wanted to defect. Anyway, they would have told me that the land I wished to return to no longer exists.

It existed in 2003 but only just. I caught the tail end of the old ways, its vapour trails, as it left and politely shut the door behind it. When I started as a trainee journalist in 2001, an editor told me it takes a few years to feel the heartbeat of the place, that strange internal chemistry of a workplace that you can only really know through the passage of time. Heartbeat is many things: it's history, it's knowing the readers, it's seeing faces and changes come and go, it's knowing what works and what doesn't, it's developing an intuition about the organisation—how it will move and how it will react. It's knowledge that can only be gained from being there long-term and having some sort of stake in the place. It's time. It's the opposite of Malcolm Gladwell's *Blink* and his thin-slicing theory where you can *get* an organisation in the blink of an eye. It's also what the management consultants don't get when they come in with a business plan.

It was 2003 and the start of a wave of redundancies at Fairfax. Some of the longest-serving staff members were taking them. Some had been at Fairfax for thirty years and had known no other employer. The company had, in some cases, outlasted marriages, friendships, their youth—the heartbeat of the place was as intimate to them as their own. When it came time to say goodbye there were maybe 200 of us around the newsdesk and some more waiting downstairs by the lift doors. From there, the departed would be driven home by Fairfax driver John Foster. As the redundees exited Sussex Street for the last time it was to a cacophony of noise, the feeling of emotional static in the air. A leftover printer's tradition from the newspapers of Fleet Street, it involved banging metal on metal, anything we could rustle up—paperclips in jars, Coke cans, knives and forks from the canteen. The noise was deafening. All else was silent. We shook our bits of tin and steel and clashed our knives and forks. It seemed so tribal, emotional, so weirdly stirring that many people banging the tin were also weeping. This was the visceral point where the present was consigned to the past.

Years later in London when the newspaper I was working at was going through a particularly brutal period of downsizing, I noticed that although long-serving staff were departing on an almost weekly basis no one was clapped out of the newsroom, or, if they were, it would be only (quite eerily) by the one or two older staff members who sat at their desks and slow-clapped as the journalist walked out. The past and present were no longer meeting—that point had passed. The romantic notion of 'Fleet Street' was dead. Speeches for the departed were given later down at the pub, but there was no *communal moment* in the workplace.

I realised what sounded like the past back in Sydney was actually the past. People come unannounced and others left publicly unmourned. No one talks about the heartbeat anymore.

There are elements that are attractive about this new way. Who hasn't dreamt of telling your boss to 'get stuffed' and rolling troubadour-like onto the road—your skills in your swag, bedding down on a new patch of workplace, then moving on when restlessness hits and the sun beckons a bit brighter down the road. But, once on that road, things did not seem as simple or as easy and it became hard to make a distinction between being free and being cut adrift. Freedom is a double-edged sword. Certainty can be stifling. In a fluid, dynamic economy why should we stick to the conservative old ways of working? Sometimes the choice is not something we make—circumstances dictate that we cannot find permanent work in our field. But what happens when we submit to the restless economy? When we jettison (or are jettisoned by in turn) the structures that once tied us to the mast, the thing we once clutched when the economy became turbulent?

In this new way there is freedom from sick pay, long-service leave, colleagues, seniority, recognition and holiday pay. To be free also means to be vulnerable. Working as a free agent, I can't get sick, there's no holiday pay, no superannuation. The other thing is, I can't really plan. The work could dry up tomorrow and nothing is owed to me to cushion that blow. Even on the good days, when this arrangement feels alright, when I feel *okay* about working in isolation, when the light is good, and I've been for a swim in the crisp ocean in the middle of the day, when I am not sick of the songs on the radio, there is a low-level feeling of anxiety in the air—the shadow of the hammer before the fall.

One man who has been tracking all the change from structure to random bits of rolling work, who has been weighing up the benefits of freedom versus certainty, who hears the stories in his Melbourne office of workers who've been discarded like faulty machinery, who are no longer fit for purpose, is Charles Brass, Melbourne-based chair of the Future of Work Foundation.

'They are finding it difficult to categorise workplace relations. We've broken it apart with virtually no rules and what we are now in is a period where the rules are gradually emerging again—it's like an explosion, it's like after a bomb goes off—it takes them a while to find all the pieces then put them back together,' he says. 'We are in the first phase.' What will it look like? 'That's a very contentious question—that for me comes to the core of the issues that most people aren't addressing. The whole economic notion of how wealth and value is created and distributed is broken and we do not have a model to replace it.'

What will it look like? A picture is emerging although it's still sort of hazy. But while I can't see it, I can feel it—it has a texture. It has a lot of movement, it doesn't stop, it is borderless, global, it's powered by technology, not respecting time. Not everyone will survive in it.

My hometown of Warrnambool, in country Victoria, is a snapshot of a region in transition from an old economy of manufacturing to a new economy of 'churn jobs' in service industries such as tourism and hospitality. Three-and-a-half hours' drive from Melbourne, Warrnambool is an attractive beachside town that employed generations of local workers in the blanket, clothing and butter factories. When the manufacturing sector started to decline in the 1980s and 1990s, Warrnambool and its workers took a hit as one by one the factories closed.

A decade on Warrnambool is thriving and prosperous; manufacturing may be almost gone but it has a strong services industry and is successfully courting the tourist dollar. Outward signs of success are all over town: the gloriously dingy nightclub of my teen years, the Lady Bay Hotel, where Midnight Oil, the Angels, Jimmy Barnes and the Hoodoo Gurus once played, has been demolished and in its place is upmarket resort accommodation. Next door is a day spa. The old feed and grain store has also closed but there's a posh deli plus more restaurants and cafés than I can ever remember being around in my gourmet-deprived childhood (aged seventeen, I did not know what guacamole was). Unemployment is lower than the state average,[31] house prices are soaring and over the summer there are help wanted signs on the café windows.

Despite all of this, I can't help but wonder: have we knocked down the big stone factories where generations of Warrnambool people once worked only to replace them with a much more flimsy structure, casual jobs that won't hold up should a storm pass through? In the shift from relying on manufacturing work to industries such as tourism there is less protection for the worker—beneath the gloss of almost full employment figures there lurk some questions. There are jobs for those who want them but how many are secure and how many are seasonal? What are the figures of full-time jobs being created versus temporary, casual or contract positions? And how many are in sectors such as hospitality that are traditionally not unionised, leaving employees with less protection?

It's summer 2008 and I'm having coffee at one of the busy Warrnambool cafés and chatting to the waitress, Sally, twenty-nine. The daughter of a Fletcher Jones (once the local garment-making institution) seamstress, she knows that unlike her mother she will not be associated with one job, in this café, for life, but it suits her for now. She tells me she enjoys her job and as a casual employee gets paid a reasonable $17.50 an hour. But the work is seasonal and in contrast to her mother she isn't guaranteed a certain amount of work per week, nor does she enjoy the benefits of sick leave, holiday pay or long-service leave. She works between three and seven shifts a week.

Sally complains that some shifts, running to only three hours and in the middle of the day, are barely worth her while. Her roster also includes on-call work, where her employer retains the prerogative to call her in should the café get busy. When she is on-call she doesn't get paid extra but she can't travel or even be away from her phone. 'Even if I don't get called up I feel like I am working, because I am always conscious that they could call me in at any time', she says.

As the weather gets colder, and Warrnambool's long and often miserable winter weather sets in, her shifts will drop or dry up completely and it will be time to move on, maybe up to Queensland, following the sun and the work. Others like her, from Lorne or Portsea or Queenscliff, the cold Victorian beach towns, go where the sun is, because that's where the work is. This is restless work, where a feeling of instability is inbuilt in the work (shift times that change each week, how much work one is given dependent on how busy it is and, as a result, wages fluctuate each week). It is also seasonal work that has a geographical churn—the worker following seasons from state to state.

Sally doesn't expect to be employed all year round by the one workplace and she reflects on her mother's working life as though it was something from another era. Her mother was dependent on the one employer, Fletcher Jones, subjugating herself to not only the workplace but also to the union and the *routine* of it all. And in the end when the factory closed down, there was a certain bitterness that came from having thrown in your lot with one employer until the fag-end of its days. Sally holds out no such notions of a paternalistic employer of her own and knows that in bad times you have to look out for yourself. 'This place [the café] won't keep me on if it gets quiet', she says. No free rides for workers, not anymore.

Naomi Klein in *No Logo* spoke of a generation of workers around Sally's age, for whom temporary work was the norm. She wrote:

> We live in a culture of job insecurity, and the messages of self-sufficiency have reached every one of us … That message has been received most vividly by the generation that came of age since the recession hit in the early 90s. Almost without exception they mapped out their life plan while listening to a chorus of voices telling them to lower their expectations, to rely on no one for their success.[32]

Employee expectations of employers have been lowered but there doesn't appear to be much mourning for this. Check out the bookshelf of any business section and there are no books telling you how to be a better employee, instead they all want to prepare you for a better life free of your employer: *The 4-Hour Workweek*, *What Colour Is Your Parachute?*, *Feel the Fear and Do It Anyway!*

They say if you want to really make it in this world, you do so on your own.

Sally, like many others caught in restless jobs, has dreams that revolve around self-sufficiency: she wants to design and sell her own range of handbags. She is in many ways emblematic of her time— nursing dreams of autonomy, creativity, even a small measure of fame and recognition, and using transitory, temporary work as a way of keeping the world at bay until she finds it.

According to *Seek*, the preference of employers for 'Part-time, sessional, project, contract and temporary work … is shaking the world of work to its roots, and the implications for unprepared workers are significant. For those at the bottom of the system, those with the least resilience, there is potential for catastrophe.'[33]

What is this potential for catastrophe? Catastrophe for whom? And when? In a recession? Is this catastrophe due for all of us who are casual workers? All of us who have internalised so thoroughly the message of the market and kept it flexible, let the ties hang loose? Those of us who have *adapted*? And what about those referred to by *Seek* as 'those with the least resilience'? Who are they? The very old? The uneducated? The unskilled? The migrants? Those that haven't *adapted*? Those among us who despite being primed for, despite it being so prized, do not cope so well with change? Those that get lost in the restless economy?

Brass reckons the winners in the new system are those who can adapt: 'anyone who can embrace it is doing well and anyone who can't embrace it is doing badly … adaptability, resilience, self-confidence, trainability—it's not about technical skills. [It's about] soft human skills of being able to negotiate.' A winner, says Sennett, is 'someone who has the confidence to dwell in disorder, someone who flourishes in the midst of dislocation … The true victors do not suffer from fragmentation. Instead they are stimulated by working on many different fronts at the same time.'[34]

It's not just the rules of work that are being rewritten; it's an entire system of values. Loyalty, service, seniority and playing by the 'old rules', where there was a ladder and it was climbed incrementally— could it be that these things are no longer prized in the new economy workforce? Or even worse, is it their opposite number that is sought by companies: short-term, restless, junior, transient?

In 2007, economics correspondent for the *New York Times* David Leonhardt wrote a piece entitled 'One Safety Net Is Disappearing. What Will Follow?'.[35] It flagged one of the biggest trends in American workplaces, that of undercutting established conventions such as seniority in favour of efficiency. This trend creates restlessness in the workforce by breaking a covenant that has long existed between employer and employee—that is, if you perform, are skilled and loyal to the company, in return your pay will steadily rise in step with your seniority. There is a narrative of incremental moves up a ladder. This is no longer the case in the new economy model of work where 'an unwritten covenant between employers and employees is being annulled' and efficiency rules.

Leonhardt's story followed the fate of workers at US electronics giant Circuit City, which in April 2007 decided to reduce staff by 3400, or about 8 per cent of its workforce. The ones to go would be older workers, who over the years of service had built up their pay rates. The company thought they were being paid too much, and wanted to replace them with cheaper, less experienced workers. It invited the laid-off workers to reapply for their jobs, albeit at a lower rate of pay. The company called it a 'wage-management initiative' that was expected to save it US$250 million. Leonhardt writes that the layoff 'offered an unusually clear window on the ruthlessness of corporate efficiency'.[36]

The decision was devastating to Eloise Garcia, sixty-six, who earned US$15.13 an hour, typical of the experienced Circuit City staff (typical also of the average American worker). Circuit City intended to replace the workers with people earning less than US$10 an hour. 'At my age, I know it will be hard for me to find a job. I just couldn't believe that after 17 years of dedicated service to them that Circuit City would do this to me,' she said.[37] Alan Hartley, a car-stereo installer, said, 'We just bought our first house about two or three months ago, and I'm afraid I'm going to lose it … I'm not sure what I'm going to do. I'm hurt mainly because I love this company. I planned on retiring from it. I feel I've taken very good care of them, and I can't believe they did this.'[38]

Part of the squeeze for Circuit City was a price war over flat screen televisions (manufactured cheaply in Asia and Mexico), which had been driving prices down but squeezing Circuit City's margins.[39] At the same time, the company had to reckon with cut-throat competition from other retailers such as Wal-Mart. Wal-Mart had also been taking steps that seem aimed at pushing out more experienced workers, like setting wage caps for certain jobs and requiring people to work nights and weekends. Leonhardt surmises that 'tying worker's pay more closely to their performance' was reflected throughout corporate America.[40]

Australian companies are also increasingly tying in pay with performance. John Shields, a senior lecturer at the School of Business at the University of Sydney, told me that the trend was to 'move away from the current CPI-based pay rises to targeted increases geared towards individuals and small groups. What this system does is widen the pay gap ... the plodders are the losers.'[41] Ian Wilson, spokesman for the ACTU, said the trend rewarded articulate and confident workers who could argue their case for a pay rise.[42] They are the workers who maybe have succeeded at branding themselves (aka A Brand Called You) over and above their colleagues/competitors.

Subverting what was conventional wisdom, we can no longer take for granted the concept that service is rewarded by employers. Richard Sennett describes how 'the head of a dynamic company recently asserted that no-one owns their place in an organisation, that past service in particular earns no employee a guaranteed place'.[43]

New York Times readers were quick to condemn the decisions of Circuit City executives, pointing out that 'experienced workers who interact with customers can generate goodwill along with increased sales. Those who work in the "back room" (or on the factory line) can contribute important suggestions for jobsite improvements. They are also typically more reliable than younger workers,' wrote Max Alexander.[44]

Other *New York Times* readers called on the government to step in and regulate the often ruthless nature of the free market. 'I am sorry, but the option that is not viable here is to let massive companies like

Circuit City treat their employees like last year's stock', wrote Robert Guido. 'At least if we want to maintain the thin veneer of living in a civilization, as opposed to a Victorian industrial slum. Placing some controls over what companies do to their employees and how they can do it, even at the cost of higher unemployment and a welfare state, would be tragic only to folks who'd like to see us return to a 6 x 12 hour work week.'[45]

I go to the St Kilda headquarters of the Australian Institute of Management (AIM) and speak to Chief Executive Susan Heron about these trends. She wears a pinstripe ensemble that could be described as a 'power-suit', an eye-catching brooch and a chocolate brown coif. Her institute trains managers and she has the gift of being able to explain the corporate world with a refreshing no-nonsense lack of spin.

What happened in the USA with Circuit City does happen in Australia, says Heron, but it's 'old-style thinking'. 'If companies do that they've got a problem anyway—they are going under. Smarter companies are going to be strategic,' she says, as we sit at the board-room table under the shadow of a whiteboard which she leaps up to use a number of times when illustrating (literally) a point.

Heron explains that 'a lot of companies use contract workers to avoid headcount', which refers to the amount of workers in a particular organisation whose wages and benefits form part of the organisation's liability. 'A lot of the time when reporting, if it looks like they have a massive headcount, it's too heavy, too many people, you're not managing well. The return criteria that the market is asking for has pushed a lot of companies in that position. The upfront cost has been "who wants to be retrenched?" but the company incurs a real and often significant cost to bring them back as contract workers', as in the temporary workers who 'assemble the cross-country roadshow'.

But isn't that unfair to employees or an irresponsible business practice?

'I wouldn't say it's irresponsible, but it's not sustainable', says Heron, recalling the last recession. 'I had this mental vision in the nineties, when we had the recession, of people on this treadmill and they would get to the end and they would fall off, lying in a heap in a bucket—spent—and I think, how short term is that? They're not engaged, not earning money, not spending.'

Since the 1990s two tiers of workers have developed: those full-time permanent staff that enjoy the perks that flow from this status— holiday pay, sick leave and long-service leave and protection during troughs in the market—and a second tier of worker who enjoys none of these benefits or the security of protection. In this second tier are workers for the 'peaks', such as agency workers, who are becoming the norm in catering, private security, construction, food processing, call centres, hotels and aged care.[46] With the current recession, many of these workers are operating in a trough—having their hours cut, or shifts removed. Unemployment has risen sharply since 2008, with many of those joining the dole queues being those previously in casual or contract work. This two-tiered workforce is also split along gender lines. You only have to read Barbara Ehrenreich's *Nickel and Dimed* or Elisabeth Wynhausen's *Dirt Cheap* to see how much second-tier, insecure work is done by women.

The two tiers do not sit neatly together; rather they co-exist in an uncomfortable dynamic. This second tier can be used to (and quite often does) threaten or destabilise the first tier by undercutting the wages and conditions of the first tier and thus making the use of the second tier more attractive to employers. Say British unions, there is 'an epidemic of undercutting in agency employment'.[47] Even writ small, agency workers say that a chasm—sometimes a coldness or unfriendliness—exists with permanent workers when they are working alongside one another. Agency people are not classified as employees but workers. It unfolds something like this: the firm hiring the worker pays a fee to the agency and the agency pays the worker's wages. Any liabilities or benefits that usually flow between employer and employee are short-circuited by this arrangement because the employment arrangement is constructed to circumvent employer responsibilities. Sickness, holiday and maternity benefits do not flow from this type of contract.

Agency workers epitomise restless work not only with their rolling shift times, and their 'just-in-time'[48] schedules but with workers unable to place and identify themselves in the most basic way: that is, they cannot even answer the question, who do I work for? With agency work the people that are hiring you are not the people that you work for. Instead there is a complex web of contractors and sub-contractors and agencies. Somewhere in there lie your rights, maybe, but if they are there, they are buried.

Sometimes they are not there at all. Agency worker Rebecca Ames, thirty-four, connected British Telecom (BT) customers to broadband services for almost four years. She sat alongside BT staff but claimed to have received barely half their pay, with a fraction of their sickness and holiday benefits. 'About 60 per cent of the people in the office in Truro were on agency work', says Ames, who left BT because she said she could not live on such a low wage. 'Most of the people were doing the same job', she told the *Guardian*. 'For a 30-hour week I was receiving around £10 000 a year. BT staff on the same hours were paid £18 000. As agency workers we didn't get annual pay rises. You don't expect to be treated like that in a blue chip company in 2008.' The response from a BT spokesman was that 'Agency workers are a valuable and important resource. They help with the peaks and troughs of varying workloads that the business has to react to.'[49]

Further, companies react to the 'peaks and troughs' of their business in the way they organise their relationships with internal as well as outside employees. Sennett contends that these employer-employee relationships are characterised by casualisation:

> Employees can be held to three or six month contracts often renewed over the course of years; the employer can thereby avoid paying them benefits like health care or pensions. More, workers on short contracts can be easily moved from task to task, the contracts altered to suit the changing activities of the firm. And the firm can contract and expand quickly, shedding or adding personnel.[50]

Back in London, June 2008, and I am told I should meet Peter C, who typifies the product of the restless economy. He is desperately seeking permanency but is unable to find an employer in his field to provide it.

Peter C started as a journalist in a regional paper in the north of England after completing a literature degree. He then moved to London where he began working for a wire service, Press Association (PA). After three years at PA and keen to break into the national newspapers as a reporter, he began doing casual shift work. This shift work varied between working online and reporting for newspapers. It spanned an entire twenty-four-hour news cycle (often meaning that if Peter worked until 2 a.m. for one newspaper, sometimes he would be rising three hours later to work for another paper on the 6 a.m. shift). Sometimes the reporting was simple and all he had to do was rewrite wire copy. At other times it was complex, with certain shifts requiring him to make news judgements and analyse complex material such as government reports. In short, the work he was doing required him to have a range of technical competencies (particularly when he worked online) as well as display a range of skills, from writing, to analysis and news judgement, often in a very short space of time—'twenty-minute turn-around', he says.

The job also required sophisticated people skills. In the three news organisations that Peter concurrently worked for he was slotted into both night and day teams and production and reporting teams and was expected to pick up the pace immediately. He tried to remain unruffled when put at the blunt end of some difficult personality quirks. That was one of his most common causes of anxiety, says Peter. When he started on shift, he didn't know his workmates; he didn't know how they worked to be able to work in harmony with them. He had not been in the workplaces long enough to *know* people—when they are under stress and how best to deal with them, and when to ignore an outburst, and when to react. He spent much of his early days in eight- to ten-hour shifts feeling tense not only because he didn't know how the newspapers operated but because he didn't know how his colleagues operated.

Peter thought it would only be a matter of months before he would be put on a contract with a newspaper and then eventually be given a staff job; that is, permanent, full-time work. Instead, four years later, Peter is still a casual journalist. The career he had chosen, the one that he hoped would provide him not just with a stimulating, well paid and interesting way of spending his life, but enable him to save for a house and later have a family (essentially to sustain him) had been turned into bits of work. With these bits, Peter was barely able to construct a normal working week, let alone a career that would give him meaning and also give a shape to his future. He felt mostly in a state of suspension, 'like I was always trying to prove myself'. His working life had become 'a probationary period' but in many different workplaces and at different times of the day and night. He might please one editor on one paper, but the next night on another paper or with another editor he might do something to annoy someone or make a mistake. He could never 'just chill out'.

According to Sennett, 'Socially short-term task labour alters how workers work together. In interviewing temps, I've found that those who prosper in this milieu have a high tolerance of ambiguity.'[51] Peter's 'tolerance of ambiguity' naturally waned over time. The editors promised him more permanent work—giving him a cycle of hope that became thinner the longer it was stretched out. But months turned into years and instead of a contract he received a roster published just two weeks in advance with his mad, seemingly random shift times. Online 8 a.m. to 4 p.m. Newspaper 6 a.m. to 1 p.m. Online 3 p.m. to midnight and Christmas Day. 'They always get me to work on Christmas Day', he complains. As someone who didn't have a permanent job, but desperately wanted one, he always said yes.

'I don't blame the editor', says Peter of his immediate bosses. 'Often it's out of their hands. Management talks about headcount issues. They want the ability to shed staff without any of the legal responsibility that goes with it.'

Technology has also changed things at newspapers. More people are getting their news from the internet and advertising revenues for newspapers are falling dramatically. The industry itself is in a state of churn, which matches news consumption. Consumers of news are restless, getting information from many different sources (online, via mobile phone, radio, TV) at many different times. Static mediums such as newspapers find themselves lost in the pattern of churn. All of these factors plus the fact that many newspapers are owned by shareholders and have the same drive for efficiencies as any other listed company mean that workers like Peter are finding it increasingly difficult to get full-time permanent work.

After eighteen months, Peter was given a six-month contract with a newspaper. Now he was gunning for a staff job, with paid holidays, sick leave, and that additional psychological benefit of full-time work—the chance of having a working *home*, a space that he could make his own and begin to carve out his future. He became excited talking of one newspaper where staff were given sabbaticals of up to six months to write books. 'Imagine that', he says. 'You can go off to the countryside, or Spain—write a book and when you're done, your job is still waiting there for you.'

Peter's newspaper of choice seemed like the most enlightened workplace—one where you didn't have to make the difficult choices (book versus job, job versus children, children versus book)—one where you could do it all. But like the old way of working, this way was dying. People who got those jobs were dinosaurs who roamed through the world in the Old Times, before the efficiencies and casual work and the technology, before media itself uprooted, diffused and spun out into thousands of directions. As they went through newsrooms with their holiday pay and their sabbaticals and their security, the casual workers such as Peter seethed. 'I work harder than them but I have to. They can slack off. I can't.'

Yes, there was a 'two-tier working system', he agrees. 'I'm not sure if it's possible anymore to get to the next tier.' Peter wants to stop the restless pattern of his working life, but can't. Instead there are just more six-month contracts and the last three months of each contract, he says, are nail biting, 'stressful', full of anxiety.

As a way of preventing his legal entitlements as a casual worker from initiating, his employer now requires him to have a six-week break at the end of each contract, otherwise his status will be converted to that of a full-time worker and he will get the entitlements that flow from that. The six-week break suits the newspaper (who editorially are left wing and often highlight the plight of disadvantaged workers) but not Peter, who has no income for six weeks. He could have got another job in that time until his new contract started, or he could have tried to live off his savings. He decided instead to sublet the room in his north London house and move back in with his mother to save money. 'I'm thirty-one', he says. 'Too old to be living like this.'

One of my university friends Chris Davis, thirty-three, is typical of a worker who is well paid and working for a highly regarded organisation, but his workplace has appropriated elements of the restless economy—no long term, rolling contracts, no job security, no benefits—and applied it to highly skilled workers like Chris.

Chris lives in Rome and has had several contracts with a large transnational IT firm, working in logistics. 'It's a luxury in a way, as it affords me the opportunity to work and live in different places and have an unusual kind of life. I was on a short-term contract in Melbourne and I hated it. I didn't have the mobility, just insecurity,' says Chris.

December in Rome and we are going to a fundraiser for war-ravaged Afghanistan. Rome, as always, is la dolce vita, but for this crowd—an educated elite of international workers—it is a Benetton ad of races and colours, and also way-station, with many of them working on short-term contracts. As with Peter C, the organisation breaks up the work, so the worker's rights are not triggered. 'As a consultant they'd only employ you for eleven months at a time. It's something to do with their liability. I don't get any kind of pension. After eleven months it's a compulsory one-month break but they repatriate me to Australia. I had four months off—it can extend out. These days the only way they employ people is through contracts.

'Everyone they employ is on contract. I'm a consultant, next up you have a fixed term [which is] like a full-time job with paid leave but it's all for a period, six months or three years. You get really good health-care benefits. If you are on a fixed-term contract for five years, they have to give you a full-time job. After that you're unsack-able. They try and get rid of you by saying, "Okay—you're going to the Sudan!"'

This is the third time I've stayed with Chris in Rome and each time feels like the last. He is always about to move on or pack up or go to the next place: Africa, Indonesia, Melbourne, Canberra. Although he is footloose and fancy free he is also a hostage to his contract—making plans only a month or so in advance in case it all falls apart. He says of his employer, 'They are serially dishonest when it comes to contract renewal'.

Chris lives in a share house near the Coliseum and he says he's been fortunate that his room has become available again after another contract took him to Brazil, breaking up eighteen months of contracts in Rome. The constant in his life is the house cat Lamiso. It's a Roman cat, blind and weeping in one eye—an incontinent veteran of many street fights, a defecator outside the bedroom door. She has the run of the house and Rome—she will outlast Chris.

'I just consider it as something I can do for a certain amount of time', he says. 'If I had a family I wouldn't do it. At the moment when I can be flexible and can have months off, I do quite like it. But the grass is always greener.'

Chris considers people who are on contracts to be better workers, as 'more dynamic people work in contracting—you are in a crowd of people who are better at their jobs than the permanent people'. As to whether dynamic people are attracted to insecure work or whether insecure work makes them 'more dynamic' is not clear. But what is clear is that this type of work does not engender loyalty, either to the company or to the people who facilitate work, such as recruitment consultants, who Chris calls, 'pimps and vampires trading in human flesh'.

He says, 'I feel less loyalty [to my employer] because I am constantly in the process of renewing the contract and it's a waste of time. In reality they leave it to the last minute to get the paperwork signed.'

But in the uncertainty, in this short-term world, planning for the long term is difficult. These are people who avoid mobile phone contracts, broadband connection, long-term leases, relationships even, because they don't know where they'll be in a few months' time. They cannot *plan*. Says Chris, 'I signed up for a twelve-month contract with my internet service provider because I'd put if off for so long. I am sick of being able to think only one or two months ahead.'

Rome after midnight is great. Fewer crowds, a mellow vibe in the bars, all those old buildings looming up from their cobblestone moorings—more alive, more sinister now that it is night and silent and the street is emptied of day trippers and romantics. Chris and I sit at the bar ordering one, two, maybe three glasses of wine. I smoke his cigarettes. As we used to do in college, we sit around and talk about life: secure job versus travel, security versus freedom and our friends back home and the choices they've made. His contract is up for renewal again and the future seems up for grabs. I'm currently unemployed and travelling. Adventure seems to be winning over security for both of us. La dolce vita—sweet hedonism—or a refusal to grow up and get, you know, a real job, a permanent job? A question haunting the edges of these conversations with Chris or any number of my friends is: are we getting too old to keep living like this? Are we such children of the market and lifestyle, such creatures of a 'dynamic economy' that we are so in tune with its relentless beat, so unable to settle, even if we intend to?

A few months later, back in Australia, I ring Chris. He is still in Rome, Lamiso has been sulking and job security is still elusive. 'This morning I was told I had a contract until the end of December, then an hour later they told me it was only until the end of April', he says. But he has finally installed the internet and this Easter is planning a trip to Cannes. 'Spring is flirting with Rome', he says. 'I think I'll be here for one more summer.' I smile, having heard that before.

It's 2008. I move back to Sydney for a while. The building has a 1920s chestnut caged lift and rooftop views of the bridge and Opera House, but I find during the day I need to escape because of the sound of the nearby jack-hammering that rattles the teeth in my head. In the Kings Cross library, cockroaches climb the walls and out the window is a canopy of browning leaves, sheltering the creatures of the Cross: the girls in high heels, smelly men in old suits with everywhere eyes, and burger wrappers, beer cans and cigarette butts that swirl in a wind that seems unsure of which way to go.

It's not the only thing that seems to be going both ways. The Labor government is operating with hurricane speed in Canberra; motion is everywhere. The weekend newspapers run pictures of the prime minister sitting on the ground, head cocked in a sort of listening pose. Click along the image gallery and it's a beautiful Hollywood actress, also at the ideas conference, click some more and it's an actor with a stubbly beard who has also played the cartoon character Wolverine listening too—and later laughing—and then it's a standing ovation for a beaming prime minister.

Yet, just as the winds of Rudd's big ideas blow in, so too blows economic uncertainty.

March and April are white-knuckle months as my parents try to sell their house after they bought a new one at the peak. Friends are the same. I stay the night with one family desperate to sell. There is furniture I don't recognise in the lounge room, hired to make a good impression. Interest rates have their third rise in as many months. Other friends who own a café in the outer Melbourne mortgage belt complain that every time there is a rise, business the next day is quiet. Their coffee machine stops for a breather. Everything stops for a breather. There is a spike in mortgagee sales and gloomy financial stories in the papers. Property prices are dropping. Confidence is dropping. Some sort of long, long bull-run is stalling. Which way is the wind blowing? No one's quite sure. This is six months before the recession hits—but of course we didn't know it then. All these things are signs—the shadow of the hammer before the fall.

In Sydney during this swirl, very few people I meet seem to have full-time jobs, the old fashioned nine-to-five kind. People I meet— doctors, journalists, graphic designers, teachers, sales assistants— have a litany of descriptors after their job title: part time, casual, free-lance, self-employed, on contract. All the combinations of how to be and how to click into the work world are played out in Sydney, a place of flux and motion. It is the only city in Australia that styles itself as a global city and as such there is more of a global way of doing things: fast and loose, transitory. Many people I meet in Sydney appear as if poised for flight—they'll do one thing for a while, but then they'll do something else, somewhere else. They are everywhere, these people that do a combination of things, and do those things *for now*. But it is part of the Sydney character to have half an ear cocked, half a bag packed, ready for the *next*.

In May, at a barbecue at the yacht club in Rushcutters Bay, I meet an animator in her thirties who has been working freelance for years. 'I've always been able to get work', she says. But then again she acknowledges that there has always been money to do projects and in the ten years she has been working, economic conditions have been buoyant. 'But they get rid of people like me, the free-lancers, when there's no work around.' Boats bob in the harbour, the last of the champagne has been poured, the shadow of fear that moved across her face has come and gone. That hasn't happened yet, when there's no work around—the thing that everyone is afraid of—the recession.

In Coogee I meet a sub-contracting clown doctor embedded in a complex labour-hire web that can occur in the relationship between corporations and charities. She is hired on a daily rate by a multi-national company that makes chocolates and donates her time and services to the Randwick Children's Hospital. I have dinner with her and a freelance graphic designer in the backyard of the designer's Coogee home. The grass in the yard is long and smells sweet swaying in the breeze. The designer rolls homemade cigarettes and clears away the pasta bowls. The women, both in their forties, talk about their jobs in the way they may have talked about men. How it's good *for now* but they also feel insecure. How it works—but for *how long?* What about the future when they are old and grey? Or when times turn bad? Who will look after them?

Although the sub-contracting clown doctor doesn't have a full-time position because 'it's a charity so there are no full-time positions', her part-time work intrudes into the rest of her life. 'There's emails every day so you have to follow up—it seeps in. There are a lot of part-time employees and you get emails from them at 10 p.m. and you think why are they there [at work] so late?' She is also affected by the seasonal nature of her work and she finds she needs to adjust her yearly spending around it. 'September to December I can earn a lot but in theory I need to work all year round.'

The designer misses superannuation. 'Having a full-time job where they pay your super is fantastic', she says. But the only jobs she has been offered have been casual or contract work that doesn't include super. She is on the second tier of the two-tier workforce. She would love to agitate these places for full-time work, 'but they've got you by the short and curlies because they know you're a single mother', so she takes what she can get. 'If I enjoyed the job and someone offered me full time I would jump at it. [But] companies want short-term contractors.'

And out of all this motion—restlessness. Says the clown doctor of her workplace, 'if you start with this company you bring your own farewell card because they are always saying goodbye to people'. Workers are not expected to stay long with one company anymore, rather they enjoy the flexibility that companies offer and find it easy to leave because they feel no ties or loyalty. We sit, uncertain for a while in the quiet suburban dark, and wonder just who is creating this restlessness: them or us?

Charles Brass meets me in his office, a suite in Little Collins Street, Melbourne, and it is evident that he has taken an intense interest in the way work has morphed into its current form. He has hundreds of work-related books on his shelf—everything from *What Color Is My Parachute?* to *No Logo*. When I mention a particular writer or idea he twists towards one of the shelves, 'I've got that here, somewhere'. During the interview he also turns to his computer and forwards me recent reports, pulls out flow-charts and explains to me what a figure of 5.2 per cent unemployment *really* means.

Brass's interest in work came from his role as HR manager at Ford, where he saw firsthand the weakening of the manufacturing industry and changes to the industrial landscape. Now he counsels workers looking for a change. I first came across Brass on the internet. His company, the Future of Work Foundation, operates a clipping service. In the stark, spare language of sub-editors, the headlines give a concise picture of work in the new economy—people working longer hours or else unable to get full-time jobs, but plenty of casual and temp work on offer.

In the clippings you can see the cycles; for example, an article from *Time* magazine in 2001 was headed 'Part-Time Recession: Now that hard times have hit, the part-timers are getting hit harder than most'.[52] And this in 1998—'Irreversible Trend Towards Contract Labour'.[53]

'One of the dilemmas of the modern world is that there are not enough jobs', Brass told me. 'In the 1950s and 1960s the expectation was a promised path. It was secure, it was stable, it was permanent and it was pretty well guaranteed. Now work is much more contingent: circumstances dictate. Some circumstances are determined by individuals, so you now have young people saying, "Stuff you, I don't want to work for you" and you now have employers saying, "Stuff you, I don't want you to work for me".

'It's less reliable, less secure, more random, more haphazard, more contingent. I'm one of those who believe there's no such thing as good or bad—it's both … the good thing is people can now construct lives. You are not locked into something just serving out time because it's all you have. The downside clearly is people find it more and more difficult to economically survive because they can't attach themselves to work in a way that attracts lenders of money—and even renting [becomes more difficult]—because they don't look stable enough. It's a trend that's being reinforced by both individual behaviour and corporate behaviour.'

Brass doesn't advocate a return to the way things were. He acknowledges a job for life for many was a form of oppression. But back in the 1960s, 'things were so much more comfortable in so many ways; everything was conspiring. We had a centralised IR system with a minimum industrial wage, tariff barriers—everything—it was a nice, cosy comfortable world that's all but disappeared. [Now] anyone who can embrace it is doing well, anyone who can't embrace it is doing badly,' says Brass. 'Every one of the things that made full-time work secure has disappeared. With contracts of all kinds replacing awards, and they all have termination clauses, it has a greater flexibility than ever before.'

When Brass worked in Human Resources, 'if you saw a résumé with more than three employers they were unstable. Now if you see a résumé with less than seven they are too boring—it's changed very quickly. Around two-thirds of people are in what we used to call full-time work—still overwhelmingly the majority, but as a percentage it's decreasing.

'There are all sorts of ways people are attached to organisations—that piece of research hasn't been done. It's so variable that research-ers are finding it really difficult to categorise. They are finding it difficult to categorise workplace relations. We've broken it apart with virtually no rules and what we are now in is a period where the rules are gradually emerging again—it's like an explosion, it's like after a bomb goes off, it takes them a while to find all the pieces, then put them back together. We are in the first phase.' What will it look like? 'That's a very contentious question. That for me comes to the core of the issues that most people aren't addressing. The whole economic notion of how wealth and value is created and distributed is broken, and we do not have a model to replace it. The notion was that businesses create wealth and people get a share by going to work for that business. Their spending of that share of the wealth created other businesses and that was the model. [But] most of the conventionally done economic stuff doesn't need people anymore.'

This fractured, broken-down system, with its piecemeal approach to work, makes many workers vulnerable in a downturn, says Brass. Those in the second tier are particularly vulnerable. 'There is no question that people are more vulnerable to economic downturn than a generation ago because then we had a centralised employment and industrial relations system and you had to deal with unions, tribunals and awards. People would be shifted in bulk—you would negotiate for 200 or 300 people to go. Now employers can do it one at a time at a whim. Gone!' Brass clicks his fingers. 'Just like that.' Brass adds that we can expect 'there will be a much closer link in time between the unemployment rate and the economy. There used to be a lag between these two and a buffer. Employers now have the opportunity to manage their workforce far more than they did thirty or forty years ago—"just-in-time labour"—and the government is aware of this.'

We wrap our talk up. Brass is taking his daughter to see a Stoppard play and I am late for a dinner in Brighton. Back on Little Collins Street I feel on a downer, I can't dislodge the dread. Brass tells me, 'We are in this end of the big cycle. We haven't had this experience of such a long period of prosperity before, so it will be interesting to see what will happen.'

What will happen? I ask nervously.

'We haven't got any mass rallies of any kind. However vulnerable most of us feel, we haven't resorted to collective action; if it gets bad enough it will be back. It hasn't been bred out of people.'

Or has it? I'm not too sure. Work in the new economy is about the individual, not the collective. We have spent the past fifteen years absorbing the reality of 'less reliable, less secure, more random, more haphazard, more contingent' work. In this decade, for the first time ever, John Howard–style enterprise workers outnumber the old-style trade union members.[54]

Who's to say we would rise up in support of our fellow workers?

The restlessness has changed us—we are a bit more hardened now.

It is a Friday night in Port Fairy and the air smells like sea mist and freshly mowed lawn. It's the first night of the annual folk festival and I'm sitting on the grass with some old school friends watching one of our number play in a band. We drink wine out of plastic cups and holler at the lead singer. After the set I am asked about my book.

I talk about the end of certainty, the rise of casualisation and the death of a job for life. Kim Grundy-Garner says she couldn't imagine anything worse than a job for life. Aged thirty-three and with four young children, the textbooks and the experts say she's meant to be the sort to hanker after security, but instead she likes variety and flexibility, being able to make decisions about her work and time. She is a naturopath who works in several nearby towns at different times and could think of nothing worse than having a boss. The group seem to give off a collective shiver. Working for someone else can often feel like going back to school—get the wrong boss and you are infantilised and stymied—better to take a risk and work for yourself.

They tell me about friends and relatives who (like Sally's mother) worked their whole lives in Warrnambool's now defunct industries, Fletcher Jones and the Woollen Mill. They had a job for life until the manufacturing industry bottomed out, but couldn't get work after the factories closed down—they'd been doing the one thing far too long. They were protected, to an extent, but that ended up being to their detriment. Flexibility hadn't been bred into them, and like patients who hadn't been inoculated against a new, virulent virus they were unable to survive in new economy conditions.

In workplace terms, they died.

The next band comes on, the conversation wraps up.

My friends are not mourning the end of certainty—they are celebrating it.

In 2005, I managed, with a great deal of cursing and assaulting the snooze button, to attend (in my capacity as the *Sydney Morning Herald*'s *My Career* editor) an early-morning breakfast seminar hosted by a recruitment company. The reason we were assembled in a conference room of a chintzy Sydney hotel at 7 a.m., with plates of untouched glazed pastries and jugs of filtered coffee, was that a new generation were entering the workforce and their bosses weren't quite sure what to make of them. A self-styled 'Gen Y' consultant, Peter Sheahan looked perky as he sang for his supper. The new workers, he said, would 'leave one job for another to get a pay rise. There's not much loyalty to the company but they do have loyalty to brands. They respond well to flat organisational structure. They are used to being entertained and stimulated and want to take this into the workforce. They don't like mundane jobs. If you treat them badly at work they will SMS, email and tell all their friends what a bad employer you are. They will have twenty-nine jobs in five industries over their lifetime.' [55]

Discussion afterwards was lively. This generation didn't want to work their way up to the top, said one manager. They expected the best jobs immediately and gratitude for even showing up, said another frustrated boss.

I later wrote a story on it and found no shortage of people to tell me that this new generation were breaking the rules before they even started playing the game. 'I did unpaid work experience for six months and got the tea, but we've had to send work experience girls home when they've said, "We're not here to get the coffee"', Mia Freedman, then editor-in-chief of *Cosmopolitan* magazine told me. 'They want to redesign the [magazine] cover.'[56]

Flexibility—that term beloved of chief executives but which strikes fear into many an established employee—has been reinterpreted by younger workers who have grown up in an insecure but relatively job-rich work environment. 'They are turning flexibility on its head', says Johanna Wyn, director of the Australian Youth Research Centre at Melbourne University. 'Young people themselves have taken the idea of flexibility on board. They're now living in a way that causes problems for employers. But it's so-called flexible work practices that have helped to cause that. I think that's quite a nice twist.'

Wyn found young people have met the market's need for flexible workers—such as the demand for casual and contract labour—by prizing flexible work conditions above job security. What's in it for me? they ask. If employers break up the traditional structures, free their workers from the covenant, send them out into the marketplace with all its winds and gales, all its vicissitudes and risks and opportunities and near-death experiences, the workers will become a bit battle-hardened, a bit less likely to throw everything they've got at the job.

During the breakfast seminar I thought: instead of wondering *what* Gen Y has turned out like, shouldn't we be asking *why*?

Social researcher Hugh Mackay says young workers embrace flexibility purely because it's become reality. 'For their parents "job insecurity" is a shock and a challenge but it's simply part of the reality for the members of this generation, and they are incorporating it into their approach to work.'[57] In other words, they were born into this manic restlessness and that has become their natural habitat. They feel at home in flux.

Adele Horin in the *Sydney Morning Herald* argues that the labour market doesn't offer Gen Y the same prospects for full-time employment as for their parents' generation. It is difficult for those without a degree or trade qualification to get full-time work; and for those who do get offered work 'entry-level jobs are invariably probational—young people are put on contracts, or given part-time work, or traineeships, rather than a permanent position'.[58] When 'probational' style work becomes the norm, when flexibility is prized above all else, you have a generation of workers emerging who have no experience or expectation of full-time, permanent work.

Workers and employers are locked in a flexibility two-step. Flexibility is what the market has started to impose on workers but, according to Hugh Mackay, it's also what workers, both young and old, want. He contends that younger workers 'want jobs where they can have greater control over the management of their work and their pattern of working—when to be in the office, when to work from home, when to take a day off, when to work full-stretch without a break'.[59]

Matt Bolte, thirty-four, of Melbourne, works as an agency nurse and describes the work as seasonal.

'I have a contract for eighty hours a fortnight but that's not guaranteed. I can only work up to eighty hours a fortnight. I ring up each Monday and say I'm available and they say, "We've got work" or not. It's very seasonal, particularly in school holidays where a lot of nurses are mums so they're not there. Right now you've got new grads starting so I don't get as much work. In the wintertime I get a lot of work—ninety-six hours a fortnight because the nursing staff are sick and the general population is sick.' But as an agency nurse, Matt doesn't get sick pay so 'if I'm sick I'm not working and if I'm not working I don't get paid'.

Matt does not see himself working in one place for very long and views the work in a transactional light: they pay him for his time, which allows him to live a lifestyle he wants. It is a priority that he is able to control his own time. 'Being an agency nurse suits me as I can pick and choose when and how often I work and where I work—if they ask me to work [ward] 6 East and I don't want to work 6 East then I don't go. I prefer working in different fields as I get a different knowledge base. Yesterday I worked on the neuro ward—it's all heads and strokes. But then I can work in the oncology ward the next day.'

Remaining disengaged from work politics is one of the advantages of agency nursing, says Matt. 'You don't have to get tied up in politics and personalities. Clashes in the ward—you can quite easily get tied up in inter-office politics, which can be detrimental.' According to Dan Pink, work politics and work friendships are unnecessary distractions in the free-agent nation.

> From infighting and office politics to bosses pitting employees against one another to colleagues who don't pull their weight, most workplaces are a study in dysfunction. Most people do want to work; they don't want to put up with brain-dead distractions. Much of what happens inside companies turns out to be about … nothing. The American workplace has become a coast-to-coast *Seinfeld* episode. It's about nothing.[60]

Matt is not so concerned about the churn that comes with agency work, as he has made a deliberate decision to focus on other areas of his life—in fact, he seeks loose ties as it means his identity is not so bound up with his employment. 'Lifestyle takes precedence over work. We live in Fitzroy and go out lots and dine out lots—I work to live and not live to work. With the group of friends I've got, we're all in the same boat. We all work to afford the lifestyle. Among my nursing friends, work is primarily there to pay the bills, to go on holidays, and another reason people do nursing is to work overseas.'

Paul Howard of Melbourne relies on flexible work so he can pursue his first love: music. On the weekends, when it's warm and there are outdoor festivals and the crowds drift in their summer clothes towards the music, you may hear him singing. The 32-year-old Melbournian rigs up a stage on the back of his ute and travels around the state strumming his sweet songs and selling his CDs. 'Baby, I'm a lighthouse', he croons. I stand with his mum. We holler and call out for more, more. But during the week he is known as 432; as in '432 come off the freeway, there's pallets to collect in Heidelberg'.

Paul works as a casual courier for a Melbourne company. 'It's five days a week but I could do one or none', he says. 'They might have a pallet for me to pick up with steel bars or just an envelope. If I want to finish work at 2 p.m. then I can. They work a run for me accordingly.'

Paul has been working as a casual courier for seven years and enjoys the freedom: 'I drive and go bang! a line for a song so I pull over, write it down. I love that flexibility.'

He is aware that as a casual he is vulnerable in a downturn, so he doesn't take his employer for granted. 'I respect the fact that my employer provides me with this opportunity because it's a rare situation and I know that by showing loyalty to them they'll show it to me [but] at the end of the day it's a marketplace. If there's $100 000 worth of work they divide things and it's better to keep on their good side.'

As a casual Paul is in charge of his own expenses. 'I have to look after my own superannuation, tax and associated costs, like fuel. I'm on LPG fuel so it doesn't get too bad.' But despite the hidden costs and insecurity, working casually is preferable to working as a full-time employee, mainly because as a casual Paul gets to control his own time. 'I would do full-time work if I was the boss. In this job no one tells me what to do and that's important. I like to be able to decide what to do from day to day, rather than say, "I'd really love to do that but I can't".

'I have a home—the mortgage is the only driving element that I need to be in control of.' And of course, there's his true love—music. 'Since I was twelve I wanted to do music. It's very tough to be a musician and also have the things that everyone else has—a nice car, go on holidays, so I will always pursue flexible work while my first passion is music. I have a musician's mind—I've never been driven by money, I just want to enjoy life without being excessive about it.' The courier job fits in with that 'as there are no gigs at 9 a.m'.

The 'flexibility two-step' is at work here with these restless work patterns—workers such as Matt and Paul demanding flexibility and getting it—and the work itself configured with a focus on flexibility.

Who are the losers in the restless economy? After all, the move towards flexibility, temping, just-in-time labour and casual and contract work will only suit some workers. It suits workers like Matt Bolte and Paul Howard who derive their identity and meaning from things outside the workplace. It suits Chris Davis (for now) because it offers mobility. It suits Kim Grundy-Garner because she doesn't like to feel tied down. But what about those it doesn't suit, such as Eloise Garcia of Circuit City, who feels she has been betrayed by her employer? Or Peter C, who needs to have a 'work home' in order to feel a deep sense of personal security?

Not everyone is enamoured with flexibility. Not all of us want to 'keep it loose' and ties weak. I meet Janet, a 46-year-old TAFE teacher from regional Victoria, who has been agitating for years for improved job security: to move from the second to the first tier. Despite being well qualified and well liked by colleagues and students, she has struggled to get permanent work. She's not a footloose and fancy-free worker who can roll with the punches and a constantly shifting job market. She is held in the region by geography and family, caring for her elderly father, who has dementia. The restless economy is not a place where she feels comfortable.

'I'm not going anywhere', she says. 'This is where I live, this is where I'm needed. It was important for me to get a permanent full-time job. There are a lot of permanent part-time jobs, particularly for women. The call centres came here in the 1990s and I could have got regular hours there but I wanted to use my degree and I wanted to teach,' she says, almost sounding apologetic about wanting to use her skills and qualifications. But for the better part of a decade, this meekness was bred into her: the only work Janet could find was sessional or casual teaching.

The education sector, as well as the commercial sector, follows a just-in-time workforce model. Janet explains: 'The reason for sessional is that the syllabus is changing—you only employ people if the hours are there. They let sessional workers go because they may no longer run programs they teach. Our ESL [English as a Second Language] co-ordinator was there for years as a sessional and she rang up to get her hours [at the start of term] and there was no job for her. It was very underhanded. She felt very dark, very let down, she didn't go back to TAFE.'

Recently a new manager meant a new way of doing things and to her relief Janet was given a contract. 'The contract is initially twelve months, then it's ongoing, like a rolling contract. Now I get holiday pay, sick pay and annual leave.' The difference in status has meant Janet now feels more engaged and secure in the workplace: 'I'm a permanent. It's great now. You have a desk—that helps. And you get invited to staff meetings. As a sessional you feel very disengaged from the whole department.'

The feeling of security has had a flow-on effect into other areas of Janet's life. 'Anything could happen with Dad. He could go downhill fast or stay the same. I can't control that, but at least now I feel settled in my work, that bit of the future is under control and that makes all the difference.'

It is not much to ask for: a desk, a pigeonhole, the chance to attend staff meetings, the ability to plan a bit for the future. But this is what many workers are fighting for. In the battles of the new economy talking ideologies is a long-ago luxury; instead our new Waterloos are *contracts*.

So how do we balance the demand for 'flexibility' from both workers and employers alike, yet also give those workers who need it a measure of security?

I am told by a number of industrial relations journalists to ask Peter Lewis. Lewis, a former journalist turned union media strategist, meets me out the front of his workplace, Essential Media. Sussex Street is an interesting part of Sydney, where the pointy tip of Chinatown and the pointy end of the NSW Labor party collide. We head to a nearby Chinese restaurant to eat glazed pork, salt and pepper squid and prawns and talk about work. Will he be as optimistic as AIM Chief Executive Susan Heron that smart companies will not treat their employees like 'last year's stock'?

Or will he agree with sociologist Richard Sennett who believes that through the 'work churn' there is disengagement, which, in turn, rents the social fabric and creates a pervasive insecurity? And I am intrigued by what he might think of Charles Brass's analogy of the work world being now in pieces and how it will come together again.

Lewis, now in his forties, tells me he was once typical of a restless worker, staying in one job for a few years then moving on, but in the last ten years he has been building up his business. When he was in the restless stage he wrote a book called *Tales From a New Shop Floor* about how young people were managing their working lives in the 1990s.

Now Lewis believes there is a 'two-paced labour market'. 'There is an odyssey period where you try everything before you see what fits and have a home base for your career. People hit a point when they have kids and it changes. The churn is for the first ten years, then after that people want to settle down.' The trick he reckons is that when people want to settle down and have job security, there will be jobs for them that give them and their family stability. 'The question is whether our employment structure reflects what we want out of life. You don't want to stop the odyssey period but go too far the other way and you can't get a sense of continuity or community.'

What is certain is that everything is changing in the workforce—the way of doing things is up for grabs. 'In Australia we are having a debate about what the rules [governing work] are', says Lewis. 'Security is the most important thing for a lot of workers, [but] you shouldn't have to write the narrative from day one.'

We part on a street corner, but not before he urges me to read Friedrich Hayek, an academic said to be one of the inspirations behind the architecture of Howard's WorkChoices scheme.

WorkChoices holds some sort of key to understanding the pervasiveness and entrenchment of restless work. WorkChoices was in part the former Howard government attempting to enshrine into policy the values of new economy work—the values of individualism, looking out for yourself and feathering your own nest. According to the *Monthly*, at its core, WorkChoices aimed to make the individual pre-eminent in the workplace.[61] Could the fact that WorkChoices was repugnant to many Australian voters be an indicator that even though we may perform restless work, we have not wholeheartedly adopted its values?

Andrew West and I are sitting in a pub in Pyrmont, eating Thai food and talking about WorkChoices. It is the end of a soggy Sydney summer but, not only that, it is also the end of eleven years of Liberal government. Now in Kevinland, I am particularly interested in whether and how WorkChoices contributed to the Liberal party's defeat.

Andrew West is the *Sydney Morning Herald*'s industrial reporter, Bob Carr biographer, and long-time observer of the political scene at both the state and federal levels. West says, 'A lot of this materialism was not something for which people necessarily strived, but if it is something easily attainable or you have very easy credit and you think the economy is coming along and you walk into a shop where you can buy a giant flat screen TV for $2000 and no repayments for the first three months then $10 a month, people think "Okay, that's easy enough". Howard made the mistake that people were locked into materialism but really they wore it lightly.'

West reckons that in the second half of Howard's reign, people 'realised while fripperies were becoming cheaper, like CD players and four-wheel drives, the most essential things in life, like housing, education and health care, were becoming out of the reach of most people'. West believes that 'Howard never quite detected these trends. If you tell me I can buy a new four-wheel drive for $30 000 with $50 per week repayments I can think, "Yeah, why not?", but Howard mistook this as the ultimate aspiration for a lot of people. [Anglican archbishop] Peter Jensen said the real aspiration of the aspirational class is to have more and better family time. Howard misread the political mood.

'Howard thought people would be prepared to endure all sorts of degraded work conditions to have the boat. [But] Australians placed a higher premium on balance. Philosophically it [WorkChoices] was about balancing the power in the workplace in favour of employers. It encouraged the worst aspects of Australian life: ratting on your workmates and crawling to your boss, and Australians particularly deplore this. As long as you know the only thing you have to sell is your labour, then people are very conscious of the potential to be exploited. People don't like the idea of being pitted against their workmates. They may be competitive in a game of darts but they are not sufficiently competitive to do their workmates out of a job or out of money by undercutting their workmates in a race to win their boss's favour.

'Fifty per cent of Australians told pollsters that Australia is a meaner place under Howard. The meanness started in the early nineties as a response to the recession: "I don't deserve what I've suffered and now I have to look after myself". That's where the more introspective nationalism came in. It was a response to globalisation. A lot of the meanness was in response to the fact that globalisation and money markets were changing the way of life.'

So have those under thirty, who may have no memory of a time before Howard, absorbed the values of the age—a sort of osmosis of materialism and acceptance of this 'meanness' as the norm?

'They might be materialistic in the sense of having grown up with broadband internet, iPods and digital TV. They say they want these things because they don't know life without them,' says West, who describes himself as a non-materialist ideologue. 'I never thought of myself as materialistic for wanting a TV. If you can get something at comparatively little cost the human instinct is to say, "May as well", but are we willing to make a serious compromise to keep getting these things? I think not.'

While WorkChoices has been shredded, and many Australians still would 'rather be fishing', nonetheless the restless in the economy and the restlessness within has altered the way we work and the values that we learn through our experiences in the workplace. It is an unavoidable fact 'that globalisation and money markets have changed the way of life'.

The old-style economy rewarded service, loyalty, mutual commitment, trust, diligence and a steady accumulation of skills and experience. Workers were in it for the long term, and there was a ladder and hierarchies that everyone could see and climb. Workers did not dwell in ambiguity to the degree that they do today. The new dynamic economy is short term, rewards adaptability, detachment, 'superficial co-operation',[62] and soft skills such as communication and teamwork, yet also a strong sense of individualism, such as the ability to market or distinguish yourself ahead of your co-workers. Says Brass, 'It's not about technical skills, it's soft human skills'.

By the age of thirty, Liza Boston was a veteran of no less than four corporate collapses. Her work history epitomises something of the times. Ambitious, educated and mobile, she's been downsized, had a dozen short-term contracts and is now, at age thirty-four, an entrepreneur. She has been a part of the churn and survived. In fact, her adaptability has allowed her to thrive. Now running her own show, Cracked Pepper, a consultancy based in Melbourne, her business concerns are also zeitgeisty: the environment, online media and corporate and social responsibility.

She tells me, 'I'm helping a lot of my friends transition at the moment'—a seer, maybe helping fellow travellers find their way through the restless economy. 'When I was at uni [studying arts/ commerce at Melbourne University] the dream was to be a captain of industry, get into a global corporation and work my way up.' To this end, she got a place on the Ansett graduate trainee program and then, aged twenty-six, took time off to go to London and work in the booming telcos market.

'The roles were really interesting. I moved into management more from marketing; it was more about the project and the excitement. I had a short attention span. It was important I worked for a big name or a big brand. They have the resources, give you more exposure, more interesting projects. I didn't really understand then what it meant, these big companies—the core of them,' she shrugs, like at the core there was something rotten, 'but at the time you don't know what you don't know'.

Boston moved in a world that operated on contract labour. It could expand or shrink with the minimum of interference from labour laws. 'Everyone at WorldCom was on a contract—they just grew so quickly—even my boss was on a contract.' WorldCom was 'putting fibre [optics] in the ground from Rome to Spain. It was going nuts … Then when that went under I read about it in *Time* magazine—I thought, what's it all about? I had dinner with the CEO and he said, "Well, we had a great time spending all those millions", yet everyone else was sad and in shock.'

The company she was initially working for in the UK, Eircom, had also collapsed and brought with it the understandable onset of existential angst. 'At WorldCom I was really shocked when that went under—it really threw me. It made me just question everything. It was around the same time Ansett went under. My whole résumé was redundant. I worked so hard at uni, and I'd been so competitive for these roles, I started to really question what it meant to work for a company, and around that time I started to question things like corporate governance. I think around that same time Enron went west and there were a lot of high-profile corporate collapses, and I thought, what are we? What sort of people are we working for in these evil, corrupt organisations? They weren't all corrupt and evil but WorldCom was. Then I started to think more laterally about companies, environments; how do we become more sustainable?' The collapses left a bitter taste in her mouth. 'I definitely saw people badly treated, particularly at Ansett; pilots committed suicide—that was a social tragedy, the hidden human tragedy.'

Boston eventually accepted a full-time job at the National Australia Bank (NAB), '[but] I still treated it like a contract. It wasn't my cup of tea.' She began taking her laptop down by the river to work, avoiding the office environment. 'I started thinking about making a transition because there was no meaning in what I did. I was having these physical reactions to it. I ended up in hospital for an operation, stress induced. At the NAB they would say they were a values-based organisation but you wouldn't find any evidence of that in the way they treat people … they make the same ambit claims about how they treat the environment.'

Boston left the National Australia Bank in 2004 and took a one-year contract with the Melbourne Fringe Festival at a fraction of the salary she was receiving in the corporate world. 'Getting there it was like landing in Nairobi, they were so relaxed, they were laughing. But it was a really confusing time. It was hugely hard to step away from the money. I am leveraged—I've got houses and cars and to walk away from the NAB where it was hugely lucrative …'

Boston describes going back to short-term contract work in the finance industry: 'On the first day I walked to 333 Collins Street I had a physical reaction in the lift. My new boss saw the look on my face said, "You're not going to come back tomorrow" and I never went back. I thought, that's it, I'm going to have to create something—a company that makes a difference. I was reading No Logo and reading about this capitalist, consumptive beast [the market], and it was about encouraging brands to become more robust and sustainable in their thinking.'

Boston's company Cracked Pepper opened in July 2006 and employs a mix of contractors and permanent staff. 'We have a lot of contract workers in here, but they are not treated like contractors. I don't think there's any distinction at all. It helps us ramp—there are peaks and troughs in terms of our workload. You have to be able to create a scalable work force to be cost effective … now I am totally on the other end of the stick.'

For Boston, there are no regrets. 'At the bank they say bring your whole self to work but no one does—but here you can be who you want to be.'

At twenty-four, Simon Moss is transitioning. Right now Moss is a portfolio worker, the type of work that has inbuilt restlessness—bits of work in bits of time in exchange for bits of money. Moss organises his life in colour-coded blocks of time, each one representing a different commitment: soccer club, exchange program, tutoring, consulting with Microsoft on a technology project. Some of his work is not for profit, other bits are paid, and then there's university on top of that.

But he is turning twenty-five, an age when in this time of extended adolescence adulthood begins, and so he is considering the switch to full-time employment. He has a lot of choice but right now he's not really sure whether to trade flexibility, mobility and diversity for security and stability. Moss arranges to meet me at Universita Café in Lygon Street, Melbourne, and says to look out for a guy in a yellow cap.

The rise of casualisation and creation of many more *bits* of jobs, rather than full-time positions, led to new thinking about how we can organise work. In the mid 1990s management guru Charles Handy predicted the demise of full-time work; instead we would evolve into our own micro-businesses undertaking a range of projects. A career could be created from many part-time jobs, he argued. This became known as the portfolio career. The idea is that you identify your skills and interests, then you obtain part-time employment, temporary jobs, freelancing and self-employment with different employers that when combined are the equivalent of a full-time position. Having all your eggs in different baskets protected workers from downturns and retrenchments, in the same way unions once promised. So if you were a graphic designer who had contracts with a vodka company and a newspaper, and the newspaper suffered a downturn, then you would still be able to draw some income from your work with the vodka company. You are partly protected not by the collective (for example, unions) but your own spread of risks between employers.

I get to Lygon Street and there's Moss in the sunshine drinking tea, wearing a yellow cap covering longish brown hair, and tapping out something on his laptop. Now is a block of time in between classes at Melbourne University where he is doing a masters degree. He is also in the real world, making it happen.

His rapid-fire conversation is peppered with intriguing nuggets: 'In Ghana we started campaigning around ritual servitude. I did a doco there which we showed through the community education work we're doing back in Australia, which was great'; 'I was in Davos on behalf of the British Council as a young person'; and 'I did consulting to Microsoft in 2004—we worked with the futures guys—it was blue-sky, open-space thinking stuff. All because I responded to an email I got through web community TakingITglobal.'

Phew. Okay. This is high-status restlessness. But an hour later I still don't know exactly what Moss does. There is some tutoring, setting up a university exchange program, running a soccer league and that murky job title, 'consulting'. The roles include a lot of the soft skills that Charles Brass believes are essential for the modern worker to survive a dynamic economy: the ability to negotiate, work in teams and communicate, plus adaptability, resilience, self-confidence and trainability.

The winners in this new economy are those who are flexible, can adapt to change and get another job as soon as the last contract dries up. In other words, they are people just like Simon Moss, who has so internalised the temporal, adjusted to work that 'drifts in time', to the whole restlessness inbuilt in the economy and the now fragmentary nature of work, that it would be strange for it to be any other way.

Moss doesn't consider work to be a job in the traditional sense; rather he approaches it as a series of projects. 'The system I've been running since 2004 is usually one major project in full swing, something small on the side, something winding up and something starting, some paid and unpaid. I have had I think the coolest eighteen months I could have hoped for. That's the space I've been working in.'

It was when Moss first caught a plane to Germany when he was sixteen that he changed from being a 'community-based person' to a global person. After he came back and finished school, 'that's when I started doing portfolio work'. The shift to portfolio work, considers Handy, is an inevitable product of the times: 'we are all responsible for our own lives to a greater extent than we were; that doesn't mean we will all be entrepreneurs, although we all need to think of ourselves much more as independent agents'.[63]

Moss describes his choice to be a portfolio worker in these terms: 'You don't need to be a slave to anybody else—maybe I am being really impatient but I want to do it my way—I don't want to tie myself to one thing. I know the sorts of things I like to do, the sorts of projects I like. This is the rule I've lived by in the last few years: don't tie yourself down to something when there are other things that may really excite you and you like. It's not that you don't commit to things. I'm young, I have no real commitment—it's only to myself, as I am not tied down to anything, mortgage, partner or anything like that. If I have an opportunity to take risks that may not work then I can do that.'

Moss identifies with the traditional definition of a portfolio worker but is also aware of the limitations of such a definition. He asks, 'In many ways does it stop being portfolio work and just become what I do? In my working life and own life there are no barriers. Work is what I do. Many of my recreational hobbies are work related and many of my friends are work related. There are a couple of friends who aren't work related so one of the things I do is carve out time regularly for them. One of my friends doesn't like the work I do. He says, "It's not my thing", so we just play stupid games and chat.'

With the merging of work and life, 'my life is one giant exercise in project management, incorporated in which is project managing time which is specifically not project related, so that's bigger blocks of time, two or three days, then it's lots of time here and there but no full days. I have just become so used to my time being arranged that way.' Moss blocks his time out by the hour and each six months he'll 'take a full day to step back and see what I am doing'. On the bedroom wall of his Glen Iris home is a list of goals. 'One is to run 12 kilometres in an hour, another is to get my driver's licence and another is to organise a two-week holiday after June 30.'

The US *Today Show* profile on portfolio workers went for the glamorous combinations: Deborah Rivera, an executive recruiter/ chef-hotelier; Rashid Silvera, a high-school teacher/fashion model; Bonnie Duncan, a dancer/teacher/puppeteer; and Alex von Bidder, a restaurateur/yoga instructor.[64]

In Sydney, the *Sydney Morning Herald* profiled twenty-something Joseph Dickson, who spent weekdays as a lecturer in the investor education department at the Australian Stock Exchange and each Sunday working at Bondi Beach as a surfing instructor. Darren Higgs was running a similarly dual career. He worked as a financial planner in North Sydney during the day while three nights a week and every Saturday he worked as a martial arts instructor.[65]

Some workers took the idea of portfolio work to its extreme— building a career with not just multiple employers but using vastly different skill-sets—such as Peter Bates, a former investment banker turned rare pig farmer, cabinetmaker and business adviser. 'None of the jobs I do relate to each other. I have no background in farming', says Bates. 'I enjoy greater security since I haven't placed all my eggs in the proverbial basket.'[66] Bates isn't just protecting himself against an employer going bust; he's protected against entire industries going under.

While Handy extolled the virtues of portfolio careers in terms of the spread of risk and flexibility, for many workers it's less about freedom and more about self-responsibility; the underlying, continuous thrum of tension in knowing that employers will no longer look after you when times turn bad. You have to build your own safety nets, be wily, adaptable, an ever-morphing form to suit an ever-morphing employment market. It is about becoming a worker in tune with a workplace in flux. As Handy says, 'we are all independent agents'.[67]

US career commentator Penelope Trunk sees portfolio careers as symptomatic of the times. 'Notoriously raised as latchkey kids, they are dropping out of corporate life and cobbling together a bunch of part-time careers to pay the bills and keep one foot on the career path', she says. 'For people in their twenties and thirties, a portfolio career is a means of self-discovery, hedging one's bets, and protecting their quality of life.' [68]

Young people who aspire to work in creative industries get the message about the need for portfolio careers before graduation so they have an armour against the 'bitsyness' of work available. Clare Douglas, a placement manager for the Fashion Business Resource Studio (FBRS) at the London College of Fashion, expects fashion graduates to have a portfolio career. An FBRS survey found that 'recruiters do not want to employ graduates who are able to do only one thing'. 'We need students to be flexible and not just go for one position. They need to be versatile and able to adapt to different roles,' Douglas says.[69]

The idea of portfolio careers—and the inherent philosophy behind it of spreading risk and encouraging flexibility—appeals to many employers. Some are even encouraging their employees to establish a portfolio career within the organisation. A spokesperson for Network Rail in the UK says, 'We need to create an environment that gives Generation Y the flexibility and variety they want in work. We have to allow people to switch jobs within the organisation and still move up the ladder. We must let them build a portfolio career within the organisation. At the moment, people tend to stick with one discipline.'[70]

Many organisations have already morphed into forms that connect with an emerging class of portfolio workers. Handy dubbed these workplaces 'shamrock organisations'. The shamrock is symbolic of the different groups of people within the organisation: the professional core of employees; the contractual fringe where all work that could be done by someone else is contracted out; and the flexible labour force, all those part-time workers and temporary workers.

Can engaging in a strategy to ward off risk itself be a high-risk strategy? For those starting their career, lack of focus on one area can mean you do a lot of things okay but don't really excel at anything. David Trapnell, head of the Sydney finance recruitment team Ambition, says people who want portfolio careers may find it hard to get top jobs. 'If you want to get to the top, you need to focus and specialise. If it's quality of life you want, you might pursue a portfolio career.'[71]

A portfolio career is the opposite of what Sennett calls craftsmanship, which is basically doing one thing many, many times until you become exceptional at it. Think of an artisan who handcrafts violins or the chef whose mastery over a dish ensures perfection or a room attendant who has perfected the art of 'hospital corners'. Sennett contends that the depth and obsession required for craftsmanship does not fit with the new flexible organisations that are 'based on short-term transactions and constantly shifting tasks'.[72] In fact, the craftsman 'stands at the opposite pole from the consultant who swoops in and out but never rests'.[73]

The popular image of a portfolio worker is some zany dude who when he isn't riding between jobs on his skateboard is having a meeting with clients about his new t-shirt range at the local café before heading off to DJ somewhere that night. He is what many of us aspire to be—mobile, operating outside oppressive corporate structures, taking their money but not playing by their rules. He is our own best self. Our free self.

Yet for every model/actor/DJ/software designer we read about, those who are most likely to work in a portfolio career are those caught in the churn, coasting at the lower end of the market, the workers who haven't even made it to the second tier but instead juggle many different jobs, shift times, managers and demands, often to the point of high stress and exhaustion. They probably did not plan to grow up to be portfolio workers, but as 'permanent work is on the way to becoming a museum item',[74] many developed a portfolio career by default, simply as a way of paying the bills.

One suspects that the real winners of the portfolio careers, who benefit from this institutionalised flexibility, are those at the top of the pile with a rich contact book and favours to pull in. They can 'draw upon a fund of social capital'[75] that resides in their networks. They are people who already have a financial safety net, and can pursue a career consulting or sitting on boards after decades riding at the top in corporate jobs.[76] Asks UK Conservative MP and commentator Michael Gove, 'What will be the fate of those in the construction sector, those who work on oil rigs, agricultural workers and all those who rely on physical strength to complement their other skills? The debate, with all its talk of how easy it is to build a portfolio career across the generations, seems to be a conversation in which working-class voices are silenced.'[77]

Most portfolio workers toil in the backwash of the restless economy. They talk about their work stretching to six or seven days a week instead of four, they are isolated, their hours are unpredictable or antisocial, and they live with the unnerving prospect that a source of income could be cut off without warning. They are a species unprotected from the whims and changes of fortune of the labour market.

At a café in central Sydney I speak to David, who has worked up to five casual jobs at once to make ends meet. A 26-year-old singer, shop assistant, singing teacher, usher and bartender, he works many jobs in order to pay high Sydney rents and also because full-time work in his chosen field is difficult to secure. 'I've worked five different jobs at once. It was hard to fit in all the shifts. I used to piss off my employers because I was running around so much. It's very transactional—you go in and do the job. Management was really harsh at some places—it was a high school mentality: "Okay, who did this? Put your hand up", but no one worked hard for them, no one gave them respect. There was a lack of commitment.'

David drains his coffee and says a quick goodbye. He has to race to start his shift at David Jones. He finishes at 4 p.m., then has a half-hour break before heading to his evening job at the Opera House. He says he barely has time to 'come up for air', nor can he remember where he was working yesterday—'It's all such a blur'. Sennett asks, 'How can a human being develop a narrative of identity and life history in a society composed of episodes and fragment?'[78] He argues that a fragmented worklife, like David's, is damaging. 'Most people are not like this; they need a sustaining life narrative, they take pride in being good at something specific, and they value the experiences they've lived through', says Sennett.[79]

The ultimate damage people suffer under such conditions is corrosion of character, believes Sennett. 'Character particularly focuses upon the long-term aspect of our emotional experience. Character is expressed through loyalty and mutual commitment or through the pursuit of long-term goals, or by the practice of delayed gratification for the sake of a future end … How do we decide what is of lasting value in ourselves in a society which is impatient, which focuses on the immediate moment? How can long-term goals be pursued in an economy devoted to the short term?'[80]

In pursuit of short-term goals, we often lack witnesses; that is, someone or a group of people who we are with each day and share rituals that were common in the old economy: a birthday cake in the tearoom, praise for a project well done, support when you are under pressure—'where the deeper experiences of trust are more informal, as when people learn on whom they can rely when given a difficult or impossible task'[81]—where people see the milestones and the mill-stones, year after year after year. But we are moving too quickly to take note of anything but the most fleeting of our movements—the flap of the horse's mane, the chalky thunder and then echo of hooves underneath as we gallop past.

Nomad workers, also described as Bedouins, are named after nomadic Arabs who wander at will around the desert. Nomad workers roam from café to café, following the path towards the wireless internet signals and tables big enough to spread out their folders, papers, phone and laptop. They are a generation of mobile workers who attach themselves to projects, not companies. Rather than lease office space or work from home, they take advantage of cafés with wireless internet, good coffee and staff that won't make them feel too uncomfortable about staying all day.[82]

Time magazine calls it 'temping gone global'[83] while the *Times* says, 'Punch-in culture is out—a surgical attachment to a laptop and a mobile phone, and a willingness to travel, are in'.[84] It's also the logical blending of two of the biggest trends of work in a consumer age—contract work and mobile work—that is, work untethered from not only a physical environment such as an office but also untethered from a country. Technology has enabled the strings to be cut with ease. Now not only can workers cobble together a career based on short-term contracts but they can construct a life in many different countries. The possibilities for what sort of life may result from these elements are endless.

Do these workers feel the 'anguish of voluntary homelessness'[85] or do they feel like a 'citizen of the world'? Are they adrift or swimming their own race?

Time magazine profiled neo-nomad Paul Finster Fleming, a 43-year-old engineer who 'has wandered the world for the past seven years. His British passport boasts stamps from 45 countries'.[86] In that time he hasn't had a permanent job.

> Fleming is a global temp worker, a modern-day nomad who jets off every year or so to a new locale, where he contracts out to companies desperate for engineers savvy in mobile communications. He is earning three to four times the salary he once made as a full-time employee of companies like Ericsson—which is why he was sounding merry on a recent morning, heading out of Seattle on a three-month contract to train engineers for his latest temp boss: Ericsson. 'Now I go anywhere anybody pays me to go', he says. 'It's a good way to see the world. I'm meeting new people and learning new systems. Traveling the world, you become unique and invaluable.'[87]

According to the *San Francisco Chronicle* the neo-nomad trend is a response to increasing job insecurity. It is a worker taking charge in an uncertain environment:

> San Francisco's Bedouins see themselves changing the nature of the workplace, if not the world at large. They see large companies like General Motors laying off workers, contributing to insecurity. And at the same time, they see the Internet providing the tools to start companies on the cheap. In the Bedouin lifestyle, they are free to make their own rules.[88]

In 2006 Ben Keene, entrepreneur and author of *Tribe Wanted: My Adventure on Paradise or Bust*, was setting up an eco-tribe on a remote Fijian island. Now based in London, he has continued to be a mobile worker. He told the *Times*, 'There'd be huge costs in setting up an office: all I need is a laptop, a mobile and a passport; it's totally transportable'. His resources are all online and free. He connects with his global team via free Skype and video-conference calls.

Nomad workers require a degree of self-sufficiency and self-reliance that sits uncomfortably with the old model of work. They also need luck, favourable economic conditions—the recession is, quite predictably, hurting unattached, freelance workers—and a degree of room for flux in their personal life that flows with the fragmentary, transitory nature of their work.

In the restless economy, many nomads find that, cut adrift from a physical place of work and locked-in hours, there is a seepage of work life into their 'other life'. 'The day doesn't end', admits Ben Keene. 'It's addictive. I'm often logging on when I'm supposed to be asleep. And sometimes I wish I had the security of a base and a team in the same time zone. I can go for two or three days without any real physical contact.'[89] Remember what Richard Sennett said we need to survive in this type of working environment? We need to 'manage short-term relationships and one's self while migrating from task to task, job to job, place to place' and 'to develop new skills, [how to] mine potential abilities as reality's demands shift'.[90]

I am in Fremantle, Western Australia, a place caught perpetually in some sort of afterglow. The sun is hot but at 4 p.m. most days a wind blows in from the sea, cooling everyone down, chilling everyone out. The beach at the end of the street is inviting. There's a café on every corner. This seems to be a nomad hotspot. There are a lot of people sitting around on laptops, having meetings at the local hive, Ginos. Lots of cafés are wi-fi zones.

At a bar on the wharf with wi-fi, brewery and book exchange, I chat to Tony, who has been typing away on his laptop. He is wearing a t-shirt and no shoes but confesses it doesn't really matter what he looks like as he never sees anyone in a business context. All the work he does is online. Like Ben Keene, he too can go for days without any real physical contact.

Tony works in the morning, swims and gardens in the afternoon then does some work at night. 'This is the enlightened way of working', he says. 'I do enough to make what I need, then enjoy the rest of life.' But he says it took him a while to get used to that rhythm. 'Work had institutionalised me. I didn't realise until I stopped working in an office for a firm how much my identity rested on it. That's part of the horror of attaching yourself to work and realising there's nothing much left.'

But what is left? Sitting in a café every day with no shoes on? Being the relaxed 45-year-old guy in the Mambo t-shirt adrift in the good life, who has cottoned on to the 'horror of attaching yourself to work' and realises to survive you've got to put yourself first? Somehow this doesn't seem like enough. If we're going to murder then we'll have to create.

In the space of only a couple of years I had managed to move from stable employment to the sort of transitory, fragmented sort of work I am critiquing. I had a permanent full-time job, which I (maybe rashly) swapped for full-time freelance work in London. This was well-paid daily work that superficially differed little from working somewhere permanently. These roles didn't include things such as sick leave but it didn't matter because I never got sick. Then I moved another rung down and suddenly didn't feel so cool about things.

By 2008 I'm working for myself as a freelance journalist. It can be rough riding along this tier. I write an article for a Scottish magazine within the deadline only to be told offhandedly that the accounts department is a bit slow and it will be months before I get paid. I want to, but do not say (because it is embarrassing) that because 'the accounts department is a bit slow' I will not be able to pay my rent this month. I swallow my pride and borrow some money from friends.

I do casual shifts at an English newspaper and, once again, because of the monthly pay cycle it's almost six weeks before I get paid. They must assume a degree of financial planning or independent wealth that I don't have. I start putting groceries on my credit card. In meals out with a group, I put the entire thing on my credit card and they give me cash. I improvise, I am creative, wily, *adaptable*—all those things the new economy tells us we should be. But there is a fugitive quality to this. It doesn't feel 'creative' or 'dynamic'—it is depressing and terrifying. It's skin-of-the-teeth stuff and it feels deeply insecure to have no money in the bank, to not know when a 'slow accounts' department may pay you. It also engenders a deep sense of personal jeopardy that is counter-intuitive to any adult.

A senior journalist friend who has been in the game for a long time tells me I need $50 000 to play. That is, I need a nest egg of $50 000 because the way things are going now, I'll wind up destitute. So it is those 'with a degree of financial planning or else independent wealth' who can survive in this pointy end of the restless economy. I find that living like this is impossible in London, difficult in Sydney, manageable in Berlin. I contemplate going back to newspapers, but suddenly my inbox is full of bad news about another round of redundancies at Fairfax: the company 'will axe 550 staff in Australia and New Zealand … as part of a plan to bolster profitability'. The job losses come just days after the company reported 'that after-tax profits rose 47 per cent to $386.9 million … while overall revenue gained 34 per cent for the year'. In briefings for analysts after the result, company executives discussed taking 'cost-cutting "opportunities" this year'.[91]

As requested by my former colleagues, I sign an online petition protesting against the cuts but my cynicism about how companies are run has sunk so deep that I now believe petitions to be worthless. No one talks about heartbeat anymore. No one reads petitions. All is chaos. Stability has given way to disorder. The horses are eating one another. A profit increase results in job losses (or in a cheeky piece of Unspeak: 'cost-cutting "opportunities"'.) In this new low I contemplate a return to the law.

Some of my London friends visit me in Berlin. It is Sunday and the streets are slick with rain. We take shelter in Café November. Over tea, talk turns to the margins we are living in. Kate, twenty-eight, is losing her job at the end of that month after three years' service because the newspaper she works for will no longer be employing all the full-time freelancers (of which there are around seventy). She tells me that she lies awake at night, unable to sleep because she worries about how she's going to pay her rent and bills.

James, twenty-five, has a job at a business newspaper paying minimum wage in return for eleven-hour days. He says no one seems to have been working there for more than two years. His employer expects a churn of eager young graduates wanting a job and willing to work for next to nothing. This is the business model: staffing costs are low and turnover is high. 'No long term' is the message. James says, 'shoot me if I'm still there in six months'.

Peter, thirty-one, is on a break from his employer who, in ways similar to the employers of Peter C and Chris Davis, makes workers take compulsory (unpaid) breaks so their rights under industrial laws do not trigger. This global company is routinely praised for its business model and makes $1 million profit *a day*. Peter doesn't think he'll return from his break. He is going to slip down a rung to where I am, white-knuckled, still pyjama-clad in the afternoon, checking my bank account online with a measure of dread and fear. Peter graduated from Manchester University, Kate graduated from Cambridge and James from Oxford but that doesn't appear to give this trio any massive advantages in the workforce. Being bright, young and well educated is no insurance against submitting to work in the restless economy.

While it was largely the working class who suffered during the collapse of the manufacturing industry in the 1980s and 1990s, this recession is hitting the educated middle-classes who have trumpeted their autonomy and personal freedoms when undertaking contract work as opposed to being 'tied down' in permanent jobs. My friends and acquaintances who have lost jobs have been bankers, lawyers, journalists and architects. The *Australian Financial Review*'s front page headline for an article in March 2009 about the recession and job losses seemed almost celebratory: 'A Rude Awakening for Gen Y'.

The rain streaks the café windows. It's cosy holed up in here; we do not want to go back outside. I realise with a kind of piercing longing that I miss talking like this. I miss sharing experiences with those that are going through what you are going through. Maybe I miss having workmates and that much-mocked thing that used to come with it— solidarity. Work in the restless economy can be a lonely beast. It doesn't encourage deep collegiality, only 'superficial co-cooperativeness'. Look at the elements of the churn again: WorkChoices 'aimed to make the individual pre-eminent in the workplace'; free-agent nation was all about 'achiev[ing] a beautiful synchronicity between who you are and what you do'; a Brand Called You rested on the premise, 'we are CEOs of our own companies: Me Inc.'; portfolio work diffuses and dilutes relationships because you build a career with 'not just multiple employers but using vastly different skill-sets'; the uncertainty of con-tract work dissuades you from pursuing long-term relationships both within the workplace and also outside it. Remember my churn jobs from the 1990s: 'a world of loose bonds and loyalties', where 'people came and went—often unmourned, quickly forgotten', of 'temporal drifts and unsettling glimpses of meaninglessness'?

If there is a 'dread of meaningless which is man's fate', I'd like to think that we are dreading things together. Is there anything more awful than dreading things alone?

Mum emails. Dad is having a special party to celebrate his retirement from work. He has been there for thirty years. Almost my whole lifetime. I can't contemplate it. There will be speeches. Can I send a couple of words over? she asks. All that goes through my mind is how it feels to be the daughter of someone who has been in the same job for thirty years and who has (for the most part) loved his work. Growing up it felt like security. I felt *safe*—it was a feeling I took for granted. I can't imagine having children without being able to provide them with a similar sense of security.

When we ate together every night, both mum and dad discussed their work days. Dad would always be energised by the day and would explain—quite often in great detail yet also with discretion—what he had done that day, the challenges he had faced and how he had overcome them, the people he had met and how they had fitted into what he did. At the time it felt like normal dinner conversation, but looking back it was also a template that he was offering the four of us: work is wonderful, difficult, stimulating, meaningful, transforming, important, he was saying, night after night after night, year after year after year, and here's how it's done.

But how, I wonder to myself, can those lessons be applied when the workplace has transformed into a place of no long term? No one stays anywhere for thirty years now, and instead of a continuous narrative we have a series of jump cuts, disconnected from any coherent story. How can we develop our character through our experiences at work (as my father has done) in the churn? Where do we do our growing?

'Work, paid or otherwise, is inseparable from living a full and rewarding life', says economist Clive Hamilton in *Growth Fetish*.[92]

My first professional job was as an articled clerk, then a junior lawyer at a Victorian labour law firm in a reasonably remote industrial town close to the South Australian border. In the town there was an aluminum smelter and workers who were injured were often sent by the union through our door. As part of their compensation claim, the workers had to make what was called a section 98 affidavit, which detailed in fairly plain English, with numbered paragraphs, the narrative of their injury: how it happened, a description of the pain, the effects the injury had on their quality of life, etc. If you want to get a sense of how paramount and meaningful work is then you should read a few of these affidavits. For each man (for they were mostly men) the story of injury and incapacity was wrenchingly personal; it felt like his burden alone to carry, his highly individual curse. I guess that's what pain and loss feels like: intensely personal.

Many of the affidavits followed a remarkably similar narrative. The workers, mostly skilled and earning good money, often had families to support. Expecting a long-term future with the company, many workers had taken a mortgage in the town. The company was the major employer in the region and provided workers with the chance to train in different areas of the smelter, learn various skills and work their way up clearly delineated pay grades. The union was a strong presence at the smelter and as such the workers enjoyed good pay and conditions. In the course of the worker's linear progress, in their narrative of development and growth, a serious injury was a violent and disruptive event. It was as if 'the social contract had been torn up and the pieces set on fire'.

Graham Greene wrote in *The Third Man*, 'One never knows when the blow may fall'.[93] And so it was with these workers. In the aftermath the worker often seemed all at sea, as if he couldn't quite believe it had happened to him.

In this industry town where a significant percentage of the population worked in the smelter, to be injured and not working was like being 'cast out', and on the outside there seemed to be no place that provided the same degree of social inclusion as the workplace and the footy club (both of which mostly required a degree of physical health). There was an injured workers support group, which was surprisingly large and well attended for a town of that size, and some workers found solace there. In all cases, the injury caused the worker not only physical pain, but a psychic pain. Work was more than just work, it was pride, it was identity, it provided a sense of belonging, not just in the workplace but in the town where you would be positively identified as a 'smelter worker'. Because of the largely long-term nature of the work it was also, along with family and friends, a scaffolding on which character was developed and meaning was derived.

The loss of their ability to work meant many of these men not only suffered loss of income and debilitating pain, but also perhaps (and this was the hardest to describe in the bald language of an affidavit) the sense of themselves as men and providers. Their status. Themselves. As I recall more than one worker saying to me; 'it's a pride thing'. In interviewing the workers, it was not unusual for the affidavit to end with a description of other ailments that seemed to inevitably develop as a result of serious workplace injuries (most of which were back injuries). These often included stress, sexual dysfunction and subsequent marital problems, a growing dependence on alcohol and prescription medication, and—waiting there patiently at the end—depression.

It also seems to me, reflecting on the experiences of these workers, that to treat lightly the mutual obligations between a worker and a workplace, to say that we can derive all our meaning from *outside work* is to tell ourselves a falsehood. That to pull back from our commitment to the workplace and to let the workplace rescind from commitments to us, to be relaxed about the 'broken covenant', is to be playing with something dangerous and irrevocable.

It is, I suspect, quite unfashionable to support the creation of full-time permanent jobs. Stable jobs. Jobs where there is long-term mutual commitment. After all, as Gen Y consultants like Peter Sheahan say, no one wants those jobs anymore. They will 'leave one job for another to get a pay rise. There's not much loyalty to the company but they do have loyalty to brands.'[94]

The old way is stodgy. It is old school. Yet there's always been a troika of journalists I've admired who've seen past this fashion for dynamic work and advocated the structural and psychological merits of stable employment.

Elisabeth Wynhausen of the *Australian* has written about the experience of working in low-wage, insecure employment in her book *Dirt Cheap*, while the *Guardian*'s Polly Toynbee has written about the UK experience in *Hard Work: Life in Low Pay Britain*. Adele Horin writing in the *Sydney Morning Herald* highlights in her columns how full-time work can provide meaning and purpose.

Toynbee uses a caravan analogy when writing about those in low-wage and insecure employment: of society being a caravan crossing a desert, where the people at the back can fall so far behind they are no longer part of the tribe. She asks, 'When the front and back are stretched so far apart, at what point can they no longer be said to be travelling together at all, breaking the community between them?'[95] That this line of thinking has now been adopted by UK Conservative party leader David Cameron shows just how apparent the problem of inequality in Britain has become. The problem is now even more pressing due to the recession. The numbers at the back end will grow, as companies slough off the casual and freelance workers during the troughs.

In 2005's *Dirt Cheap*, Wynhausen talks of the Australian low-wage experience: 'Now we seem more inclined to blame people for lagging behind. And there are more lagging behind than ever before.'[96] Wynhausen contends that 'ruthless restructuring', which has aided workplace efficiency, has had serious consequences for millions of Australian workers, particularly the '2.3 million casual workers who are largely denied the perks of permanency—respect, security, predictability, paid holidays and sick days'.[97] Similarly, Horin describes how low unemployment 'masks the reality of job insecurity, people churning in and out of work, the hours people work ... and the scrabblers at the other end who piece together a life from 2 or 3 casual jobs'.[98] She argues that 'prosperity in part has been built on the back of the stressed and overworked'—the casual workers.[99]

That 'more [are] lagging behind than ever before' in 2005 at the height of prosperity begs the question: what's going to happen as the recession plays out?

Prosperity ... ah, remember that? How quickly things can shift. In April 2009 OECD chief economist Klaus Schmidt-Hebbel said, 'The world economy is in the midst of its deepest, most synchronised recession in our lifetimes, caused by the global financial crisis and deepened by the collapse in world trade'.[100]

The focus of the Australian government, as with many governments around the world, was to try to douse the effects of the global financial crisis through a range of policy measures, ranging from cash handouts to the injection of funds in training and job creation. Reserve Bank governor Ric Battellino declared that Australia was going through 'a very substantial decline in economic activity', which would result in a large rise in unemployment.[101] ANZ senior economist Katie Dean told ABC Radio that jobs would be shed but also that workers would lose hours and move from full- to part-time work.[102]

Remember Sally of Warrnambool? As a casual worker she is vulnerable to her hours being cut. So is Peter C. They were on the margins in the good times, and now, in the bad times, they face being further pushed out. Contracts can protect workers to an extent (but that protection lasts only for the life of the contract—a reprieve from anxiety for what: a year, six months, three months?). But it is only permanent, full-time stable work that can deliver a greater sense of security to workers—the sort of work being described as extinct, as a 'museum piece'.

As the global financial crisis hit everywhere, the way we operated during prosperity needs to be examined. We cannot assume that a restless, fast-moving economy will carry us swiftly to where we want to go. Sometimes this restless economy and our restless, rootless modes of work land us in a place where we don't want to be. A place where we feel highly insecure and vulnerable, where we are definitely not 'relaxed and comfortable'.

Being solely at the whim of the free market seems dangerous all of a sudden when the free-market system appears on the verge of collapse. It's not just jobs that are vulnerable but our idea of ourselves as agents of our own destinies. Of being people able to plan and dream. The *Guardian* newspaper interviewed workers (or ex-workers) whose retirement, travel, marriage and baby plans had been put on hold or scrapped due to the uncertain economic situation. The newspaper concluded that 'The casualties of this recession will be counted not just in job losses or bank foreclosures but in something less tangible … the recession is now pressing the button on ordinary dreams'.[103]

At the start of the slippery slope of the financial crisis—around September 2008 (when Iceland's banking system crashed, many of England's banks became nationalised and Lehman Brothers collapsed)—analysts interviewed on the BBC World Service were considering whether the crisis marked the end of rampant free-market capitalism. Lying in bed with a late summer flu in my Berlin flat and hearing the BBC talk seriously about the end of capitalism seemed surreal. Was it some fevered dream? For these experts in the eye of the storm, the problem was that the money markets and banks were incapable of self-regulation.

In April 2009, Australian Prime Minister Kevin Rudd took a similar stance. He attacked the ideology of 'extreme capitalism' that held that markets 'were self-regulating, that government regulation of such markets was interference and that the unrestrained pursuit of self interest was not only morally legitimate but equally to be morally encouraged'.[104] British Prime Minister Gordon Brown's response was to call the boom the Age of Irresponsibility, and encouraged Britons to revive the Blitz Spirit. He was perhaps forgetting that a previous incarnation of his government, New Labour, rose with and was intensely entwined in the boom, in everything from tax policy to cultural spin. Remember the boom-time branding—Cool Britannia? 'We are intensely relaxed about people getting filthy rich',[105] New Labour apparatchik Peter Mandelson said in 1998.

In this sudden shift in the economic and social climate, politicians are doing a volte-face, but what about the workers? We are not in a position to be so nimble. Where does the recession leave the solo worker—the restless worker in a restless economy? The mantra from worker and corporation alike for 'greater flexibility'? Right now it means greater flexibility to be dumped when times turn bad.

Only a few years ago, the restless worker was said to be empowered by the long bull-run of prosperity and a slew of self-help books that said work was about self-actualising and if you could brand and market that self-actualised self then riches would follow. What happens to those workers out there in the market at a time of such turbulence? I think of them standing outside when a sudden storm passes through and they are without shelter or even an umbrella. There's debris flying around, rubbish blowing out of bins, dirt and dust swirling up the streets, the wind blowing hard every which way. Those stranded outside in the storm are scared. What happens to those workers—out there in the market at a time of such turbulence?

Vulnerable is a word that springs to mind.

So which workers are the winners and losers in the restless economy? The winners have been those who are flexible, adaptable and don't expect too much from their employer. They are detached and they understand the phrase 'no long term', as opposed to the phrase 'heartbeat'.

A consultant who managed downsizing at IBM said once employees 'understand [they can't depend on the corporation] they're marketable'.[106] They create their own personal brand so that in the marketplace, even in their own workplace, they stand out. They offer something different or distinct from other workers. They are in competition with others they work with, while also being superfically cooperative. They are focused on their own individual trajectory rather than being truly engaged in teamwork. In the restless economy, a cynical worker uses work as a vehicle to get from A to B—to pay the rent, fund dinners out and travel. They don't want to be tied down to the politics and the pettiness—it's not in the job description, not a factor in the hourly rate. A job is stripped down to its most basic function. Your money in exchange for my time.

Just as companies have contracted workers out so have we contracted out companies as a crucial player in our inner lives: shaper of our stories, integral to our identity. 'I'm a Fletcher's man', 'I'm a CUB worker'; no one says that anymore—now identity is signalled through the products we consume, not where we work, such as 'I'm a Mac person' or 'I only wear Nikes'. Employers are no longer our intimates—one company there with us on life's journey; paternalistic, protective, also indulgent, to an extent, of our personal peaks and troughs as employees, during the times, maybe for months running, where we will not be as productive as when firing on all cylinders. A company that will allow us our fallow periods because they have seen us pull an all-nighter to complete a project or they know we have a baby with colic so may not be as alert, or they are aware of a recent bereavement and so, without fuss and without overt acts of sympathy, they quietly cut us some slack. In return we do our best for the company even though there may be *nothing in it for us*; in this old way, the interests of the worker and the workplace were entwined.

This kind of give and take only occurs in a relationship that has lasted for years; when each has proven itself to the other, when a pattern of reciprocity has been established, when there exists a covenant of mutual commitment. It is unlikely to happen when the employee is a casual or short-term contractor. There is no room for subtleties or peaks and troughs, for cutting each other some slack. There is none of the accommodations of a long relationship, the bagginess, the room, the act of listening to the other's heartbeat.

The old-style economy rewarded service, loyalty, mutual commitment, trust, diligence and a steady accumulation of skills and experience. Workers were in it for the long term, and there was a ladder and hierarchies that everyone could see and climb. Workers did not dwell in ambiguity to the degree that they do today. The new dynamic economy is short term, rewards adaptability, detachment, 'superficial co-operation'[107] and soft skills such as communication, teamwork and co-operation, yet also a strong sense of individualism such as the ability to market or distinguish yourself ahead of your co-workers.

The new economy suits workers that survive very well in the churn. Those who swing monkey-like from one contract to the next, and cope well with its unpleasant cost to the psyche: feeling adrift, the insecurity, anxiety, transience and instability. These workers have internalised the message of consumer culture, their identity is separate from their workplace (such as Matt and Paul), they may have seen their parents downsized in the eighties, and as Naomi Klein said 'rely on no one for their success'.[108] They have taken a measure of things (as children, their ears to the bedroom door, hearing their parents talk in worried, hushed tones about 'recessions' and 'lay-off') and have morphed sylph-like into forms that best suit the market. They know there are no paternalistic employers anymore where the weaker or more eccentric workers may have seen out their days with a measure of shelter and protection.

These are the winners: the free agents, entrepreneurs, nomad workers, consultants and portfolio workers who, like shapeshifters, can adapt to the ever-moving forces of a 'dynamic economy'. When interviewing the creatures of the restless economy, they exuded a strong sense of being in control, of steering their own ship despite the fact that they are unprotected when the economy takes a hit. But like good students they have absorbed the message of the market—be self-sufficient. It is their only way.

Peter Lewis is right. If you are footloose, fancy free and highly educated, casual or contract (churn) work can be brilliant. It gives you mobility, allows you to travel, and that all-important thing in our consumer society—the opt-out—not having to stick with something that is boring, or where you are poorly treated, or if there is a better offer just around the corner. It's about choice. The tedious today is tolerable if there is the promise of a better tomorrow—of flight and a future of new faces.

We can remake ourselves in new jobs and different workplaces. The old reputations that we may have carried albatross-like through our old workplaces ('she's slow, she's a gossip') do not haunt us in those first bright, clear few weeks. Although it's a double-edged sword—we also have to start again. We erase the past, our shining successes, and some of our status. We start new jobs without histories, other than the promises we made about ourselves in the job interview.

Being fleet of foot in a lightning quick economy, where workplaces aim to be gaunt, will give you a run on the inside track. But what happens when you dream of permanence outside the real estate agent's window? Or when you have children? Or when you look around and realise that the air of impermanence and instability that characterised your working life has seeped into your personal life? Where you don't own any furniture that isn't used or disposable— where certain crucial aspects of your life seem to be on hold because you don't really know where you'll be in six months' time? Where your no-strings-attached working life has morphed into a no-strings-attached life?

Work in the new economy, churn work, creates a feeling of insecurity, a dread that when something happens, there will be nothing to protect us. This makes us timid. Look at Peter C and Janet waiting around—sometimes for years—for contracts. They want a chair in the staff meeting, access to the tearoom, to fully engage with work— such small things, such modest requests.

We do not have the security of full-time employment and instead work on rolling contracts or day rates. We fume, but usually to ourselves as erosion of the union movement means there is often nowhere to go with our complaints except to the manager, who has 'headcount issues' and anyway is probably at the mercy of a higher boss, who is at the mercy of company controllers, who are members of a global empire located 2000 kilometres away. Distance and detachment—a disconnectedness characterises each relationship in the control chain.

We put in our timesheets and stew in our dread and anger but there's not much we can do about it. The most detached workers are literally as well as figuratively homeless—they work in cafés, 'paying their rent in lattes'. For the nomads, their notion of a workplace has been turned into 'central command' but it is a place that has been hollowed out of workers, it is an empty body, a sack of skin. There is no heartbeat.

We could, like Liza Boston, fight our way out of the churn and become entrepreneurs, but that takes an unusual strength of character to succeed. Liza herself now acknowledges that 'the shoe's on the other foot' and she uses contract workers to 'ramp' with the peaks and troughs. Many contractors, such as Chris Davis and agency staff such as Matt Bolte, say they wouldn't have it any other way but their ties to their employer are loose. Distance—once again—characterises the relationship. It is like in my churn jobs of the 1990s, where the 'employer has divested all sense of purpose and energy in the development of the employees'. The works gets done, and done well, yet a mutual apathy or drift characterises the employer–employee relationship.

Charles Brass optimistically believes that in a downturn there will be a return to collective action. Yet I am not sure. We have been architects of our own situation—our emphasis and insistence on flexibility has helped create the conditions towards our vocational homelessness—we have cut the workplace adrift from our lives, we belong nowhere. Somewhere in the prosperity years, the Howard years, we became flabby and lazy, we took the flatscreen TVs and the four-wheel drives and the credit cards and absorbed the messages of individualism that seemed so pervasive and *of the times*. It became difficult to focus on the weaker members of society, being so focused on ourselves—and so those trailing behind the caravans fell even further back. In a downturn more of our tribe will join them at the receding rear. Yet will we care? Solidarity has been bred out of us until it has become an embarrassing word.

Sennett's concern is that work in the new economy degrades character. The things that once built character—mutual commitment, long-term work that strengthened ties and developed skills—are not a feature of work in the restless economy. 'The conditions of the new economy feed instead on experience which drifts in time, from place to place, job to job', he writes.[109] I share the same concerns yet I also see a larger sadness. Work in the new economy atomises us—and makes us lonely. There are no longer shared stories, because our shared experiences are so fleeting.

All our witnesses have been shot.

TRAVEL

When did mobility stop being a blessing and instead turn into a sort of terminal restlessness?

For me, it could have been at the airport check-in counter when I said I was taking a plane to Sydney, only to be told I was already in Sydney. Or maybe it's when I consider the twenty-five houses I have occupied, in fifteen cities over the last fifteen years, or the fifty-five different beds in nine different countries over the last year, as I moved from place to place in a kind of manic, geographical ADD. Or the sudden career changes, or the dreams of immigration that occur every three months now, just after I become settled wherever I am.

I always told people that I wanted to move 'home to Melbourne' but I had been saying that for a decade and some sort of turbulence or restlessness inside me wouldn't allow me to settle—it worked like a motor I couldn't switch off. At age thirty-four, the big question in my life is not, thankfully, who am I? but the stranger question of which country do I want to live in? And what part of that country? And once there, what will I do? Then, will I stay or will I keep searching for the next thing that's going to hold my interest? And yet how, paradoxically, travel has lost its sense of wonder, its allure declining incrementally with each slow-walk through the airport's metal detectors, each long, empty hour waiting in a departure lounge.

Trying to work out the answer to the question of where I should settle has inadvertently led to an almost frenzied circling of the globe, checking out this place and that—each place more enticing and glamorous and promising than the next. Until choice becomes impossible because of too much choice, and the inevitable paralysis of indecision means that the process of moving around—just to see 'what's out there'—is repeated and repeated and repeated. The savings I have are not funding a meaningful 'journey' but a sort of cursed and ragged voyage where I do not feel like a footloose and fancy-free adventuress so much as like Odysseus himself—bobbing out on the sea for eternity, unable to dock.

There are travellers I meet on the way—people who pop up in Sydney and London, Berlin and Hong Kong—who are following their own internal migratory calling. They are always appearing in unlikely places like characters from a Jason Bourne film—or maybe cameos in a documentary about globalisation—the nation-stateless workers such as the lawyer I had dinner with in London who trained in Melbourne, but was soon to be transferred from London to Shanghai and harboured dreams of moving to Sydney. Over Peking duck he talked of 'experience fatigue'. Or the business school graduates on six-week to twelve-month project placements, gritting their teeth through lonely nights and spreadsheets in monogrammed hotels. Or the hospitality workers who circle the globe with only carry-on luggage in an endless summer, until their restlessness defines them, or the ski instructor dude, the travel-fatigued consultant, the jetlagged foreign correspondent, and the banker whose friends call him the International Man of Mystery. Their life is not about the here and now, but always in thrall to the *next*.

Sometimes the nation-stateless say they feel settled right now, but other times there's a bit of anguish not far below the surface. At a late-night party, standing by the drinks cabinet, the 2 a.m. question is asked—where do I want to live? Where do I belong? Everywhere and nowhere.

The people I meet in all these places, at all the parties, become friends. But there is a sort of anguish in this too—of always leaving, an endless round of leaving-dos, of dipping meaningfully into someone's life, for a time, before going again. Skating the surface of your own life is one thing but skating the surface of another's sometimes seems like gross negligence of the emotional kind, an absconding. Forget what anyone says about social networking sites such as Facebook. They allow you to check in, but there is nothing in the software to enable you to go deeper, into the marrow of other's lives, where the real stuff happens. When you leave, you leave. The only way to truly connect is to be there. Drawing each other in with a hug, eye contact across the table, that old look, that meaningful frown that can only be deciphered after years and years of what certain PR mavens call 'face-time'.

So skating, skating across the surface we go until we meet again and try to reconnect. How successfully we have absorbed the message of the market to keep it loose, to revel in weak ties, to be fleet of foot in a fleet-footed, often turbulent economy, to keep moving!

Mobility is not just enabled by the devices we carry, such as BlackBerrys, and the technology we use, it is a state that we aspire to, it is the default setting of the modern age. Nor does the word just imply movement, but instead it is a condition that is always whispering about an enticing 'next'. It's always about the next place and when that place is reached, we are craning our necks towards the next.

Consider those characters representative of another gilded age—Tom and Daisy Buchanan, the too idle, too rich couple in *The Great Gatsby*; self-absorbed and always vaguely unsatisfied. Says the narrator Nick Carraway, 'I felt Tom would drift on for ever seeking, a little wistfully, for the dramatic turbulence of some irrecoverable football game'.[1]

Tom and Daisy keep moving but they are always pining for the past. Their drift hits a modern note although now 'turbulence' is not a reminder of an 'irrecoverable' past, but a way of getting to the future a bit quicker. Why? Because that is where the promise of happiness lies.

Today, mobility is available to the masses. Air travel is cheaper in real terms than it's ever been before, with greater combinations of more routes allowing us to tailor our dream holiday to our precise desires, and thus take in everything from Montreal to Minsk, to a shopping trip to New York followed by a guided tour down the Amazon.

One friend recently observed how much our relationship to travel has changed in ten years, how 'you don't even have a going-away party anymore because everyone is always going away'. His god-mother, also at the table, guffawed and said that when *she* first went to England in the 1960s, it was by boat and it took six weeks. It was literally the trip of a lifetime, because you were only expected to go the once, if at all. That this conversation took place in Latvia, where I had arrived for a weekend break from Berlin, where another friend had flown in from London and where my friend and his godmother had just arrived from Australia, illustrates the point that a lot has changed since the 1960s.

So what is restless travel?

It's being transferred by your company to the Singapore office at short notice. It is deciding on Thursday to book a flight from Sydney to Melbourne for a shopping weekend. It is the pursuit of travel as a goal on par with getting an education and maintaining good health. It is the family that promises their kids a holiday in Japan for the 'cultural experience'. It is the new and growing breed of super-commuters who travel more than two hours a day to get to and from work: Torquay to Melbourne, Pittwater to Sydney, rural France to London. It is the teacher who dreams, over recess coffee and tour brochures, of the

Middle East. It is people like myself, who when based in Europe will regularly hop from country to country on budget airlines and when in Australia help support what is one of the busiest airline routes in the world: the Melbourne to Sydney run.

It is people like my father who once he turned fifty and had spent his entire life in Australia then seemed to disappear regularly for stints in an eclectic variety of places: Belgium, Boston and East Timor, the trips getting increasingly closer together until he was fluent in the distances between gate lounges at LA airport, euro to pound sterling exchange rates and international road rules. People who believe mobility to be a birthright and exercise it fully believe deep down that they are citizens of the world, that there is no country they cannot go, no impediment to movement. Only time, perhaps, and money, both of which can be made and allocated. The earth is flat and seems spread before them like a picnic blanket, covered in treats to be sampled and enjoyed. They spread themselves out and taste it all.

Concerns about talent leaving Australia for overseas, a 'brain drain', were met with extensive research by Graeme Hugo, Dianne Rudd and Kevin Harris, who argued for an Australian government policy of maintaining active contact with the Diaspora. Their findings were presented in a 2005 Senate committee report on Australians abroad:

> We live in mobile times. Impediments to overseas travel and employment have increasingly been removed and most governments of advanced economies are facilitating the movement of skilled persons across their borders. As a consequence, there has been a massive increase in the international transfer of highly skilled managerial and professional workers. It is by no means a uniquely Australian phenomenon.[2]

One in five Australians are overseas at any one time.[3] Why are so many of us travelling? Why are so many of us deciding to relocate overseas? Because we can. Because 'impediments to overseas travel and employment have increasingly been removed'.[4]

Ryan Heath, twenty-six, is from Coffs Harbour but currently lives in Brussels, where he works as a speechwriter for the European Union. He has also lived in Sydney, Oxford and London and worked in Canberra. He says his mobility is due to having plenty of choices. 'I felt that I had choices available to me about where to live and work, and like many people with choices I took them. It wasn't a deliberate rejection of Australia, though anyone who leaves is implicitly saying they need more of something. My move was a positive embrace of what the world has to offer and the fact that historically low travel costs and technology make it a realistic choice.'

Some people are Departure People. Every time you see them they are departing for somewhere else. Friendships with Departure People are enormously fun. It involves a lot of going out for drinks, because they are always about to leave somewhere, and increasingly bleary toasts made to travel and adventure. It's hard to feel old or jaded around Departure People as they carry with them the hope of the Next.

I am living in Sydney. It is crawling towards mid-year and winter. Some Departure People ring me from Berlin. Come over, they say. Crash with us, we'll have an apartment by then. They talk about the sunlight and ping-pong in the parks and all the people writing, painting and strumming guitars.

Mmmm, tempting.

It's getting cold in Sydney, the days shorter—soup is beginning to appear on restaurant specials boards. The cafés in Macleay Street still set up their outdoor tables but provide soft blankets so one can rug up as if on a camping trip by a log fire.

Another friend in Berlin, Luke Lalor, calls. He tells me about all the cool people he has met in Berlin, how there is a wine bar in the old east Berlin where you only pay 'what you think the wine is worth' rather than a fixed price. The enormous, high-ceilinged apartments, the cheap rents and the cafés.

He has moved from Canberra to Melbourne to Sydney to Munich to Berlin. He writes on my wall in Facebook:

Come to Berlin, Come to Berlin, Come to Berlin come to berlin
come to berlin
COME TO BERLIN
have i made myself clear?
:)
xx

A week later another friend, Sophie Dougall, who had spent the last two years in the sun working at a luxury Whitsunday resort, had also chucked in her job to move to … Berlin. She says she 'didn't feel ready to go back to Melbourne and settle just yet'. I ponder the curious magnetism of some cities—how sometimes you don't know anyone in a city and then a month later ten people you know have decided (separately) to move there.

The next day I walk down Macleay Street, after sitting shivering under a blanket, outside a café, eating soup. 'What have you got on Berlin?' I ask the chap behind the counter of the bookstore. 'Ahh, Berlin', he says. 'My best friend just moved there. He's doing his PhD and writing a book. Full of artists—lots of Australians.'

I buy a Wallpaper* city guide and go back to a café to crawl under a blanket: Brandenburg Gate, the Reichstag, swimming pools in the Spree, the zoo behind Zoo Station—Berlin, it sounds good. I look up airfares. I can feel the roar of the jet engines underneath, the first fresh whirring of turbulence and the old feeling of restlessness starting up again, and hear some lines by Philip Larkin in my head:

> Yet still the unresting castles thresh
> In fullgrown thickness every May.
> Last year is dead, they seem to say,
> Begin afresh, afresh, afresh.[5]

The world is packing its bags and taking a trip, moving on to the next place, checking out the neighbours. The latest United Nations World Migration Report estimates the number of migrants has more than doubled in the past twenty years: from 84 million in 1985 to almost 191 million in 2005.[6] By 2050 there are expected to be 230 million migrants worldwide.[7] For those of us in countries not affected by war or famine, persecution or strife, the question is *why do we go?* Why are we so keen to constantly uproot ourselves and move about? Why are travel, relocation and the upheavals that come with it so highly prized?

Could it be that we don't want to 'miss out on something' and that, by staying still, there is the sense that the fun is always happening elsewhere? Transcendence is to be found in travel, in what Freud called that 'oceanic feeling'[8]—a feeling of insight, beatific expansiveness that is not to be found by sticking close to home. In our restlessness is the best place always the next place?

'Katoomba', shuddered my friend Patrick, 'is full of damp.'

Yet, I like it, particularly on mornings like this: early winter, cobalt-blue sky mornings, cold and clear as a bell, the Blue Mountains' air crisp with eucalyptus scent and chill winds.

In the old, faded grandeur of the Carrington Hotel, I am here to see author Steven Toltz speak as part of the Sydney Writers Festival. His book, *Fraction of a Whole*, was written while Toltz, a Sydneysider, lived in Montreal, Vancouver, New York, Barcelona and Paris, working as a cameraman, telemarketer, security guard, private investigator, movie extra ('or warm prop'), English teacher and screenwriter. As for the jobs, 'it was a case of swinging from the bottom of one ladder to the next'. Chair Malcolm Knox asked about the 'anxiety of not climbing the ladder'. It was writing, answered Toltz, that kept him going, the only thing that seemed to be a constant in a life of churn, and 'unstoppable restlessness'.[9] Toltz's pattern was to spend one year in Sydney then another overseas. Much time was spent in Barcelona living in a room where he wrote by the light of an unreliable bulb.

Toltz's motivation for moving so much was that when he turned twenty in Sydney he realised, 'if I lived to eighty I'd have spent a quarter of my life in the one place. That was a horrible thought.' This freaked him out. His restlessness was spurred on in part by realising that there was a lot of the world to see.

How many of us are haunted by the spectre of stasis? The proverbial pram in the hall, the 'horrible thought' of having spent too much time in one place?

Remember my friend in Rome, Chris Davis? Originally from country Victoria, via boarding school in Melbourne, Chris has lived in Dublin, London, Indonesia, Brazil and Rome. He worries that he'll stagnate in Australia.

'I can't remember who the author is, but someone was telling me the other day about an Australian guy who wrote a book about living in Paris for several years. Apparently when he returned home to Australia for a visit, he wrote that he was terrified of staying still for too long in case someone tried to renovate him. I think that however condescending this comment is, there is something there that I can relate to. Many of my friends back in Australia are in some kind of pre-retirement phase. They rarely leave their house, watch what I consider to be a staggering amount of TV, and are more likely to spend their time bitching about microeconomic issues than those that may affect someone they've never met. I am often surprised at how little many of my well-educated friends know about the world.'

Johanna Leggatt, thirty-two, of Queensland, has lived in Sydney, Florence, London and Brisbane and says spending money on living abroad and travel 'is far more appealing than home ownership in an outer Sydney suburb [that you still can't afford], and not being able to travel, take time off work and enjoy yourself because you're tied to your bloody home repayments. Europeans don't get as hung up on the quarter-acre block phenomenon like Australians do, and that is immensely appealing.'

Sydney-born and -raised Richard Lane, twenty-eight, who for the last eight years has lived in London and Berlin, says, 'All my friends back home may have put down roots—good for them—but I don't consider them the better trees. If anything, scampering about a bit has hopefully made me more rounded. It's certainly made me feel more a citizen of the world. London's obviously close to Europe and has an unparalleled job market but beyond that … how shall I put it … it feels like things here matter—on the world stage. To someone in the early stages of a career, that can be very compelling.'

D, a 37-year-old lawyer from Melbourne, says, 'I was thirty-five and realised that if I did not move to the UK soon I probably never would. There was also an unhealthy dash of ex-relationship-related angst mixed together with a decent dose of all round professional and social exhaustion that made the move inevitable. In short, it was simply time to move on.'

Luke Derbyshire, twenty-nine, of Geelong, has lived in Japan and now London. He says he moved from Melbourne because of 'adventure and the lure of the pound. For me London is like the centre of the galaxy. It has so many opportunities for work, travel, culture and history. To have a pint at the pub where Madness played their first gig, to enjoy a curry on Brick Lane or to jump on the Eurostar for a business trip to France is second to none.'

There are romantic reasons to travel, there is escapism, there is fear of staying still and 'being renovated', there is self-fulfilment, there is even transformation or maturity but in the Long Boom, never before did Australia wave goodbye to so many economic migrants, bright young people fleeing the country in search of riches only dreamed of on home soil.

You see them in airport lounges. Young people in sharp suits with a confidence that many other people (people who strain for the announcements about gate lounge changes, or fret that they have forgotten *something*, who pack liquids in carry-on luggage and fumble with their boarding pass) lack. These travellers are *prepared*. They travel without the usual measure of anxiety that signals not so much class and money or education, but those who are at ease moving around the world. It is the difference between those who are surfing on the crest of the great wave of globalisation, and the rest of us who are caught floundering in the backwash.

Those surfing on the crest have their Qantas club memberships, laptops, BlackBerrys and pills for sleeping on the plane. They have the name of a good little hotel in Malaysia that does a great rooftop pool and laksa, and the names of the late night bars in Soho so that a fellow whose body thinks it's 6 p.m. can get a drink in London at 3 a.m.

They have friends everywhere and often run into them at places of transit—airport lounges, taxi ranks, hotel check-in desks. They arrange to meet for drinks in unlikely places—'Next week I will be in Miami, but I'm stopping for ten hours in Hong Kong. Do you want to meet there at the same bar as last time, or else I'll just see you in Crete at Georgia's wedding?' Their unexpected arrival at a house party often prompts guests to say, 'What are you doing here? I thought you were in Rome.' Or Indonesia, or Mumbai. It is not so much that people expect them to be at another party, rather they presume them to be in another country. But the people in this world are hyper-mobile and to travel across several countries to attend a party does not raise too many eyebrows.

'Gold Collar Workers' is how the 2005 Senate committee report labelled these workers.[10] They are 'young, highly skilled, well-educated, high earning Australians'.[11] More than half are between the ages of twenty and thirty-four and, overwhelmingly, their favoured destination is the United Kingdom.[12]

These expats are the New Colonialists and perhaps do not see the irony of their situation. Going back to the Old Country in a sort of reversal of (literally) fortune from Victorian days when the Brits lit out for the colonies and plundered the New World's wealth and resources. This time the New Colonialists hit the mother country in the capacity not of speculators or administrators or explorers, but commodities traders, corporate lawyers and hedge-fund managers. The global recession has dented their confidence and, in some cases, cost them their jobs—or they have had to forgo their bonus. But for those still in the game, the spoils are in the form of salaries and bonuses. The plundering occurs through creative use of non-domicile tax status and offshore banking.[13]

The Old Colonialists of Somerset Maugham novels shielded their faces from the sun and perspired through ennui and gin and tonics. Their wan English longing was for their children in boarding schools, lawns, dew-drenched roses, black cabs, red buses and rain. New Colonialists shiver through the seemingly never-ending winters and spend nostalgic nights in wood-panelled pubs; their longing is for parents in beach houses, summer holidays, swimming in oceans, mangos and light, making even more melancholy the long evening's gloom. When they've had their fill and the boom wanes, the New Colonialists return home with a nice stash. On the way home there may be stop-offs in Asia, going where there may still be a bit of give in the market.

This beast born from hyper-mobility, this New Colonialist, was a construction that emerged from this restless era that I call GEMs (Global Elite Meritocrats). GEMs are young professionals, who through talent, hard work and top-notch education, are on the rise in their chosen fields. They see the job market they compete in as global—a job offer in Sydney is weighed up against one in New York or Hong Kong. Their motivators are money, status, experience and travel.

GEMs are usually educated in a mix of overseas post-graduate courses after obtaining an undergraduate degree in Australia (they are often products of the Hawke–Keating policies of the Clever Country). They have careers that transcend international boundaries, such as those in finance, marketing, engineering, policy, IT and the media. They believe themselves to be citizens of the world, and if they don't hold more than one passport, they have an immigration lawyer on the case to keep them abreast of the passage of their Highly Skilled Migrant Visa through the Home Office, or the progress of their US Green Card or E3 visa. On their computer favourites is a currency converter and a big part of salary negotiation for their next posting concerns which denomination they will be paid in. Right now it's euros, a few years ago it was popular to be paid in US dollars, but whatever the exchange rate you can be sure a GEM will know it as soon as Travelex.

GEMs spend their money on travel, holidays, education, technology and good restaurants. They keep a savings account so they can buy property, often close to outright, in their home countries. Their friends are similar high achievers from other developed nations who they may have met at business school, or on a secondment in Frankfurt. They all holiday at a chum's pile in San Sebastian or housesit at a mate's place in Paris or organise complicated leasing arrangements on boats around the Greek Islands or villas in Mexico. A large percentage of a GEM's income goes towards travel, including regular flights back to Australia for Christmas and weddings. James Button, writing in the *Age* on successful Australians in London, spoke to one political staffer who flew home to Australia for three days to MC a friend's wedding. 'I still have to get the carbon offsets, they're worth five trees', he said of the journey.[14]

Depending on the economy, GEMs will stay away for a while, then return. The skills, education, values and knowledge they bring back with them has and will continue to have a dynamic effect on Australian culture, the economy and how the country is run. In 2008, the *Sunday Times* in Britain reported that 'previously expat Aussies appeared in no great hurry to return, but now the country is seeing a mass homecoming at a rate of 34,000 a year—bringing cosmopolitan ideas from around the world with them'.[15] A deep recession in the USA, Europe and the UK, the end of the Howard years and technology were factors the *Sunday Times* article suggests for the mass homecoming. The internet, in particular, has helped Australians to be closer to the rest of the world—able to live in one place and work in another.[16]

Freelance production manager Cassandre Khoury, thirty-nine, is a 'boomerang migrant', thinking of returning home. 'I've been in London for five years', she says. 'I want to start my own production company and I know I could make it happen in Australia, but not here. It feels as if there are more opportunities over there [Australia] now.'[17]

GEMs are the lucky children of globalisation and have a lifestyle that many graduates aspire to.[18] They are at the other end of the ladder of those other children of globalisation—the kids in the factories making trainers for the transnationals. Cheap airfares, technology and—during the good times—a strong job market also contributed to the growth of the GEM class, and the stimulation of our restlessness.

The ascendancy of this new class—the GEMs—has been aided by foreign governments hungry for skilled workers, and the emergence of transnational companies that see recruitment as a global rather than local enterprise. A characteristic of a GEM is a desire to work for a global company and enjoy all the perks that come with that— status, enhanced mobility, expense accounts—plus opportunities to be posted to branch offices in different parts of the globe. One only has to open to the jobs pages of the *Economist, Australian Lawyer* or Friday's *Australian Financial Review* to see jobs for economists in Kenya, computer programmers in Hamburg or tax lawyers in San Paulo. The internet has also made searching for jobs overseas as easy as looking for jobs locally.

In Australia, recruiters such as Hudson and Michael Page International tempt top graduates and junior lawyers and bankers with ads promising a life of sarongs and sangria for those working in the tax havens of the Cayman Islands or Bermuda. You can go to the recruiter's offices in Sydney, Melbourne or Brisbane and interview for a job in Dubai, Hong Kong or London. A global lingua franca or verbal shorthand has even developed around so-called international law firms—they are called the 'magic circle' in London, five or six of London's leading law firms[19]—while the Big 4 are the four largest international accountancy and professional services firms worth packing your passport for.

As for the move to work overseas, an entire service industry has sprung up to make it go smoothly. Tax experts, visa and immigration advisers, shipping companies, mobile phone leasing outfits, mobile broadband providers, furniture storage warehouses are all enablers of restlessness. Their ads fill the back half of magazines such as *TNT*, a freebie magazine in London, fat with advertising, which caters for expat Australians, South Africans and New Zealanders. If you are good enough, talented enough, educated enough and have the cash—the impediments to mobility such as working visas and getting your stuff from one side of the world to another seem to magically disappear.[20] 'The tyranny of distance has pretty well collapsed', says Paul Wellings, a dual citizen and vice-chancellor of Lancaster University. His university now hires regularly from Australia. 'As the internet has kicked in it is possible to be sitting in Toowoomba thinking, there's a nice job for me in Lancaster', he says.[21]

Professor Graeme Hugo of the University of Adelaide says the reason for the surge in Australians working overseas is the behaviour of 'a new generation of young people who see the labour market they are competing in as global'.[22] London, the centre of the global economy, has lured financial, IT and media talent from around the world. A survey by Hugo of 660 Australian graduates in London showed 'they felt increasingly that none of the really challenging work for global companies happens in Australia'.[23]

Mobility and ease of movement has this century become a characteristic of the middle classes, while another sort of mobility is symptomatic of poverty. Think of people packed like pellets into border-crossing lorries and leaky boats, and people smugglers—the language of immigration for the poor is very different from that of the GEMs where cocktail party chatter is of good immigration lawyers, relocation packages and highly skilled migrant visas.

The movement of less advantaged groups, says Hugo, 'has become increasingly constrained by the erection of greater barriers to entry than was the case in the past. Hence, while the option to move may be there for many of the poor, the unskilled, etc. they are often confronted by greater barriers than is the case for the empowered elite skilled groups.'[24] If they wish to be mobile, they face a mass of red tape and high fees for legal advice for visas or are forced to become 'irregular'[25] (aka illegal) migrants in order to circumvent the income and education bias to true mobility.

One of the tests for getting a highly skilled migrant visa in the UK requires that you reach 75 points to qualify.[26] Points are awarded for a high level of education: applicants need a minimum of a masters degree to meet the threshold test. With each band of income you climb, your chances of being classified 'highly skilled' also rise—the presumption being that 'skill' is synonymous with salary. A banker, tax lawyer or fast-moving consumer goods brand manager under this definition is skilled—a master craftsman, teacher, researcher, scientist or social worker is deemed unskilled.

America's young and talented are also being lured to European postings.[27] The *International Herald Tribune* (*IHT*) reports that the prestigious Massachusetts Institute of Technology holds a European Career Fair on its campus just outside of Boston in order to match 'eager students' with 'equally eager foreign multinational companies'. Organisers of the 2006 event collected almost 5000 résumés from candidates wanting to work overseas.[28]

According to *IHT*, young people are driven to go overseas by their careers, not the prospect of new cultural experiences. 'Today, a shrinking world with better communications has propelled a new wave of young people abroad—this time with laptops instead of bedrolls. For this new generation of expats, career advancement, not cultural exposure, is the bottom line.'

Over drinks at the Opera Bar on Sydney Harbour, I speak to banker Rex Ollie. He has worked in the finance industry for ten years in London, Stockholm and Sydney. He says, 'It's pretty Darwinian. I don't have a particular affinity for the companies I've worked for because it's an abstraction. It's the way it is with all the global companies.

'I don't think there's any type of brand loyalty to companies these days', admits Ollie. 'Everyone is an opportunist and all the companies are so homogenous that moving from one to another is just like musical chairs. It's more interesting to talk about a class of company. I would work for any investment bank but I wouldn't work for a domestic company. I would only work for a company that's global because I'm motivated by travel, and having a global brand is important. Every company pretends to have global exposure but some of them are spread a bit further than others. That's definitely a factor.'

Later that week Ollie and I meet a mutual friend, T, for lunch in Bondi. T works for a global bank based in Tokyo and says that if a banker applies for a job who *hasn't* had a lot of different jobs in a lot of different countries, usually over a short space of time, then he (for it is usually a he) is viewed with suspicion. The best CVs are crowded.

This global, fast way of working—these hyper-mobile careers— epitomise the life of churn. You might start your career at twenty-four in Perth, then move to Sydney when you're twenty-seven, realise that to make more money you need to go to business school in America or France, which you do, then re-enter the workforce but in a different capacity and maybe a new market so you go into management rather than strategy, in Milan rather than back in Sydney. The recession is putting the brakes on lavish entertaining, but during the boom clients were entertained in a lavish manner with cocaine, boozing, expensive restaurants and titty bars. Weekends were spent decompressing with serious bouts of European travel or guilty gym visits. All this before you're thirty. Relationships buckle under the strain of constantly uprooting yourself and long hours. Friendships are conducted online and local culture is given only a cursory look; instead, unwinding takes place in some expat bar with other people like yourself who provide not only camaraderie for the often lonely life of working away from home, but also the ability to network—and see what other jobs are out there in GEM-land.

But for all the apparent ease in friendships, the drinking culture that rewards sociability, the bonhomie—look underneath and there's not much incentive to relax. In the fast-moving world, in the restless economy, you are a loser if you stay still.

James Starling, thirty-one, lives in London, where he works as a currency options trader. He was born in rural South Australia and has lived in Adelaide, Melbourne, Sydney, Buenos Aires, San Paulo, Paris and London. He says, 'I grew up on a sheep farm in south-east South Australia. Boarding school at thirteen probably established my independence and hence made it easy to just drop everything and move first from Adelaide [high school] to Melbourne [uni] then Sydney [first job] and later from country to country.

'I moved from my home country ostensibly for work and study, but that begs the question: why did I want to work and study abroad? Same reason backpackers travel—adventure, different life experiences, see the world, learn other languages, see other cultures, but mostly because Argentine chicks are hot, and traders in London get paid more.

'In any place I lived, sport was a great icebreaker. I played rugby in Argentina and France. France was easy because I was at biz [business] school and everyone was thrown in together so it was easy to find people also separated from their previous life and friends. You make new mates in that environment. I still keep in regular contact with a few friends from Argentina and Brazil, regularly see friends from biz school all over the world, like in Miami where I am now, even though I studied in Paris. It's a bit because I went to INSEAD [a prestigious business school in France], which differentiates itself from other biz schools by seeking to be more cosmopolitan—you need three languages to graduate and students came from 70-odd countries all over the world.'

I ask him if he plans on returning to Australia. 'Yes, back to the sheep farm, though maybe on a six months in Oz, six months in Europe kind of basis. And not for ten years, until I retire from trading FX.'

Starling is relaxed about being a global worker. 'Paul Kelly says it best with that song about how all fucking cities are the same. It's pretty true of my experience; there are different languages and some cultural differences sure, but when you get down to the root of it, I live the same life with similar friends no matter what city I'm in. I do miss Australia from time to time, but even at work about 10 per cent of the people I work with on the trading floor are Aussies or Kiwis so our culture has a strong influence on the culture of the workplace, which makes it easier. Two or three of the top five guys in my department are Aussies or Kiwis so we definitely punch above our weight and that means work operates in an Aussie fashion, which suits me but no doubt makes some of the other nationalities a bit less at ease. Their problem.

'I don't worry much about what goes on in Oz generally, don't usually bother to vote. My seat is the safest Liberal seat in Australia, though, and I'd usually vote that way anyway, so don't expect it would have made much difference. I do keep up to date with local weather and things affecting my farm though, like those wankers from PETA and general tree huggers, but then living abroad and having a more high-powered job than even exists in Australia means I have access to info, people etc. that I wouldn't otherwise and I can channel that back home to our advantage.'

In his book *Growth Fetish*, Australian economist Clive Hamilton warns that 'the archetype of the new flexible, mobile worker—the "symbolic analyst" or the "bourgeois bohemian"—provides no model for the future'.[29] This flexible, mobile worker makes up around a fifth of the workforce and 'can sell their services anywhere and are happy to do so'.[30]

Hamilton is critiquing this new rootless, restless and opportunistic worker as a symbol of unfettered economic growth. Mobility has freed this worker from much of the constraints and pressures of being a *citizen*—of the basics like voting and the acts of citizenry that flow from that, holding the powers that be to account, building community life, involvement in activism—of caring.

Instead a GEM's nation-state is their global company and their ties and loyalty are to the company. An elaborate super-structure caters for the GEMs so they can be in the country of their choice, yet outside it. They exist quite literally on a different plane and can skate, skate across the surface of things.

In a story published in the *Herald Sun*, Australian expatriates were ranked third wealthiest in the world, with almost 40 per cent earning more than $200 000 a year. Only the Brazilian and Irish expats earn more. The places where expatriates were likely to earn the most and also save more than they would at home were India, Hong Kong, Singapore, the United Arab Emirates (UAE) and the USA.[31]

The top locations for luxurious living were UAE, Singapore, India, Hong Kong and Belgium. In these places expats had 'access to private health care, access to more than one property, gym membership, ownership of more than one car, private education for children, and the ability to employ staff such as cleaners'.[32] Britain, unsurprisingly, finished at the bottom in this category, where only a certain breed of oligarch, soccer star, supermodel or hedge-fund manager could afford the trappings and the ease of the mega-rich.

But for globalised workers sent to Asia or the Middle East, Sodom awaited.

When Mel Kingston's boyfriend was sent to Beijing to work for his management consultancy, she accompanied him, packing up her home in Hobart. It was a typical 'corporate fuck-up', she explains. He was sent to Indonesia on a short-term project that never seemed to end and was flown to Beijing to 'help out on something for a bit' but ended up 'running something for quite a long-time—four years in the end'.

As such the couple didn't plan the move and were unable to prepare for the upheavals in their lifestyle by learning the local language. They spent their time in Beijing playing catch-up. 'We didn't have a conversation at any time [about relocating to China]—it was just a bastard act of the corporation. It was really tough not knowing the language', says Kingston.

When they arrived, they quickly connected with the expat scene. 'We hung out with other Australians and Brits and the odd American. There was one couple who were Chinese friends that my partner met through work. But it was very hard to have Chinese friends and I don't think many of the foreigners did. When we had that [Chinese] couple around for dinner, they were very nervous. They had read an etiquette guide to prepare, yet [ultimately] we were able to be friends with them because he had studied in America and the cultural differences were not as great as if he had never been outside China.'

Despite the uncertainty and the fact that 'we never really knew how long we'd be there [China] so we never could plan anything', Kingston and her boyfriend tried to make the most of the experience by travelling and enjoying how far their expat salaries went in China. They, like most other expats, had a lifestyle that would be unattainable in their home countries. Several times a week Kingston and her boyfriend went to a salon to get their hair washed. With eyes closed, head back, a dreamy smile and a slight groan of pleasure, Kingston mimics what happened when she got her hair washed. 'They gave the best scalp massages', she says. Must have been hard to go back to washing your own hair, I comment (somewhat wryly). She agrees. 'The next posting was London and we could barely afford a curry there.'

For an expat in China it was like the last days of Babylon. 'We would go out for drinks at all the big hotel chains, the Hilton, the Marriott, le Meridian, The Renaissance. The champagne brunches were amazing … free-flowing Veuve Clicquot and oysters and cray-fish. It was hedonistic, it was amazing, totally decadent. We had Christmas lunch at the Hilton and Easter at the Marriott and we'd go for drinks at fancy cocktail bars, even the nice Chinese restaurants. Whereas we've never been to the most expensive restaurants in London and I'll probably never go.'

An English friend, Michelle, is scathing about the expat life. Growing up with a pilot father meant different stints in different parts of the world. Now in her thirties, she is equally peripatetic, spending part of the year in South America, the Philippines, England and Dubai. But the expat scene leaves her cold. 'Often expat workers have very little experience of life in that country—they eat in the expensive restaurants, stay in expensive hotels, and if they meet any locals they are likely to be workmates who have been educated at Harvard Business School or in Europe. They live in compounds. They're sort of on the surface of the country.'

Compound living, by its very nature, is resistant to integration, into the idea of going deeper into the local community, of getting your hands dirty in the local real estate market, and all the complications and entanglements that community life entails. But compounds feel nice: safe and clean, with the cool, hard glamour of five-star international hotels and business class travel. Compound people have an air about them, as if to say, I'm not a wide-eyed tourist, I am here on business and I must keep moving.

The things in a compound, the clubs and the saunas and the golf courses and the swimming pools and concierge and taxi service and cleaning staff and chrome and leather coffee bars are the things of surface and movement. It is a 'swirling dream-life of objects'.[33] This life is slick and textured like those commercials you see on CNN: handsome man in a suit on an escalator; jump cut to him being served an espresso by a gorgeous girl in a blinding-white apron; then his BlackBerry beeps and it's his son sending him a picture of his first day at school, he scrolls through, then he smiles as he stirs his coffee; jump cut, another airport somewhere else, another pretty girl also wearing a suit smiles at man as she goes up the other escalator; jump cut to the logo for an oil company or an airline or an insurance firm or management consultancy or a country even (which brand themselves like products these days). But, whatever the product, the message always signifies movement, restlessness and perpetual motion. Success, implies these images, is not to be found at home, but elsewhere, always elsewhere.

In the churn and travel, Kingston misses family life. 'I have two nieces—one I have seen for ten days and the other who I haven't met at all. I'm pissed off I haven't met her.' When a close relative died in Australia, 'I really missed my family. I thought they were the only people that *got it*. I wrote a poem about it and sent it to my family.'

In Hong Kong, I am staying at a residential compound called Bel Air. It has a guardhouse and a boom-gate and a man at the front desk called Carl who'll walk with you to the lift and, with a white-gloved hand, push the buttons for you. Going up this high, you can see the buildings of the compound rise up and out, like phoenixes along the coast. It looks better from the inside than out, when you're in one of those chilled apartments and all you can see is the water. Cargo ships drift by and the occasional Chinese junk.

In the evening the sun sinks languidly into the sea. It's a gin and tonic moment out there on the balcony every night at eight o'clock. Out the window, but within the compound walls, is the largest swimming pool I have ever seen. It goes on and on for blocks—surely corners of it have their own postcode. The pool is empty except for some lilos drifting desolately in the blue—everyone must be at work. Pool boys rearrange empty deckchairs and hose down the deck. The water is a light, gorgeous colour and promises certain refuge from the swampy heat, from the sour-smelling air, yet I resist. To swim in a pool like this, just the once, would render every other swim for the rest of my life a poor facsimile, a trip-rope trigger for the memory of the Bel Air swim. No other pool would ever be as empty, or as luxurious. I go to the gym instead, also vast and empty. A bored girl folds towels and mixes large jugs of water with floating ice cubes and lemon slices. Someone in a maid's outfit polishes the weights machines. All is calm and bright. This is my own personal CNN ad break. I look at myself as if outside myself; in the air-conditioned gym to escape from the heat, yet flushed and sweating on the cross-trainer. I feel weird ... I feel something else ... and the only word that I can think of that fits is *privileged*. I also think this could be addictive.

It seems there is no other city in the world more attuned to the churn, more emblematic of its features and rhythms, than Dubai.

Since Dubai began a marketing and development push around the start of the century to attract expatriate workers and investment (as part of this expansion, about 50 per cent of the world's largest cranes were concentrated in Dubai),[34] it's been flooded with foreign workers, many from Australia, Britain and Ireland. Dubai nationals are now a minority group in their own country, where more than 85 per cent of the estimated 1.8 million residents are from overseas.[35] In the world of churn and hyper-mobility, Dubai is all colour and move-ment, transience and escape, a place that is never the final destina-tion, but a place to stay for 'a while', a bubble and a Babylon where expats feel 'untouchable'.[36]

As well as being a place of cranes, chilled, bright shopping malls and faux beaches where there is a sense that it is cut adrift from both the desert and its Islamic foundations, Dubai, for foreign residents, is a world of 'pumped-up salaries', and 'tax-free wealth', where expats have the chance to climb a few rungs up the career ladder. It is a place for excessive boozing, a 'playground for adults, with residents in their 30s and 40s drinking and clubbing every weekend like they're 21 again',[37] a place for fleeting sexual encounters and 'superficial relationships'.[38] It is a city where the natural rhythm is restlessness, where there are always new faces arriving and, as such, good times.

The UAE Police Chief, General Dhahi Khalfan Tamimmay, has bemoaned the loss of traditions and rituals through the influx of foreigners: 'I'm afraid we're building towers but losing the Emirates'.[39] But the new expats, a typically transient bunch who stay for between three and five years,[40] have been creating their own rituals.

One of the most notorious expat rituals (for the UAE is a Muslim country, where alcohol consumption is frowned upon) is the Friday brunch: 'an institution among Middle East expats for years', says the *Guardian*. 'On the holiest day of the Muslim week, five-star hotels entice customers with all-day feasts and unlimited alcohol from as little as £10.'[41] On one expat website, foreigners traded tips on the best brunches, especially those with the longest drinking times and the ones that 'left a few bottles on the table' (so the drinking could continue) after brunch had finished, usually by mid-afternoon. Advised one expat on the message board: 'Been to Marina @ Jumeirah Beach (below 360)—Veuve Clicquot. 12–4. Fantastic food & glass never gets near empty. Cannot remember the price—about 460 I think?'[42] The brunches provide respite from working hard a long way from home and the usual support systems: 'In such a transient scene … the boozy afternoons are an opportunity for social bonding'.[43]

'It is the new land of opportunity', commercial property lawyer Nick Armitage, who has been based in Dubai for two years, told the *Daily Mail*. 'We live in a bubble, a kind of fantasy world of luxury living and, if you want it, endless partying.'[44] A 32-year-old London businessman in the UAE on a working trip told the *Sun*: 'This is the wildest city on Earth—I've never seen so many birds and so much booze ... If this is what goes on in a Muslim country, I'm converting to Islam.'[45] According to the *Daily Mail*, 'What the expats are interested in is having a good time—and almost everyone you meet has an anecdote about their shameful excesses.' One taxi driver recalled how he often picks up foreign men and women 'so drunk and abusive that he simply decants them at the police station, where they are detained until they sober up and are then escorted home'.[46]

Consistent with the world of restlessness and churn, nothing lasts here, including relationships. 'Dubai is commonly known as "the graveyard of relationships"', Lauren Whittacker, a 29-year-old lawyer from Devon, UK, who originally moved here with her fiancé, told the *Guardian*. 'After a year, we were finished. The pace of life here put too much pressure on our relationship and it caved in. The same has happened to so many couples I know. Now, meeting anyone who isn't after something superficial is nigh-on impossible.'

When it comes to integration, expats prefer to sit on the superstructure, not penetrate the depths. One young woman, who works for the Dubai royal family, told the *Daily Mail*, 'There is no integration here at all. It may sound insulting, but nobody is the slightest bit interested in making friends with the Arabs. It's just not done.'[47]

There was trouble in the Dubai expat bubble when in 2008 Britons Michelle Palmer, thirty-six, and Vince Acors, thirty-four, were arrested for having sex on the beach following a 'typical day spent drinking and eating to excess at one of Dubai's weekly Friday brunches'.[48] After police in the Muslim country warned the couple to stop canoodling—twice—an intoxicated Palmer lashed out at the police and the pair were arrested. As a result of their one-night stand, they faced up to six years' jail, but were later released. The case was responsible for some lurid tabloid headlines but highlighted how the fantasy-land lifestyles of many expats can clash with the realities of the host country.

Those who know Palmer and Acors speak highly of them, saying they are kind, hard-working people who behaved no differently from many of the other expats in Dubai. It's just that they got caught. It is, in its own way, a cautionary tale about restlessness—that in the whirl, it's easy to forget yourself and forget where you really are. Like the fake beaches and the champagne fountains, so dream-like is the experience and so unreal.

Swirling around the story of Palmer and Acors are other stories that link to some kind of central narrative in this hyper-mobile world: expats falling fully clothed into swimming pools; the 'bizarre "Ireland in the Sun" development, reportedly bought by three Galway-based developers for more than 20 million euro';[49] the bar at the York Hotel, 'a veritable United Nations of prostitutes—[where] Chinese, Ethiopian, Russian, Nigerian—barter their services. Inevitably their regular punters are expats.'[50] These scenes appear almost Great Gatsby-esque in their lavish excesses, and may not all be harmless. Some British newspapers predict that this kind of Western hedonism will trigger terrorism attacks on Dubai, so offensive and inflammatory is the behaviour to local Muslim sensibilities. That is, if the expats stay.

Dubai is not immune from the global economic crisis. Growth has slowed,[51] and, according to *Time* magazine, 'The large foreign banks that had been financing Dubai's real estate boom have pulled out, leaving behind a significant burden on local banks, who have turned to the UAE government for help shoring up their liquidity'.[52] The government has 'overleveraged and overextended itself' in its mad rush to be the leading centre for business in the Middle East and is 'obsessively keen' to hide its problems from the public.[53]

In 2009 there is expected to be a 15 per cent reduction in population in Dubai.[54] Questions are being asked—is this dream world built on the shifting sands of the restless economy?

In 2008 American urban theorist Mike Davis published a book called *Evil Paradises*, a collection of writings about how globalisation that accompanied the long boom has created 'new geographies of exclusion and landscapes of wealth'. In this new world order, 'the rich are dominant drivers of demand ... skimming the cream off productivity surges and technology monopolies then spending their increasing share of the national wealth as fast as possible on luxury goods and services. The champagne days of the Great Gatsby have returned with a vengeance.' Davis describes how the wealthy live in 'gilded dream worlds', enjoying the mushrooming of elite brands such as Porsche, Bulgari, Polo Ralph Lauren, Tiffany, Hermès or Sotheby's and desperately trying to 'consume all the good things of the earth in their lifetime'. Those excluded from such wealth can watch 'the great binge only on television'.

Davis is scathing about this growing inequality and its human and environmental cost. 'On a planet where more than 2 billion people subsist on $2 a day or less these dream worlds enflame desires—for infinite consumption, total social exclusion, and physical security and architectural monumentality—that are clearly incompatible with the ecological and moral survival of humanity'. [55]

We're all trying to get a taste of 'all the good things of the earth', wanting to linger a bit longer in 'gilded dream worlds'.

Twenty years ago budget European airline Ryanair flew 644 000 passengers a year. Today it will carry more than 57 million a year.[56] Ryanair, EasyJet and low-cost airlines in Australia, such as Virgin Blue and Jetstar, help put the churn into travel by opening up more routes, and making it more affordable for more people to travel to more places than ever before. It is only factors such as the fluctuating costs of world oil prices and the global financial crisis that seemed to put the brakes on their rapid, environmentally damaging expansion.

How does churn travel feel?

Cheap and nasty.

For taxes only (around £26) I flew from London to Paris in July 2007. The airport was hot, crowded, strewn with litter and the walls glowed from screens showing rolling (non) news watched by passengers who seethed in a toxic combination of boredom and anger. The restlessness was partly dulled, and the anger somewhat anaesthetised, by drinking the large balloon glasses of wine at the bar, or eating a meal sodden with fat and carbohydrates from the food court, or wandering around the shops buying perfume, magazines, jewellery, booze and handbags. We milled by Gate 40 for an hour as our plane was delayed. It was late landing at Rome, throwing the whole tightly coiled schedule out of whack. Late in Rome meant late in London meant late in Paris.

Cheap fares mean cheap overheads, and as such planes have a mere 25-minute turnaround time in each airport. They are barely cleaned. One can imagine the staff farewelling the Romans in London before straightening their skirts and their smiles and greeting new passengers bound for Paris. Jammed into my fluorescent yellow Ryanair seat, with an advertisement for insurance perched centimetres from my nose, I unhinged the tray table, which sent someone's crumbs (Roman crumbs perhaps? or crumbs from earlier in the day—maybe Rigan crumbs?) onto my lap. People complain about the 'service' or lack of on such airlines and that airline staff are rude and abrasive. I observed the flight attendants, who looked tired, skin dehydrated, squeezed into unflattering fluorescent uniforms and probably unaware, mostly, of even where they were. If there was glamour with flying, it has gone now. Travel has come to the masses—mobility has been democratised.

A Facebook group for expat or international kids states that you know you're a modern-day army brat if you can answer 'yes' to some of these questions:

- You can't answer the question, 'Where are you from?' (And when you do, you get into an elaborate conversation that gets everyone confused and/or makes you sound very spoiled.)
- You have a passport, but no driver's licence.
- You watch National Geographic specials and recognise someone.
- You run into someone you know at every airport.
- Conversations with friends take place at 6.00 in the morning or 10.00 at night.
- Your life story uses the phrase 'Then we went to …' five times.
- You can speak with authority about the quality of various international airlines.
- You sort your friends by continent.
- You have a time zone map next to your phone.
- You have the urge to move to a new place every couple of years.
- You go into culture shock upon returning to your 'home' country.
- You don't know where home is.

Child psychologists now specialise in treating the 'increasing community of nomadic kids who are growing up internationally. Some child psychologists refer to such children as third-culture kids, or TCKs (Trans-Culture Kid).'[57] The official definition of a TCK is

an individual who, having spent a significant part of the developmental years in a culture other than the parents' culture, develops a sense of relationship to all of the cultures, while not having full ownership of any. Elements from each culture are incorporated into the life experience, but the sense of belonging is in relationship to others of similar experience.[58]

Many TCKs enjoy a privileged life with high living standards—plenty of travel and private schooling—but they often fail to absorb or become involved in the local culture or make friends with local children. This may be partly a product of their segregated lifestyle but also because they are 'aware of their transience'.[59]

On an expat website there is advice for parents of TCKs for whom the question 'Mummy, where do I come from?' is not a prelude to a conversation about the facts of life, but a complex untangling of various geographical and national alliances that may have an answer like this: 'Your mummy is half Italian and half English, your daddy is English and you and your sister were born in Dubai'.[60]

We are often told that this state of restlessness is something we will grow out of. I know that's what I thought—that my twenties would be like a portal from which I would emerge into the bright, strong, clarifying light of adulthood. Then the restlessness would stop. There would be clarity and, in this clarity, peace and contentment. Of course, that is the great, dark lie about adulthood—that at some threshold, at some fixed point things become clear and a path is marked and lit and visible as if it were a runway lit up at night. We tear down it and whoosh! we are airborne.

Of course this state didn't stop. If anything the churn picked up pace, but I wasn't to know this at the time. In preparation for meeting this flight path on my thirtieth birthday—for the smooth ride that would be the rest of my life—I rattled the cage of my twenty-ninth year. I thought it would be the last time I could. I moved to Barcelona from my flat in Sydney's Bellevue Hill, with its salt-smeared windows

from the drifts of Bondi and which I shared with a thoughtful archi-
tect. In the thick of the good life, we'd spend Saturday mornings
lying prone on Bondi sand and Sunday nights cooking roast dinners
for our friends who would get taxis home at midnight after drinking
too much red wine. Dinner conversations were typically discursive:
refugees, being locked out of the property market, holidays in South
America, some documentary on SBS about crystal meth, that thing
at Belvoir that was 'quite good' …

We sometimes went to parties held on the cliff at Tamarama,
where the girls in the bathrooms yammered too loudly about their
work in fashion and PR, and crowded into the cubicles to do coke
off the back of each other's hands, or parties in shabby chic terraces
in Newtown and Darlington where red wine flowed like, well, red
wine. There were mornings swimming in the Bronte baths or at
Icebergs and car trips down the south coast. It felt like the good life
and probably was.

I swapped that life to share a bedroom, not a house—a *bedroom*—
with five others in Barcelona in the dodgy end of La Rambla for three
months. It smelt so bad that I used to sleep with a scarf over my
nose. Then I guess I started to smell like the room so I didn't notice
it so much anymore. I went *sans* scarf.

At the end of my street, prostitutes of indeterminate gender
loitered with intent under scaffolding that hid a gorgeous Gaudi
building. Want to see restlessness made manifest? Then stand on
La Rambla on a summer's Saturday night and try to hold steady
against the tide. Waves of people move up and down the boulevard
from the port. The Spanish complain about the English who are
drunk and chanting, vomiting in the street, wearing ugly clothes
or costumes denoting they are on a stag/hens night (because they
instruct you to 'suck me off'). They are brought over to the continent
on cheap Ryanair flights, and they tear through the night, willing it
to bring good times.

Everyone complains about the beggars—children and women with heavy hips and skirts that make music as they pass, trying to sell you in tones approaching anguish (but try to make out the words and you can't, as they are in another language or maybe no language at all) some little pamphlet or another. Everyone complains about them; keep a hand on your wallet they would say, while old Spanish matrons approach me in cafés and admonish me for leaving my bag splayed open, primed for violation by the first pair of desperate hands that pass by. Theft too is a sort of churn—goods passing from one person to the next with intimations of violence. The feeling it creates, too, of impermanence, of instability, the subtext that you don't have ownership, ever, only the illusion of ownership.

Even though summer passed too quickly, there was a heat about the nights there, as if everyone in this part of the city had created their own churn, an entire weather pattern based on body heat that, in turn, was based on beats coming out of the clubs and bars. If there was a quiet part of the city I did not seek it out. Instead I felt attracted to the bars without signs, where there were rumours of things happening there that were utterly, utterly … lawless. Tell me more, I would implore one of my housemates, an Irish barmaid, who had, at the age of twenty-two, seen *everything*. Long blonde hair and tired green eyes, the summer season had fatigued her. But this bad Barcelona fascinated me and I wanted to get to know it better. In time I did. I was there for three months ostensibly writing a novel but what I wrote was a poor Hemingway homage, my characters tantalisingly, frustratingly just out of reach. I went out instead. I *pardeeed*.

One night, closer to morning, the light emerging near the port almost tearing into the night but not quite, I got mugged on the way home from a hip-hop club. After the initial act of violence there were bits of my blood and bone spread not so neatly near the shrouded Gaudi building where the prostitutes usually stand. The hour was so dead and dark, so utterly suicidal in its unsociability that not even a happy hooker graced the corner. This is how adventure ends, I thought—in a Spanish hospital with a 25-centimetre facial scar. Restlessness can sometimes carry you along, but can also spit you out with radical-looking injuries. 'Grace to be born and live as variously as possible' is the epitaph on the grave of poet Frank O'Hara, but still … I left Barcelona, pronto.

It was on to Tokyo, where I lay on the couch at a friend's apartment while he went to work. He brought back large cartons of Starbucks coffee and we watched re-runs of *Dawson's Creek*. With my black eye and stitches, I looked like his domestic violence victim. We went out, gingerly at first because of my appearance, to restaurants, ones that sold golden dumplings, another with boiling sake and eggy chicken.

A week later in Kobe with my brother we sat in some *onsen* (hot springs) up in the mountains where the world was so still I thought it could shatter. Later that week when my bruises had gone down, a group of us rented a room for karaoke and sang old Madonna songs, and I felt okay again—like something was over and I was lucky to get through it with only a scar.

Later, returning to Sydney, I took a flat by Bondi Beach and lived alone and I thought quietly. I was now thirty. 'Enough already', I said to myself on those sparkly winter mornings. 'Now it's the quiet life for me', except it wasn't. Restlessness is not something you can sweat out of your system like a cold, but part of the way things are now, the rhythm of life.

Maybe Bondi was a bad place to be. Maybe Bondi fed my restlessness. Down by the beach with people moving in and out, absurd fashions like cowboy hats and thongs with white suits and aviator sunglasses and people drunk all the time or on drugs or the conversations overheard in cafés about frequent flyer miles and personal trainers, or the people making movies or the people starring in movies, the lingerie models and the short film makers and the skateboarders and

Japanese surfers and t-shirt designers and coke dealers and advertising people, and six-month leases and illegal youth hostels. And the way you would be checked for weapons with a metal detector passed across your body when going for a beer at the Bondi Hotel. And the way panic and an almost visceral feeling of dread would descend on a Sunday afternoon at the Bondi markets when trapped against some ethnic jewellery stand by a crush of people, a virtual mosh pit of wankers, who had come to a standstill because there were too many people trying to move in such a confined space.

It was only then, in the late Sunday afternoons surveying the tides of people trying to spend their way into the good life, that I thought—the beat goes on—even if we don't want it to ... the beat goes on.

Restlessness is global, as people everywhere who can get up and go, at least for a little while. This style of churn-migration is characterised by 'continuously circuitous traffic moving in and out of certain countries.'

Figures show that, of those leaving Britain for Australia, two-thirds are British migrants and a third are Australians going home. Similarly, of those moving to or back to Britain, about two-thirds are Australian, a third British. In other words, the historical migration pattern dominated by Britons moving to Australia for good is finished. In its place is what Professor Hugo calls a 'circularity of flows', involving people moving back and forth, often for relatively short periods.[61] However, this 'circulation is now occurring on an unprecedented scale', which Hugo says is due to a 'revolution in transport' that has seen the 'real costs of international travel plummet and their speed increase'.

As a result of this 'revolution', 'it is now much more possible for people to work in one nation while keeping their "home" in another country than was ever the case previously. Moreover, the cheapening of international telephone communication and the emergence of the internet has enabled temporary migrants to maintain intimate and regular contact with their home area.'[62] In other words, you can live or work in one country but call another country home, because technology and regular communication do not make you feel as if you have *left* home.

Neil Swidey wrote about Scheherazade Quiroga, a 28-year-old Venezuelan who left her parents' home in Caracas to begin a masters degree in Boston. Each night at 9 p.m. she Skypes her mother in Venezuela and talks for two to three hours at a stretch. 'I don't feel the distance so much', she says.[63] Swidey suggests that one of the drawbacks of the way technology can be used to help people retain close relationships with home is that they miss out on the cultural experiences of a foreign place that, in the past, may have helped them 'to learn deep truths about themselves'.[64] Such deep truths may emerge not from being more connected, but cut off, which can lead to being more open to strangers and new experiences, rather than the comfortable routine of Skyping home.

This new reality, where increasing numbers of people are living and working in one country but still call another one home, has also led to the strange phenomena of having a second home or holiday home in another country. This is particularly the case in Britain. 'Extreme commuting'—travelling between one country for work and another for weekends—took off in the 1990s through the transport revolution (with low-cost carriers like Ryanair and Easyjet). According to the *Sunday Times*, 'an estimated 425 000 Britons now have a second home overseas'.[65] It is cheaper to commute from London to a house in Toulouse, France, than it is to hop in your car and drive a couple of hours away to Somerset in the West Country.[66]

When I advertised a room in my Central London house in 2007, a number of the applicants were 'part-time Londoners'. They lived in the city during the week, flying back to their homes in France, Spain or Italy on weekends. These people weren't aristos, Eurotrash or trustafarians—they worked in middle-management jobs in middle-class professions such as publishing or academia (my house being close to several major universities). Their churn (imagine the horror of those Ryanair flights, feeling terminal in the terminal, *twice a week!*) was funded by bank loans for the second homes, cheap flights put on credit cards and a sort of glib, or perhaps desperate, belief that the good times would always last: the flights would remain cheap, fuel costs would stay low, the flight routes would remain open, the interest rates wouldn't rise and their property values would continue to soar. The economic conditions would continue to feed their restlessness. Of course none of it was to be; the recession put the brakes on this particular manifestation of restlessness. When fuel prices started to bite by mid 2008, routes were slashed and second home-owners were left stranded. 'I just won't be able to come and go as often', says Jo Chipchase, a PR executive who lives in Brighton but has a second home in Spain.[67]

Nowhere is the restless pattern of migration more apparent than in the UK, where governments and services are struggling to keep up with shape-shifting demographics.

In 2008, the *Daily Telegraph* reported with some alarm that Britain was being drained of its citizens, with one leaving every three minutes. This churn and restlessness went both ways, though, with 'Britain experiencing the greatest exodus of its own nationals in recent history while immigration is at unprecedented levels'.[68] Danny Sriskandarajah, of the left-wing think-tank Institute for Public Policy Research (IPPR), describes the churn of immigration in the UK as 'revolving turnstiles and not over-run floodgates'.[69]

Why have so many Brits left? A spokesman for the Paris-based OECD attributes it to a combination of job opportunities for very highly skilled Britons and their own desire for personal development by working overseas. Sriskandarajah agrees, noting that almost half of those emigrating do so for work.[70]

According to the *Daily Telegraph*, things in Britain are even more churny, as official 'figures do not include hundreds of thousands of east Europeans who have come to work in Britain'.[71] In 2009 there was estimated to be more than 750 000 'irregular' immigrants in the UK[72] but lack of records made it difficult to know how many people are working in the country. The effect of this level of churn is that government can't keep up with the cultural and demographic changes it brings. By the mid 2000s, English was no longer the first language of half the primary-school children in London, and the capital boasted 350 different language groups. According to British historian Andrew Marr, these new migrant groups 'radically changed the sights, sounds and scents of urban Britain': veiled Muslim women became common sights; 'Russian voices began to be as common on the London Underground as Irish ones'; and shops brought in Polish food to appeal to the newly arrived Polish workers.[73]

The lack of official information about these new immigrants has had a far-reaching impact. The Bank of England complained about setting interest rates without knowing the numbers of workers in the country. The allocation of funding for local services such as children's services and housing was impeded by not knowing 'where or for how long migrants are settling'.[74]

The cultural differences that some new immigrants bring placed strains on under-resourced areas. Julie Spence, the Chief Constable of Cambridgeshire, revealed how the steady flow of Eastern European migrants with 'different standards' was placing a huge strain on her rural police force and claimed to need a hundred extra officers to deal with the influx of immigrants. 'When they arrive they think they can do the same thing as in the country that they came from', she told the *Telegraph*. 'There were a lot of people who, because they used to carry knives for protection, they think they can carry knives here. And their attitudes to drink-driving are probably where we were 20 years ago.'[75]

The global financial crisis has caused a re-examination of the hyper-mobility that thrived in the era of prosperity. 'Politically they've [the UK Labour government] been absolutely clobbered on migration', says Tim Finch, head of migration at IPPR. The administration's view on the issue 'was very much part of their let-it-rip, free-wheeling, free-market, globalised approach to things. Along with everything else about that, the whole thing collapsed in smoking ruins.'[76]

In 2009, the British government tried to limit those entering Britain by making a working visa more difficult to obtain if you are not a EU citizen, and the education standards required and minimum salary for highly skilled professionals have been raised.[77] But the recession, believes *Time* magazine, is just a blip on this pattern of churn: 'in the long run however the recession will not put an end to migration. Foreign workers have been integral to the workings of the global economy.'[78]

Attempts in Australia to control the settlement pattern of migration also appeared fruitless. The plan to keep migrants out of Sydney and distribute them to some of the more sparsely populated areas of the country proved impossible to manage, partly because most bright young things don't come from Britain to live in the drought-affected inland communities. The dream is of Bondi Beach and tan marks and mojitos and the sound of the ocean pulling back and forth from your window each night and being surrounded by people just like you—other iron filings attached to the magnet of the common dream.

Governments can plan and set quotas and devise strategies but they cannot reconfigure the common dream. They cannot de-Bondi Australia. They have done too much of a good PR job selling that particular dream, that particular Australia, that now everyone wants to buy it. The highly skilled migrants, the bright young things coming over here, have been so thoroughly reared on choice, so used to seeing 'destination' as just another consumable, that to compel them to do something not of their choosing is not in the spirit of the Age of Entitlement.

Churn migration has also destabilised poorer countries. According to a United Nations report, many of the world's least developed countries are losing large parts of their already shallow pool of skilled professionals, hindering their ability to pull themselves out of poverty.[79]

In one year alone, 15 per cent of all skilled people in less developed countries emigrated.[80] Haiti, Samoa, Gambia and Somalia are among those that have lost more than half of their university-educated professionals in recent years. In Bangladesh, 65 per cent of newly graduated doctors seek jobs abroad. In Ethiopia, only two doctors are available for every 200 000 people as the country's doctors flock to the West. In countries such as Britain, the USA, Canada and Australia, between a quarter and one-third of all practising doctors were trained in another country.[81]

As a result of our restlessness, cities seethe and bubble with all this movement and their demographics totter on permanently shifting sands.

What is the effect on our cities of all this mobility? It is a certain measure of excitement, a lot of chaos and, more worryingly, growing inequality. Governments can't plan, planners can't plan. Services such as public transport, policing, hospitals and housing can't keep up with the churn. Melbourne is experiencing its biggest growth surge since the 1960s, with its population now increasing by almost a thousand a week.[82] The consequences include public transport, services and schools struggling to keep up with the growth. Housing affordability has emerged as a major issue for many young people, who have been forced to move further and further out of the inner city due to rising house prices and increased demand.[83]

Global cities such as London are the most affected. As porous as London is, it too has its limits. Publications ranging from *The Spectator* to the *Guardian* have recently featured stories by stressed-out British journalists complaining that they have been priced out of housing in their own neighbourhoods due to the influx of GEM-style economic migrants pushing up housing prices.

A growing inequality has affected housing affordability in Britain, with much of the middle classes no longer able to afford to live in the areas they grew up in.[84] The lifestyles of those who have bought houses have been curtailed by the burden of their mortgages. 'Never have the middle classes looked so rich on paper—house values topping a million—and felt so poor', wrote Madeline Bunting in the *Guardian*. Lloyd Evans complained in a *Spectator* column after buying his first house: 'In theory, we're halfway to being millionaires. Yet we don't have a car, we can barely afford a holiday, and when we go for a drink, we sit on the green outside the pub, quaffing Tesco £2.99 Frascati to save money.'[85] Even in the middle of the Long Boom, hospitals in Central London had trouble attracting nurses, schools teachers and other essential workers because these workers had been priced out of accommodation that was less than an hour's drive to work.

Those who stretched their budgets to afford mortgages in Central London watched in horror during late 2008 and early 2009 as housing values dropped by up to 25 per cent. Historically, low interest rates were introduced in Britain to counter-balance the credit crunch. During the boom, these global cities were caught in a wealth cycle where the city attracted investment and therefore growth, yet this growth was not shared equally among inhabitants. Inequality became pervasive. Tax breaks designed to attract investment (such as the City of London's non-domicile tax status, which led the IMF to go 'so far as to define the City of London as effectively a tax haven')[86] did attract investment, which attracted workers, which attracted further investment, leading to a cluster effect, with the city becoming a ghetto for the rich and upwardly mobile.

As such, for members of this elite it is no longer difficult to uproot yourself and start again in a new country, particularly if you are based in a global city, which is likely to be crowded with high-flying old school chums or former colleagues. Says Ryan Heath, 'About one-third of my friendship network moved to London between 2003 and 2007, so with that and regular visitors, and two trips home a year, I often saw more of my existing networks *after* I left Australia!'

During my time in London, it seemed the volume of particular cliques of Australians in London (the media people, the politics people, the law firm people) created a kind of feedback loop (or 'cluster-fuck' as it's sometimes known) where the people moving to London were not drawn by simply the city itself but by the city's vast expatriate population—all their friends were moving there, or their boyfriend was being transferred there—and the buoyant job market. The more talented people that moved there, the more talented people that followed.

This strong social capital lubricates against upheaval, insulates against having to break into local networks, friendship groups and community organisations, and provides an alternative to the often uncomfortable and initially submissive process of integration. Keep in mind that the word diaspora traditionally meant 'strong identity and mutual solidarity in exile'.

In global cities it becomes increasingly the local population who feel exiled.

There is a consumer element to this pattern of migration. It's a choice thing. The GEMs could choose where they lived, and increasingly they flocked to global cities.

Professor Hugo argues that migration today is a significant issue for a majority of countries as increasing numbers of people move between nations.[87] However, it seems that some nations, or places, are more attractive than others. Academic and author Richard Florida notes that 'the reality of the global economy is that certain places offer more opportunity than others'.[88] In his book *Who's Your City?*, Florida considers the scale of relocation of 'highly skilled, highly educated and highly paid people' to global cities where the lower and middle classes are exiting is unprecedented.[89] Further, he believes that talented people need to live in these cities 'to fully realise their full economic potential'.[90] A disproportionate number of the world's (both of the First and Third) richest and brightest citizens, its citizens with the most *potential*, are moving to a more select, narrow number of destinations (known as global cities), thus making their numbers more concentrated than ever before.

We're talking about the creation of GEM-lands in these global cities. The creation of these lands has consequences. They are the modern-day sites of restlessness, places that restless people pass through—stopping for a year or two or three then moving on. These cities have shown not just huge spikes in migration, but a type of circular migration, with people moving in and out through those 'revolving turnstiles'.[91] In London, New York, Hong Kong, Beijing and Sydney, where the churn is particularly dominant, the native inhabitants struggle to afford to live there. Instead, the indigenous population of these cities is supplanted by transient global workers, usually highly skilled, moving in for a time, maybe two to four years, and then moving on.

For example, Sydney, which has emerged as Australia's global city, has increased its share of the nation's immigrants from less than 25 per cent to 30 per cent while its share of the Australia-born has declined.[92] Clive Hamilton observes that the influx of newcomers is 'tempered by the efflux of thousands of Sydneysiders leaving the city each year, mostly heading north, driven out by declining amenity and house price inflation'.[93] He compares crowded Sydney to the experiment of too many rats in a cage; in the crowded spaces going mad, getting aggressive, anaesthetising themselves on drugs and alcohol and eventually eating their young.[94]

Moreover, in the global cities the workforce is becoming segmented as 'low status, low income and low security service jobs' are created.[95] Low status jobs include nannies, cooks, nursing home attendants, shop workers and cleaners. The local population doesn't want to do these jobs because they don't pay enough and are perceived to be low status, so they provide an opportunity for 'less skilled migrants'.[96] The rapid churn of population in global cities not only displaces the stable indigenous population (such as the poor *Spectator* writer who must drink supermarket wine on the lawn facing the pub, as he can no longer afford to drink in the pub), but in its place is a shifting and transient international population that comes with its own in-built master–servant operandi; the 'new highly mobile global elite' and the less skilled migrants.[97] In other words, a 'geographic sorting of people by economic potential'.[98]

I got a stark eyeful of the less skilled migrants one wet and blanket-hot Sunday in Hong Kong in 2008. I was meeting an English friend for lunch in what he described as one of the best dim sum restaurants in the city. And it was—oh, the feather-light dumplings, the notes of jasmine in the tea, the fat prawns encased in batter, the sticky rice wrapped in toasted banana skins with a bronzed nugget of duck inside, the chilled air, carbonated water and view out onto Victoria Harbour. But outside in the wet heat, sitting in sarongs on concrete, were hundreds of women, plaiting each other's hair, chatting, eating food from plastic containers, listening to tinny music on tape decks. Some of the more androgynous ones with spiky hair were dancing and flirting and changing the songs on the tape deck.

'They're like ladyboys but they're the female version', my friend Dean explained. We discussed the terminology: mangirls maybe? Or bois? This was a world without men. This was also a world without money. These women were all over the city, sitting mostly under concrete pylons, or in the doorways of tower blocks. My friend explained they were mostly Filipino domestic workers and Sunday was their day off. This was the 'new geographies of exclusion and landscapes of wealth' that Davis was referring to in his book *Evil Paradises* made corporeal.[99] The workers couldn't afford the restaurant where we had lunch, or the cinemas or the bars so, with nowhere to go, they met in the concreted public spaces. The other six days a week they serviced the expat class and sent the money back home. The remittances, the money sent back home, dollops here and there, have had a significant effect on the global economy. The World Bank 'estimates remittances to developing countries totalled $305 billion in 2008, triple the amount of development aid provided to poor nations'.[100]

A number of Hong Kong–based expats defended the upstairs–downstairs arrangements, saying the women were feeding whole families from these salaries back in their home countries. I also got a few lectures on the ripple effects of globalisation—the big picture that I hadn't seen was that the banker getting paid an enormous salary can afford Filipino help, which then means the Filipino woman can send money back home, which feeds her family and enables her son to go to university. It also means that inadvertently the banker is sending the Filipino child to university. Which is a good thing, isn't it?

Globalisation means the wealth doesn't just trickle down, it sprays itself all over the globe, to corners that it hasn't reached before. And that's a good thing, isn't it?

'There are real social consequences of globalisation', said the then head of Macquarie Bank, Allan Moss. 'It's perfectly natural that people want to talk about that ... It's a worthwhile debate.'[101] But it doesn't seem to be a debate we've been having.

Moss made this statement in 2005 after a Macquarie Bank profit announcement that showed that he earned $21.2 million, making him Australia's highest-paid executive of a share market–listed company, earning roughly 400 times the average weekly wage in NSW. A day later, in Sydney's *Daily Telegraph*, readers' letters were split over Moss's huge salary package. 'It cannot be ignored that Allan Moss and others steer financial juggernauts generating masses of money and employing thousands of people. It's called the free-market economy,' wrote Paul Roach from Greenwich.[102] Greg Unwin from the Gold Coast disagreed. 'Irrespective of what Allan Moss may be worth on the international remuneration gravy train, there is a moral issue in paying people such outlandish salaries.'[103]

What was missing was the outrage, the people throwing chairs through the bank's Martin Place HQ, motorists driving through Macquarie-owned tollways and private roads and *refusing to pay*. Instead there was a shrug-it-off inevitability about social inequality. As Bunting says, 'except for complaints about soaring executive pay from dogged critics, there has been a peculiar tolerance of Britain's super-rich elites' mushrooming wealth'. We grumble, like the *Daily Telegraph* letter writer, about the 'moral issue' of 'outlandish salaries' but we do not act.

During the boom there seemed to be a strange inertia around the issue, as if the words 'It's called the free-market economy' were so absolute and powerful that it was like being check-mated. The words assumed a triumphant position and debate was blocked. It's only with the global financial crisis that people are now questioning finance sector salaries and the real social consequences of globalisation.

The Free-*Movement* Economy is on track to deliver the same sort of outcomes as the Free-Market Economy—a sort of 'outlandish' topsy-turviness where it's winner takes all. Key cities are dominated by this new class of worker, which is a sort of constantly moving populace (imagine a Chinese Dragon) that is 'skimming the cream off productivity surges and technology monopolies then spending their increasing share of the national wealth as fast as possible on luxury goods and services'.[104]

As a result of the global economic downturn, there is further restlessness as this tide of 'less skilled' workers is in retreat. *Time* magazine describes how current circumstances have affected the plight of these workers. They were a 'vast, restless army that fanned out around the world in search of better lives during the opening years of the 21st century—an army that is now on the move. As jobs disappear and opportunities dwindle amid the economic crisis, millions of expatriate factory workers, bankers, household servants and construction crews are facing dislocation and despair.'[106]

Richard Florida wonders about how 'the growing division between the mobile and the rooted affect the very fabric of society'.[105] The growing division is easy to see: some people will sit in the heat under the pylons and eat lunch on the ground, while others will sit in air-conditioned restaurants supported by those pylons and be faced with choices of food of such ambrosial delight that the only thing to do is to eat it all.

Let's look closely at the Chinese Dragon. Moving it along (shaking our hips, showing our passports) are those of us that are members of the Free-Movement Economy. How is the churn for us? It must have something to recommend it, or why would we up and go at the pace we do? And why, when we aren't upping and leaving, do our dreams revolve around flight? Why are we fuelled by such restlessness?

Are there pitfalls to hyper-mobility? Loneliness in hotel rooms, existential crises at the baggage carousel—all of that—and more?

Keep in mind the questions I asked myself at the start: is it better to live broadly or deeply? And is it possible to do both?

On a Tuesday night in August 2008, I moved to Germany. I had been in living in south London for a couple of months, and before that Kings Cross in Sydney and before that Port Fairy in country Victoria and before that Bloomsbury in Central London. All these places and countries and moves in the space of around seven months from late 2007 to mid 2008. Not surprisingly I had been feeling unsettled all year, more so than usual. I attributed the cause of restlessness as vaguely geographical in origin. If I could just be in the right place, it would all work out, I would feel *settled*. So muddled was I that I couldn't see that frequently moving was the cause of my being unsettled, rather than the cure. And so it was on day two in Berlin I woke up with a sickness that seemed unshakeable. It wasn't a hangover—even though when friends picked me up from the airport we had a warmish beer on the U-Bahn from the airport, 'because you can drink on public transport in Germany' (and you can't in Australia, the UK and the USA). Instead it felt something like this: I woke up in the morning and wanted to be sick, and spent the whole day feeling like any minute I was going to throw up, and went to bed feeling the same way. Sometimes headaches accompanied the nausea, other times it was just the nausea, a feeling in the pit of my stomach similar to what I used to get before going into an exam. The sickness made me feel anxious and withdrawn. Even though I was living in one of the coolest areas in Berlin, I didn't want to leave the house.

I Googled the symptoms but, really, there was no need. I knew what the churning stomach was. I call it motion sickness and I get it every four or five years when there's a lot of change or upheaval in my life. It is, of course, anxiety but anxiety of the low-level kind that doesn't impair function but instead suffuses everything with an awful kind of dread, a low-key hysteria, a portent of disaster, a feeling of no, everything is not going to be alright.

I did finally venture out early on a Saturday evening. It was a balmy August night and all along Karl Marx Strasse—the old East German monument to itself—was a mile-long beer festival packed with Germans of the old school. There were mullets and perms, streaked hair and platform sneakers, steins and bratwurst, death metal t-shirts and the strains of a cover-band singing Foreigner from a far-off stage. It could have been fun but for the gallons of sweat pouring off me, the way my heart sped up and chest tightened, the way my stomach was churning so much I thought I would be sick, right there on the footpath outside the Pilsner tent. Will the churn in myself stop only when I stop? I wondered. I sat on the train home clutching my beer festival souvenir mug ('Berlin Bier 2008. Viel Vernügen!), still drenched in sweat, inexplicably afraid, trying to remain still. Almost there, I told myself, almost there ...

An article for AFP portrays, somewhat breathlessly, the glamorous socialising of expats at an organised mixer:

> Midweek in Paris. A private room at a posh bar/restaurant is packed with bright young things in designer suits sipping champagne, nibbling fancy canapés, air-kissing with aban-don and gate-crashing multi-lingual conversations. This may look like an upscale networking convention or a college reunion: in fact it's the latest time-saving social device for jet-setting expats.[107]

This scene is a far cry from the nerdy organised friendship circles that mixers usually entail that

> conjure up images of social misfits, lost in a far away land, desperate to chat to anyone within earshot. But these people

don't fit that stereotype. Rather they seem to be movers and shakers who have found that their new foreign posting brings a fat compensation package and a plush company flat, but a social diary full of windows. The lack of an immediate social circle can be difficult for members of the cash-rich time-poor generation used to things moving quickly. Serious about their careers, long office hours and frequent business travel are the norm for these expats. And traditional friend-finding locations such as conversation groups, night school and exercise classes take up too much time and do not guarantee quality contacts.[108]

Quality contacts ... could there be anything sadder than a young man freshly arrived in, say, Paris visiting a wine bar in the Marais, maybe tasting pastis for the first time, inhaling that first lungful of Gauloise drifting in from an outdoor table, his ears prickling with bits of a half-recognised, half-dream-like language. A night—indeed a new life of possibility—unfurls like the smoke and he is on the prowl for *quality contacts.*

What does it take to survive such restlessness and hyper-mobility? To be a 'member of the cash-rich time-poor generation used to things moving quickly'? To have a 'social diary full of windows'? Do you need a strong stomach? A cool head? Well, you have to be prepared, yet also flexible. Self-reliant, yet socially gregarious. You have to have strong social networks but you also have to believe in the primacy of what American sociologist Mark Granovetter terms 'the strength of weak ties'.[109] Weak ties are those with people you don't know too well; the friend of a friend who is based in Paris and may know about apartments, someone from your old job who has an ex-boyfriend living in New York, that type of thing. People in the churn reach out for what's there, no matter how weak and tenuous the link. They have learnt to be comfortable connecting with people they don't know too well or haven't built up a trust with yet because they know *that's what you have to do.*

Says Philipa Bourke, a journalist originally from Adelaide, 'While living in the United States, I had reached the point where I could pack up my life and drive into a small town, or to a massive metropolis, and set it all up again. Usually there was another journalist, an old buddy or friend of that friend, or a stranger, to cushion the move.'

What else do you need to 'set it all up again' to 'cushion the move'? Good social skills, the ability to fit in anywhere, adaptability, a portable life and not a lot of baggage. American companies are increasingly sending their young, single employees on overseas assignments because *it costs them less.* But one of the most important things you need to survive—and even thrive amid such restlessness, the thing that comes up in the interviews I have done for this book—is the ability to take risks. Not just being able to *take* risks, but being *relaxed* with risk-taking, chilled, living in a margin that others might find too uncomfortable. This new elite are resilient, flexible, dynamic and mobile—all the things that the economy, the loose world of contract and no-ties work tells them they should be, in fact the *very thing* the economy is. Funny that.

One young engineer who had been transferred from America to Berlin and had struggled with feelings of loneliness that he was gradually overcoming told the *IHT*, 'When you take a risk, that's when things start to open up', he said. 'It's definitely improving.'[110]

Richard Sennett analyses the current 'risk culture' in *The Corrosion of Character*. He argues that when we take risks we are 'letting go of the past, dwelling in disorder … living on the edge'.[111] Risk-taking and restlessness are closely connected. They involve not staying still, always moving on to the next. Sennett contends that it is not so much where you are moving to that is significant but that you are not staying where you are.[112] This kind of risk is motivated by fear; a fear that if we do not do something then we won't prosper and we will be left behind.[113] 'In a dynamic society passive people wither', he writes.[114]

Once risks were the provision of particularly heroic people; now, according to the management manuals, all of us are required to be risk-takers, whether we like it or not, whether we are *comfortable* or not.

As well as risk, ambiguity is inbuilt in the restlessness cycle and in the lives of the hyper-mobile. All of this may end tomorrow; the company may collapse, the contracts may not get signed off, the visa may be denied, the deal may die, the work may suddenly shift like a zephyr from France to Dubai, and so then should the worker. We must learn to work well with uncertainty, and change is to be expected. But how can this then not lead to a feeling of deep instability? That identity, and indeed a life, is built on shifting sands?

Clive Hamilton warns in *Growth Fetish*, 'We should not mistake mobility for freedom ... Travel and detachment are seen as being the core of identities marked by a sophisticated global outlook, but they are identities that frequently suppress the anguish of voluntary homelessness.'[115] This detachment is as a result of being unmoored from a fixed identity—from a group, a nation, a geographical, fixed point, a tribe, a home. The modern worker might be wordly and cos-mopolitan but they dwell in a fractured, fragmented, restless world that lacks a continuous, linear narrative.

For the hyper-mobile, the sheer geographical breadth of their lives, the access they have to different experiences, new countries and education marks them out as a new elite; yet their restlessness, their adaptability, the fact that their first loyalty is to a company, as opposed to a nation-state, means that in gaining a more worldly perspective, deep associations of tribe, community and family are sacrificed. Breadth is achieved at the cost of depth.

We clip ourselves free from people who have known us for twenty-five years in order to meet the people with whom we have 'weak ties'. We search for fresh faces. The world we move in is characterised by some as 'Darwinian' or 'a bubble, a kind of fantasy world of luxury living and, if you want it, endless partying'.[116]

To survive in this world of hyper-mobility it's important to not be too rooted or too attached to anywhere or anything. The hyper-mobile, the young and the restless, are detached from the politics of their home countries, social issues, family concerns and local, community issues. In their adopted countries they also stand outside. They are detached from many of the arguments that citizens have with each other and with those with power, including debates about issues such as civil liberties, police powers, how taxes are distributed and spent, how the churches and the companies and political parties behave, the accountability of corporations and governments to the environment and sustainability. Activism, or at least interest, springs from engagement, but the hyper-mobile are forever outside, never getting in too deep because, according to one management consultant friend who is regularly and frequently posted around the globe, 'you never know when you are going to leave'.

Ambiguity doesn't allow for deep connections, because there is always the likelihood that such connections may become severed, and when you are required to sever something deep there is always a certain amount of pain, grief even. For the restless, disengagement from the business of nation and community, even family, is a necessary state, a form of energy conservation. In the end the hyper-mobile belong everywhere and nowhere. And so onwards they skate, across the surface of things.

Being an expat in Italy means Chris Davis (who has lived in Melbourne, London, Dublin, Rome and Brazil) doesn't feel the need to get too deeply committed to the issues of a place. He says, 'I like being a foreigner. I like being the person with the funny accent. I like that I can remove myself from the political situation in both my home country and my adopted country, making myself just an observer in both. It's probably not a politically responsible thing to do, but party politics shit me.'

Likewise, even those who are entirely integrated into their new country practise a strong, self-protective sort of detachment, allowing them to walk away if the risk eventually fails. David Gabbe, thirty, from Sydney, has been living in London for seven years and says, 'I think it would be tough to be any more integrated than what I have become without repudiating any link with Australia, which I hasten to add I would never consider. I'm one of the longer serving members at my workplace. I have a broad spectrum of friends, have very few Australian friends in the UK and I share a flat with people from Scotland. I participate in many activities outside of work and home, most importantly singing, which is my real passion. I've developed a taste for tuna, sweetcorn sandwiches and spend far too much on high-quality produce from Europe. I read the *Times* and the *Guardian* and I love UK television almost more than it's polite to admit. I've been to the Last Night of the Proms six years running and managed to get on TV each of those times. I drink real ale semi-regularly. I work for London Underground and know London perhaps better than most Londoners I've met.'

Yet part of him is detached and holding back, fearful maybe of missing what a wrench it will be when he moves back to Australia. He tells me via email, 'There is an "anguish" which I always feel I'm trying to suppress. Instead of building on the foundations of my first twenty years of life, I basically went away and started again. New society to deal with, new friends, new job in a new field. I know that I could have been better off financially, perhaps even more emotionally stable, if I had stayed in one place and applied myself to the pursuit of whatever it is we're meant to want. Family? House? Financial security? Instead I've blown my twenties on experiences and short-term gains. I feel it's all temporary because I'm sure I'm headed back to Australia one day—though that could be a fair way off—and that I shouldn't get too attached to anything or anyone over here.'

The experience is as Sennett says: being continuously exposed to risk can eat away at your sense of character. You are always 'starting over.'[117] There is in each move a denial of past experience, yet if each new 'home' for the restless feels temporary there results a certain disorder in the existence, of floating above, unconnected and unwilling to invest in the time it takes to make deep connections.

Andrew Hewitt, a 26-year-old political staffer in London, is originally from Sydney. He moved because of better job opportunities in London. 'I was feeling limited in my career opportunities in politics. In moving to London I am now a parliamentary adviser for an MP who is also on the House of Commons Defence Committee. I would never have reached those career goals if I stayed in Sydney.'

But Hewitt 'doesn't feel integrated as such, I am lucky I don't have a broad Australian accent so most people don't accuse me straight away of being "foreign"'. His way of coping is to keep the ties loose, to not put down too many roots that may be too hard to pull up: '[I feel] chilled out because, for example, I don't have a credit card and have little to no debt, but I do miss the multi-faceted network of friends I had at home ranging from close and "best" friends to simple acquaintances I meet on the street and chat briefly to'.

Says Barbara Waley, a PA, 'I moved to Dublin then London because Sydney feels small and parochial after a while and you get restless'. Yet she does not feel integrated in England. 'The few English people I socialise with, I know through Australian friends. I am pathetically non-integrated and I am like one of those immigrants everyone hates. I complain a lot about how poorly the English do so many things (like service), and how much better everything is at home. English people would be justified in telling me, "If ya don't like it, why don't you just feck off home".'

I ask Barbara if she plans on returning to Australia. 'Definitely. The idea of returning home is always with me, creating a constant sense of impermanence. I constantly miss my friends and family and feel torn between two places. Either way I go I am missing out on something.'

Part of taking risks is not having too much to lose, of keeping things loose so if they don't work out, you can walk away with a minimum of fallout and fuss.

Yet, the resistance to stability—a characteristic that seems to be the norm among the GEMs, the Departure People, the hyper-mobile— creates its own problems. It involves, as David Gabbe says, not getting 'too attached to anything or anyone over here'. Or, as Chris Davis says, being able to 'remove myself from the political situation in both my home country and my adopted country, making myself just an observer in both'. Or as Andrew Hewitt (whose neutral accent saves him from being 'accused' of being foreign) says, 'I don't have to settle my roots'. Or James Starling stating, 'I don't worry much about what goes on in Oz generally, [I] don't usually bother to vote'.

Faced with a transient population, skilled at practising detach-ment, cities and their indigenous population respond in kind. Ryan Heath says, 'In London there are definite social walls erected against outsiders. It sounds ridiculous because London is actually very porous but because of that openness in society and the sheer pace of it all, there tends to be a certain closedness to private life. No one in par-ticular is a target, you just can't expect to be drawn in to a close-knit group of friends quickly. It takes a persistence that I didn't have.'

P, a 33-year-old lawyer, who has lived in Melbourne, Sydney, Hong Kong and London, found that although the world he moved in was fluid and dynamic, certain barriers were erected in defence against the churn. 'London is a very closed place in terms of personal circles of the locals. They are not unfriendly, just not that welcoming,' he says. 'There are always exceptions to the rule of course and they are normally pleasant enough to work with. In Hong Kong there is a language and cultural barrier that exacerbates your separation from the locals. It is extremely difficult to integrate, although again people are pleasant enough to work with.'

Another lawyer, D, aged thirty-seven, told me that he 'never actually made any friends in London that would count as proper friends. The test for "proper friends" are those that would get an invite to my wedding (should I have one) and/or my funeral (when it eventually comes around). In London, the English generally only spend time with the people they went to school and then possibly college with (e.g. think of the "incestuous" social circle in *Four Weddings and a Funeral*). It is this very queer separation of the professional and private lives that is so odd. Everyone disappears on a Friday night to have their weekend with their other lives and then re-emerges on a Monday morning to be asked how their weekend was (almost by way of a closing ritual). This is not only my experience, but probably that of every Aussie I have ever spoken to.'

Richard Sennett argues that the failure to build long-term relationships in the workplace affects emotional wellbeing. Constant short-term and project work does not allow workers the time to 'develop trust' with others or a 'sense of place'.[118] In fact, the continuous change associated with this kind of work 'leaves us floating and uncertain'.[119]

Remember T, my lunch date in Bondi, and his prototype of the financial analyst who when in full flight has several jobs a year, is not punished by the banks for being flighty and rootless, but rewarded with high-paying work? According to Sennett this is precisely what suits modern capitalism: 'the imperatives of growth make everything expendable and the capriciousness of consumer tastes requires businesses to be ever-more lightfooted'.[120]

Says P, the lawyer, 'Both [in] London and Hong Kong I have at times understood just a little of what it is like to be an outsider, to have the roles reversed from my life in Australia where thousands of immigrants and visitors must experience what I experience on a regular basis. It is often small but telling things. Noticing that the English partner treats you differently from the homegrown English associate, spending more time teaching them because we are seen as short-term fodder not worth nurturing. Meanwhile the English associate leaves at 6 p.m. regularly while the office is abuzz with antipodeans and Americans post-9 p.m. … The English partner's view becomes self-fulfilling prophecy and we leave. In Hong Kong the locals talk about my wife and her other expatriate colleagues in front of them in Cantonese (as we have found out from a kindly tattle tail). Some of the best jobs are often excluded from those who cannot speak the local language, even though corporate business here is often done in English anyway. We are guests in the respective countries and from our perspective are lucky to be here in the first place, so it is something you just have to take.'

Or how about the 'short-term fodder' that American companies send abroad as it's cheaper, and advances in technology mean they can be 'kept on a shorter leash' by head office?

Margaret Malewski, thirty, the author of *GenXpat: The Young Professional's Guide to Making a Successful Life Abroad* told the *International Herald Tribune* that competition for overseas postings was 'fierce'. But 'while people of all ages are often lured by the prospect of jetting between foreign capitals, the reality of living abroad "unaccompanied" may be less glamorous than it appears at first. Young singles may be free of family complications, but they also lack the support system that family brings. Learning a new job, setting up house in an unfamiliar land and learning to navigate a new culture entirely on their own can broadside young professionals.'[121]

A former marketing manager for Procter & Gamble based in Geneva, Malewski used to return to an empty fridge after twelve hours at the office. 'I went straight to bed and slept until morning', she writes. 'This scenario repeated almost daily for well over a month.' The *IHT* said, 'not surprisingly, loneliness and burnout can become the companions of young overseas workers'. Those engaged in project work might move as often as four times a year, Lisa Johnson, of Cendent Mobility, says, with little time to explore the culture around them or form social networks, 'unaccompanied expats, on short-term assignments, tend to work longer hours with no social network to support them. We tend to see higher levels of stress and illness in this group.'[122]

As well as the physical cost there is a psychic cost to hyper-mobility and the risk-taking that accompanies it. Sennett explains the effect of risk taking on our psyches: 'The good risk taker has to dwell in ambiguity and uncertainty … the less powerful individuals who try to exploit ambiguity end up feeling like exiles. Or, in moving on, they lose their way.'[123] More broadly, the psychic cost is the lack of shape our lives have by moving broadly across experiences but not settling in deeply to a smaller number of experiences. In restlessness there is change for the sake of change, movement for the sake of movement, constantly refreshing things because of fear of missing out on a new, and possibly better, experience. Austrian economist Joseph Schumpeter called it 'creative destruction'—where constant reinvention that destroys what comes before is a necessary part of economic growth and innovation. He writes, 'incessantly destroying the old one, incessantly creating a new one … [The process] must be seen in its role in the perennial gale of creative destruction; it cannot be understood on the hypothesis that there is a perennial lull.'[124]

With hyper-mobility, a sort of personal creative destruction occurs with each new move.

Sarah Gilbert, an Australian recently returned to Sydney after years in Buenos Aires, who has also lived in Canberra, Amsterdam and New York, tells me, 'the more places you live and manage to make a home in, the less you feel you really belong somewhere. That doesn't anguish me really, as I guess I was pretty conscious of that bargain from early on. I really value the freedom of feeling like I can make myself at home just about anywhere, so I don't mind trading in a bit of the sense of belonging. That belonging feeling can be illusory anyway. Home isn't always as comfortable as it might seem. Living in Latin America has exposed me to the reality of people who love their country but can't help but try to leave due to repeated economic or political upheaval. Things at home can change fast in most parts of the world. It's good to be able to adapt and go wherever the opportunity lies.'

Johanna Leggatt, who has lived in Sydney, Florence, London and Brisbane, says, 'I don't feel integrated into English society, but then that doesn't bother me. I like the feeling of being an outsider, peeling back the layers of a culture that is alien to me.'

We often underestimate the importance of belonging. The deep need to be understood, not just in the basic literal sense (which even that you cannot take for granted when abroad and want to buy a loaf of bread), but also in a human, emotional and elemental way. To know and be known. To understand and be understood. Something awful can happen to us if we aren't understood in this deep way, if we don't belong, if we stand for too long outside things. We freeze over. The experience of being in the world without feeling *understanding* can seem very cold. We feel disconnected from those around us, haunting the margins, floating across the surface, disengaged. Is any of this real? the disconnected ask. Do I matter? An existential lightness descends; this lightness feels like a yoke. It is terrifying.

It is as Isak Dinesen described one of her characters, a shell-shocked war veteran having a breakdown: 'I was constantly in flight, an exile everywhere'.

Floating and uncertain, disorientated, the anxiety of being constantly on the move, of having no anchor, the denial of the past, of lived experience in each new place. The children of globalisation would never admit to it, but the feeling of tumult rises up. Insomniac at 2 a.m., or jetlagged, tongue-tied through language barriers, or over-worked, or uncertain or having too many drinks with a 'weak tie' at 9 p.m. and feeling somehow *lonely*—our restlessness can sometimes look more glamorous than it feels.

According to Vavine Tapinai, thirty-one, an Australian who lives with her musician husband Matt in Los Angeles, the anguish of voluntary homelessness 'is something I deal with often. While being a foreign visa holder in the USA, I can never truly feel at home. I haven't bought a piece of art since I've lived here and nor have I bought a hardcover book. While I thoroughly enjoy our life here and feel somewhat settled and resigned to the fact that I will have an American baby, I do not yet feel at home. I have struggled greatly with this feeling.'

There are dreams of moving to Mexico to 'raise our children there for a spell [as] we have always been keen to raise our children in a non–First World country until they are old enough to understand', but 'this will only exacerbate the problem, surely. But while I have spent many an anxious night awake feeling lost, so too I have come to realise that my husband is my home.'

The problem with hyper-mobility is that once you keep moving, you are constantly leaving people behind. You can do the hard yards of getting established in one area, but it seems no sooner does that happen than you are moving again and starting the whole cycle over. It is a cycle that can be wearing. The people in the new places don't know the stories, and never really want to hear them, they 'don't see the other places'.[125] They weren't *there*. Under these circumstances it can be hard to maintain a sustainable self. The narrative is too jumpy. The pieces don't fit. People see only fractions of you, not the whole. It is as Joan Didion described in *The Year of Magical Thinking* when a widow after a long marriage failed at dating someone new because he didn't know the songs.

Naomi Mapstone, an Australian journalist for London's *Financial Times*, has lived in Canberra, London, New York and now Lima. She says, 'I spent seven years in London and I now think of it as a second home. Most of my friends are there, and when I moved to New York I was actually homesick for my friends and my regular haunts there rather than Australia. In New York I had a good circle of friends who were mostly a mix of American and Europeans. I'm definitely not integrated yet in Peru—it's been three months and I am still learning the language. It's also a very different society to New York or London or Australia—much greater levels of poverty and inequality, and different safety concerns, so for the moment I spend a lot of time in an expat bubble. I'm looking forward to a time when my Spanish is fluent and I can call this place my own too.'

When I ask her if she'll return to Australia again she replies, 'I don't know! The longer I stay away the less certain I am. In a way a move home to Australia would be like starting from scratch all over again. [But] I worry about my parents getting old, and missing out on my brothers' lives.'

Susie P, twenty-seven, moved to London from Sydney because of 'boredom at work—the same job for five years'. But despite saying she's integrated in London, she admits, 'I'm perpetually homesick, feel very far away from friends and family and like I'm permanently on the road. The hardest thing about moving to the UK from Australia was the feeling that I was starting all over again. The goal was to achieve success in my field in a much, much bigger market—to be a big fish in a big pond, etc. The problem was that when I arrived my credentials didn't matter and it looked like I may not even make it into the pond at all. For the first time I knew something of how those Pakistani taxi drivers feel who are actually doctors in their home country but their qualifications aren't recognised abroad. Before I arrived in the UK I worked at a national newspaper in Australia for five years, reporting politics and on foreign assignment. But as far as management at Fleet Street newspapers were concerned I might as well have spent my career working on the Fijian Post.'

Eventually Susie 'did get a job, and it's a good one, very respectable, but my position is not as senior as it would be if I was still working in Australia. I miss my contacts back home, and the feeling of belonging. I fantasise about returning and working in a senior role with people who trust my ability and skill and where it doesn't feel like they are doing me a favour just letting me walk into the building.'

Those caught up in relentless restlessness fear returning to base-camp because it means re-establishing themselves.

Matthew Philp, thirty, from Sydney, has been living in New York for the past eight years. 'I have visited Australia several times since moving here but I actually don't wish to return and live there. It's not out of the question but I'd have to actually have a job offer that was suitable. I wouldn't want to return to Australia to simply start from nothing and try and integrate myself again.'

Caitlin Macleod, thirty, has lived in Melbourne, Canberra, London, Cambridge, Bougainville (PNG) and Honiara (Solomon Islands) yet feels 'nervous and intimidated at the prospect of moving back to Melbourne … I feel occasionally panicked that I am growing older and still living like I was ten years ago, that I am not at home, and that I am missing out on time with my family (who seem so much older every time you see them), buying a house (that impossible dream) and having a family. Every year I am away makes it harder to go back as my peers who stayed at home become more settled and grown up and so

I wonder if we'll have anything in common anymore? Will my life over here count for anything when I return? I feel much more nervous and intimidated at the prospect of moving back to Melbourne than when I moved to a war zone, or big-city London.'

While travellers in their teens and early twenties feel homesick, older travellers like Matthew or Caitlin feel its opposite. It could be called 'homesickness' but instead it manifests itself as a dread of returning home. They feel prodigal, 'nervous', inexplicably afraid.

Philipa Bourke has lived in the USA and Japan. She says, 'I had had a peripatetic childhood, after being born in the US (making me a US citizen) and being raised mainly in Australia, as an Australian, living there again as a child on two subsequent occasions. The uprooting of my family for these stints had a massive impact on us.

'I was living in New York on 9/11. I was working directly behind the World Trade Center and was inside the WTC at least four times a day. The experience in the aftermath was much greater, however. What was a sensational and traumatic collapsing of global boundaries started me directly on a path toward "home". When I arrived in New York in the Clinton years, it felt like the safest place on earth. That feeling, a feeling of a broader home or shelter, was destroyed for me with 9/11 and subsequent developments. In the three weeks just afterwards, I often paced the rent-controlled, beautifully renovated one-bedroom apartment I had just moved into feeling completely invaded and violated.

'Ironically, the city's formality dissipated and the sense of New York as a village or a kind of home enabled me to stay there for four years. In the end, though, I wanted to leave partly to finally or fully escape 9/11. Around 2003 I tracked down and hosted a panel for new Australian artists on the make in lofts in Soho and the East Village that formed the foundation of subsequent exhibitions. I did not consider myself to be of them or among them. I found some of these expat Aussies brazen, opportunistic and ego-directed at quick success or fame or money. But I felt like I had put my time, my life in fact, into being serious about understanding American culture. I spent a year in a small town as a reporter. Americans, whose humility overwhelmed me once I got below the surface of American stereo-types, had tamed a lot of that out of me and the process had not been an easy one for me.

'I also had been in America for seven years or so by then and the experience of Japan had erased my sense of belonging. I had re-learnt my Westernness in America, foolishly assuming it would be home and it would be more "like Australia". Japan taught me that being "integrated" was not ultimately possible for a foreigner. It didn't have to be one's aim. I learnt the degrees of separation and closeness that I needed to have in entering cultures and cities. I am adept.

'Gradually, however, the risk-taking inclination subsided a bit in me and over time, the loss of the sense of shelter in the USA—I am not talking about owning a home—but feeling as if I could not have, even with my citizenship, the haven of a safe place, or the protection of a community or society that was without the very real problems it does have (the cumulative effect of and starting with the Oklahoma bombings, 9/11, Iraq and New Orleans), an economy that could guarantee that etc., all added up to a feeling of lacking a home, or precisely the shelter of a home in the immediate and sovereign sense, as dated as that term would be now.

'I would not call it "anguish of homelessness". That would imply to me a longing or emotional state that I think I may have endured at some earlier point in my expat life without knowing it, while living in Japan. I would call it a creeping anxiety, perhaps. It eventually enters your psyche in the sense that you feel like you have fewer buffers to life or misfortune overall. All told, I am not at present too wedded to the idea of "home".'

There seems to be a certain magical thinking in those of us who have gone from Canberra to London to New York to Lima, from Colac to Melbourne to Dublin to London to Brazil to Rome, or like me, from Warrnambool to Melbourne to Dublin to Sydney to Spain to London to Berlin to London, that we can, at some unfixed point, go back to where we came from, to make what the therapists and poets and palm readers call 'a full circle', no matter how wide the arc may be. It is James Starling wanting to 'one day go back to the farm'. It is me promising that one day I'll move back to Melbourne. It is Naomi and Caitlin wanting to spend time with aging parents. It is Susie 'fantasising about returning and working in a senior role with people who trust my ability and skill and where it doesn't feel like they are doing me a favour just letting me walk into the building'. Going back, back, back.

There is, inbuilt in these dreams, the hope that no experience was wasted, that no risk was too ridiculous or unyielding, that you can return to your home after having squeezed the marrow out of the world, out of *life*, and yet have a new appreciation of what you always had in your backyard.

There is the hope that it's not all been in vain.

Yet restlessness changes us. Full circles are for poets and palm readers, we do not come home the same person we were when we left, and home is not the same place we left. Completion is the greatest myth. There is always some peace to be made somewhere, and regrets. There is a psychic cost to 'dwelling in a continual state of vulnerability' to a 'creeping anxiety' of having fewer buffers—and there are stories that never get told.

This may be the cost to our psyches ... the untold stories.

In Berlin I have found a flat on my own. It is the first time in a long time that I've lived alone. Sometimes when I feel the anxious, churning feeling coming back, I lie on my bed and think of what I would do and where I would go if something bad happened. A broken arm, a toothache, a stolen credit card … or worse. I touch the wood of my nightstand out of superstition, what would I do? I have three friends here in Berlin, all of whom I would trust with my life. And there are some more a plane ride away in London, then the rest—a 24-hour flight away. Various people, at various points of distance. I lie on my bed and imagine all these people like lights on a map, flicking yellow and illuminating, blinking like lighthouses, in reassurance.

Six months earlier, and it's a bright sunny day, the end of the summer of 2008 and my Italian class is sitting in the garden of Community House in Port Fairy on the far south-west coast of Victoria.

'*Da dove vieni*? (Where are you from?)' asks the teacher. There is a jumble of answers—Griffiths Street, Port Fairy, Walsh Road, Warrnambool, just off the Princes Highway before you get to Tower Hill. The teacher qualifies this.

'That's not what the Italians mean by it. It's how far back do you go? Where are you from? It is your accent, the food you eat, the football team you support, your values and politics … Where are your roots? Where are you from?'

Aha! Our answers are different now, we think about it more carefully, it seems more personal than just spitting out an address. In the churn it's not a question that gets asked very often—*where are you from?*—because the answer's not as simple as it once was, or maybe there is no answer … we can go everywhere, do everything, but actually be from nowhere. Remember, according to Facebook's expats group, a defining feature of being an international kid is that you can't answer that question.

In 2004 when interviewing singer Shane Howard in a lean-to, makeshift recording studio on his block of land in Killarney, south-west Victoria, he recalled asking of himself, 'How far do your feet go down?' He was talking about a time in Ireland treading on farm-land that was connected to his mother's people. 'How far do your feet go down?'

What this question meant was how far back in this land do you go? How deep is the connection? For him the notion of *home* meant not just being up to your ankles in mud, but your ancestors rotting in the earth, piled on their ancestors, hipbone to hipbone, past the dirt, past the peat, right down to the chalky stuff below.

To be fleet of foot, to be international, to be in the churn and a hostage to its restless tempo means to leave a light footprint on the places you pass through, not necessarily in the environmental sense but in the emotional sense. When you are 'just passing through' you have little or no impact, your presence is meaningless except in a commercial sense where you may add a few dollars here and there to the local economy. Your feet do not go down far at all.

At the Warrnambool Hotel, I met a man who didn't like Noosa because he didn't 'know the faces', so after a while he moved back to the place where he knew the faces and hasn't left. 'Knowing doesn't mean liking', he told me as he stamped out his cigarette. 'But at least knowing means knowing.'

I nodded and said, 'I know'. Because I did.

One of my oldest friends, Jo Beattie, had a very old grandfather, Pat Glover, who lived in Port Fairy. He was appointed the town's *Senachi* (Gaelic for storyteller) at the region's folk festival. He was an amateur historian, a lively talker and had a sharp mind.

A few years ago, I was back from Sydney and he was recently widowed, so I dropped around with a bag of cakes. We made tea in a kitchen that felt like the past. It was an old person's house with the comfortable chairs and matching poufs, china cups and saucers, the smells of Vicks vapour rub and the gas heater. We talked about the even more distant past, as he remembered it. He told me about the strange time *before mobility*, when nobody went anywhere except to war if they were a man, and to Calcutta or Port Moresby if they were a nun. No cars meant people were trapped on their land and with each other. No television meant that there was little access to a 'common experience' outside your own and your neighbours. You had nothing to compare your life to that didn't exist outside your turf. It was a world contained and in it brewed something strange, rich and seething.

The stories I liked hearing most were about the triangle of land that stretched from Port Fairy up to Koroit around to Killarney then on to Warrnambool. Born of isolation, every few miles there would be a different dialect and customs, a rich and strong community life, *stories*. It was a world replete with a cast of characters—the virgin bachelor farmer, the aloof Protestant family, the abstentious publican, the alcoholic priest and his yearning, unfulfilled house-keeper. Everyone was at a fixed point in that fixed world and life unfurled from that.

This steady point, this world; rural, musical, melancholy, Irish Catholic, insular, alcoholic, unworldly, poetic, cut-off, working class, sentimental, clannish, dreaming of a County Clare that they had never seen, that had pretty much vanished. Some Warrnambool people with their undiluted Irish blood (such as myself), still look fairly homogenous but now they are great travellers, and there'll always be one, anytime and everywhere—lurking behind the Pyramids, bemused at a Sevillean bullfight, throwing coins in the Trevi Fountain, being turfed out at closing time in the pubs of Donegal.

Yet remnants of the Old World remain. A few years ago, I was somewhere, another state, I'm not sure which one, and someone was channel surfing. They flew past an old face on the ABC. It wasn't a face I knew precisely, but one I *recognised*. It was a Western District Irish Catholic face: a potato face, a face from where I am from.

'Go back to that!' I ordered. It turned out to be a 7.30 *Report* story on two elderly bachelor farmer brothers from outside Warrnambool who didn't have a car and were on the farm milking every day so they never went anywhere. They had never been to a capital city, or been on an aeroplane or taken a holiday, or eaten at a restaurant, or been to the theatre. I remember in the segment they were saying their favourite food was stew in a tin saved for a special occasion. A few weeks later I saw the elderly brothers again in a magazine supplement. The magazine had sponsored them to go on a plane for the first time and ride the escalator at Melbourne Central. They were photographed riding down in their farming clothes, looking underwhelmed.

Everything is so different now. But is it better? Or not? Did people lead richer lives with fewer 'new faces' in it? With less opportunities and less mobility? Without a means to feed their restlessness?

Had I been born in that time I would have probably been faced with three options, none appealing: stay at home aging with aging parents, marry and stay on the land breeding a football team of children, or leave and join a convent. The choices were stark. School friends told me of grandmothers who rebelled against the limited roles assigned to them but the rebellions were never heroic, just bleak and pointless—drinking, madness, asylums. Being cast out, as in the words of Matthew's gospel, 'into the outer darkness'.[126]

But I wonder: within that limited range of choice, might there be the possibility of great depth? Real happiness rather than just fleeting moments of gratification, and the picturesque contentment to be found by the modern-day traveller, the hyper-mobile on the banks of, say, the Seine or strolling through the Tiergarten on a sunny day.

I imagine these people from the 'un-mobile' past may have enjoyed quiet, deeply mined riches, the riches that come from settling with what you've got, of making the best of it. They weren't driven to distraction by unlimited choice, all the possibilities that consumer society lays on. Those lives are probably unfathomable to those who now move so far and so fast, through whose cerebral cortex so much information passes, where the stimuli is so great that how they experience the world is through a fast-moving flicker fest (disparate images bursting at speed onto the retina: the frost on the grass at Avalon as you board your flight at dawn, Buckingham Palace lit up at night as seen from the back window of a black cab, a rickshaw somewhere, the Chrysler building glinting wickedly in the sun) not a thousand-yard stare.

I wonder if our modern obsession with self-actualising—providing deepest parts of our potential with the most precise match (that's why we have vegan, bassoon-playing bisexuals who work in New Age crystal shops in Copenhagen)—is necessarily the road to fulfilment? Is all this running around, this hyper-mobility, this worship of the NEXT really a better option?

Might I have had a simple, uncomplicated happiness had I been forced to 'settle', had I been given only two or three choices, or no choices? If I had stayed put. What would have happened then? Would I have made my peace with it? Deeper or broader? I'll never know. I was born into the era of a new Babylon, came of age in the longest bull-run of prosperity, during the height of Western consumer culture, where abundance and choice were synonymous with the times.

Where are you from?

It's a question that can elicit a complicated and qualified response.

My home, no matter where I am living or what I am doing, remains a stretch of land, around twenty kilometres long, that runs from Warrnambool, down the Princes Highway, through Killarney, past the cemetery with its Celtic crosses and the deep green potato fields, running parallel with a blue strip of sea, punctuated by dunes, to Port Fairy.

None of this land belongs to me in the traditional sense—I am *sans* property— yet in a deeper sense it all belongs to me. This sense comes with a feeling. It occurs after having been away for a while and I first glimpse that strip of sea or the car takes the bend around the volcanic crater of Tower Hill. It triggers a series of physiological reactions: my throat tightens, my breathing gets a bit shallower, I strain against the seat belt to take it all in—the sea and fields and the soft, milky light. I unwind the window and inhale the air damp with sea mist. My usually static heart shifts a bit in my chest.

I took a break from my restless wanderings and returned home for the first six months of 2008. Back home I saw old friends, and the years melted away. Going to the pub in Warrnambool I didn't meet anyone new, I just re-met people I used to know. We talked about the last ten years in lumps: 'Yeah, new business, and baby and uni, but I dropped out, and then went to Malaysia but didn't stay'.

On weekends Dad made the trip from his work in Ballarat to Port Fairy. Sometimes we drove out of town and he pointed to various plots of land where his family once lived. Mostly dead now, their names are a clarion call from childhood: Mary, Sheila, Nell, Jack and Joe. During this time, I listened to old Cold Chisel, replaying *Flame Trees*, a bittersweet ode to hometowns. Reconnecting, reconnecting … old school friends, old friends of my parents, shortcuts through the town remembered, people remembered, shopkeepers, faces in the street, no one seems unfamiliar. I am ten again. Or I am twelve or twenty-four. Going home I feel ageless.

It is with the friends of my parents that I have the most fun. In their late fifties and early sixties, they are less uptight than I remember. They order pizzas and drink wine; they tell bawdy stories, argue about politics and laugh a lot. The serious business of raising children and working is done, and now the task at hand is the serious business of enjoyment. Conversations are conducted in the shorthand of long friendships. One expression ('progressive dinner') brings the table down in raucous laughter, while other words are studiously avoided because they provoke unwelcome associations or old fights. These are people who have knocked around together for so long that they *know* the terrain of each other and can navigate it. These are also people who have known me all my life, who have known me before I even knew myself. Because of this, with them I feel (and there is only one word for it) safe.

I spend a lot of time with my mum. She returned to the coast at the start of the year and has resumed teaching at the school where she taught for many years, where my three brothers and I went, and before that my dad and before that his parents went. After five years teaching in Ballarat I ask her how she's settling back in. 'It feels good to be back among your own mob', she replies. I know what she means.

I go back to reading the local daily paper. As is the habit of many local people, I start my reading on the classifieds page to feel the true pulse of the region—who has been born, who has got married, who has died. This is the news, not what is on the front page. All the names come back to me, they are mostly Irish names. I know them, or I know their siblings, or my brothers know them, or my parents know their parents. Or they knew my grandparents. It is not so much a web of associations as a blanket that covers everything.

Many of the death notices are from clubs and associations: public gratitude for service, a public acknowledgement of loss. In these notices are the songlines: the old school, the football club, the long years of service at the club or school canteen, or at the tennis club, or arranging the flowers at the church, the clubs and the groups and the sporting teams, the surf club and the parish. These are people that do not so much measure their community association and service in years or decades, but generations.

In April a good friend's mum dies from cancer. She's from a dairy farming family in a town about thirty kilometres away and my friend tells me that for weeks later they couldn't close the freezer because of all the casseroles and sausage rolls neighbours had brought to the farm.

The funeral is on a day of ragged and wild weather, trees down over roads, warnings to stay inside broadcast on local radio, rain dirty and lashing the windscreen. In the town, the church is overflowing; it is a Catholic mass and everyone knows the words. On the way to the cemetery, cars as far as the eye can see crawl along the midday road with headlights shining, the streets are eerily quiet, the town has stopped.

Later that week mum tells me about her childhood in Geelong—Irish Catholic with some of the rituals of the old Ireland still intact. She tells me about her parents going to wakes in the neighbourhood: rosaries, vigils, vespers and complines. With a bottle of poitin and rosary beads, they went and kept watch on the dead throughout the night—*a wake*. Through the night, the alive would tell stories about the dead.

I wish we'd kept that tradition alive. I could do without the corpse laid out in his Sunday best on the kitchen table and the rough alcohol and the chanting of the rosary but I could do with the stories. What did Didion say? We tell ourselves stories in order to live.[127] It is through stories we are known to others and maybe ourselves. It is through stories the dead are kept alive a little bit longer.

Stories are casualties of our restlessness. When we move on, or glide across, when we do not stay in one place, or with the same people long enough to penetrate into some deeper, truer place, when we cannot negotiate the terrain of each other, because we haven't been around long enough to know the roads in, then there can be no shared narrative. There might be for a while, but it is constantly ripping and tearing, wrenched and staccato, stopping and starting. Afresh, afresh, afresh …

The strong heat of summer and swimming days starts to fade. I go to bed early, after putting down my book and, from the verandah, drowsily watching the sun disappear. Once a week mum and I have fish and chips and sauvignon blanc down at the river. It is a tentative new ritual we both enjoy. Other nights we watch the real-life weight loss show, *The Biggest Loser*. Often I forget what day it is and have to look at the newspaper masthead to get a handle on time. Easter comes and goes and it's about a month later when mum, also drifting in a state of beach ennui, asks me what *did* we do for Easter? I have to pause and say, 'I'm not sure. I can't remember.'

Sometimes I thought it was remarkable and yet depressing how easily the past slips away when you return home. The mad dashes through Paris and London, the hardships of not finding work, the relief when you do, then the joy of spending the money: cocktails at the Savoy and high tea at the Dorchester, some club in Hoxton, shoes at Topshop and a weekend taking the Eurostar. I do not even dream about this glittery, near yet far-off past during these long coastal nights. Back home, I am with people with whom I share an ancient history, but not a recent history. When away, I am with people who share the recent history, but not the ancient. I was becoming aware of a vast unexplored interior hinterland, that although it's a human need to *explain yourself* to someone, it's impossible if they weren't *there*. There were the stories, but they couldn't be told.

I also think that everyone feels like that at some time and I also think this is what's meant by loneliness. To know and be known. To understand and be understood.

It was in this dislocation of returning home (everything so famil- iar, everything loved, yet …) I spent time agonising (as I cradled the newborn babes of my friends, inhaling the scent of baby head like oxygen) that some wrong turn had been taken. That I should never have left here, that here's where I should have gone deep, here's where I should have put down roots. The smell of rhubarb stewing on the stove, the damp and hopeful gardens, the new, matching furniture; swinging back into the rhythms of childhood friendships, and the strange comfort this brings. How could I, at those moments, not feel that the times in Sydney and Barcelona and London were a feckless folly? I couldn't smell a baby's head without the Pavlovian response of regret, not necessarily about children, but all that came with them: a home, security, a lineage, going deeper, deeper, deeper, back into the place from which you came. Among many of my young mum friends is the observation of how much having a baby brings back crystalline the deeply buried memories of their own childhood: the nicknames, story books, nursery rhymes and bath times.

But then the baby would cry, and later that night there would be nowhere to go that I hadn't already been, and the four TV channels would be showing either AFL or a documentary on salinity or the state budget, and every book on the shelf had been read so the itch started again. The restlessness, the need to keep moving, the seductive energy of the churn.

It is June. I have moved back to England. New people are in my old house in Bloomsbury so I move to South London. Yet I return to Bloomsbury almost daily, ostensibly to research a newspaper travel piece on the area's parks and squares. As I stretch out in the sun in Russell Square it occurs to me that the story was a ruse, that I was simply buying more time, just a little bit more, in a place where I was very happy.

Around that time the English newspapers are full of gloomy stories about the economy. House prices have their biggest fall since the 1970s, the price of foodstuffs rises like dough. And dough is getting expensive! Fusilli pasta has gone up by 100 per cent.[128] The pound is weakening against the euro. Fuel is becoming unaffordable, so people sell cars or car-pool or cycle. In preparation for a winter where gas is expected to rise by 26 per cent,[129] the newspapers print guides on knitting, which prove to be very popular. Suddenly Britain does not feel like the new Babylon anymore but some sort of World War II throwback with homemade clothes, ration books, no heating and thrice-weekly baths.

I read that in this climate, my old friends, the GEMs, are deserting Britain. The *Guardian* reports that 'Australians working in the City and in other white-collar professions are leaving Britain in droves for the safer economic climes of their home country'.[130] God, the GEMs are boom-time sluts, I think, shaking my head. They see no point in sticking around during the bad times and so the churn brings them home.

'Farewell fair-weather friends', waves off a blogger in the *Times*.[131] The *Times* headline calls them Walzing Matildas, 'They are the boomerang migrants. Thousands of Australians who settled here are returning down under to escape the UK's economic slowdown and its spiralling cost of living. The Australian authorities have seen a 50 per cent jump in the number of their citizens returning home from Britain since the credit crunch last summer.'[132]

I speak to Professor Hugo in April 2009 about the effect the recession may have on freedom of movement. He says the data wasn't available, but anecdotally there seemed to be some evidence of an upturn in Australians returning from the USA and Europe. 'There have been other recessions but they didn't impinge so much on immigration. But this one's different because of all the countries that are affected.' He also says it's difficult to separate the seasonal movement of people from those coming back as a result of the recession.

The cost of living *has* gone up in the UK. Bloomsbury becomes my Paradise Lost. I have been cast out by spiralling rents. I don't learn to knit—I move to Berlin.

Berlin, Berlin. I struggle with the language. It doesn't seem to stick. I can say 'cappuccino' and 'Coca Cola Light' in the cafés, but they are English words and don't really count. My language difficulties make me feel shy. I miss small talk. I long to chat to the bored-looking clerk at Kaiser, my local supermarket. In the mid-afternoon hours, long and lonely, we both idle in the pasta aisle. He looks like he could use the company as much as me.

One day walking up Auguststrasse drinking a Coke Zero ('Coke, danke', I say to the clerk, and that is all), a beautiful hippie boy with cobalt blue eyes and brown dreads stops and starts talking to me. It feels like flirting, but it sounds like … German. I say in English 'I don't speak German', and he gamely backtracks in (limited) English. 'I was just saying you are drinking a black drink [the Coke Zero] and you are black.'

'What?'

'You are black.'

'Oh, you mean I am wearing black.'

'Oh, yes, that is what I mean.' Correcting him is suddenly not sexy. I walk on, embarrassed. I miss words, speaking them to strangers, and seeing what sparks ignite and connect from them. I can't play the game without words.

Later that night after a game I can play (ping-pong) with my Australian friends at Prenzlauer Berg Park, I tell them about the cute hippie boy. 'He was trying to tell me I was drinking a black drink and wearing black, but instead he told me I *was* black.'

Dave laughed, 'That's something we've been meaning to tell you Bridge …' he paused, 'you are black'.

'Really?' I looked down at my arm, fooled for a minute. They are laughing. 'Yes, really.'

I freak out when I find out my new sublet in Kreuzberg, Berlin, includes a cat. How will I be able to just *take off* if I have to feed a cat? I wonder. I am meant to be going to Italy for a travel story. I dream about a new invention that I call the Automatic Cat Feeder. You program it from wherever you are and the bowl rotates to reveal a new day's portion of cat food. Of course there would have to be some way of keeping each portion fresh—maybe an automatic tin-opener could be attached? I ponder that, and plan my fortune: pet care for the hyper-mobile.

Time passes and summer turns to autumn (or in my case travelling between the hemispheres, summer turns to summer turns to summer turns to summer). I get a bike. It gets stolen. I get another bike and ride around the Sunday sun-dappled streets of Berlin. Indoctrinated by Australian road rules as I am, and as subversive as this feels, I follow the German custom and forgo a helmet. Instead I wear a man's Panama hat with tartan trim, which gives my head the illusion of safety, hop on the rickety green bike and hope for the best.

Riding the bike turns everything into a gorgeous, colourful slow blur. The technicolour graffiti (Kaiser King, Yuppies Fuck Off, Deuthzjeland Uber Alles, Kapatalism Rules), the pots of flowers on the outdoor tables of the cafés, the techno pumping like a sonar from the dress shops, the girls and boys with pink mohawks and lime-green sunglasses, the dog wearing blue ribbons, the caramel-skinned children with high hair and mauve balloons, the hippies in the park with their lollipop-coloured hula-hoops, the brass band near the flea-market dressed like the Beatles dressed like Sergeant Pepper, more Panama hats, more cowboy hats, bikes everywhere, more dogs and children and pots of bright, bright, bright geraniums. And on my bike I sail past it all, aware suddenly of that 'oceanic feeling', an expansiveness, a blooming, a fluid kind of happiness that is very connected to being in a new city, and gliding through it. On my new old bike, *gliding*, I make my peace with being on the surface of things.

CONCLUSION

I'm sitting in the doctor's surgery in the QV building in central Melbourne. The blood-pressure cuff is tightening around my arm and I'm trying to chill out, thinking of meadows and streams, unicorns and rainbows. The pressure tightens and the doctor, an elderly Chinese man, is telling me about the people (city office workers, just like me) who come into his clinic. 'So many people are lost, they are lost in their lives, they do not know how to live. They believe in nothing. There is so much unhappiness.'

They aren't depressed, the doctor tells me, but they aren't very happy either. 'They are searching for something but they don't know what.'

Lost people, searching without knowing that they are searching, and without knowing what to find. What a muddle. I imagine them all, coming into the QV building just like I have, rushing, then taking a seat in the quiet waiting room and then, in the hush, in this sanctioned space, some sort of levee within breaking.

'Now with rising unemployment people are anxious about losing their jobs. Jobs that didn't make them happy, money that didn't make them happy,' says the doctor, shaking his head as the pressure cuff suddenly eases and I start breathing again.

So the boom didn't really make people happy or provide answers—will the downturn be just what the doctor ordered?

I reckon it could be.

The global recession was like being woken up (shaken awake, gripped by the shoulders) from a deep, strange dream. The dream was the last fifteen years of the Long Boom. Real life, of course, went on. People hooked up and got hitched, took ill and died, moved from one job to the next, followed their dreams towards islands and horses and Spanish lessons. The usual human experiences remain unchanged throughout history: our dramas and our dreary days, our passions and paranoia, our pet projects, our children, our triumphs and troubles.

The continuous background to this, constantly playing out, was an era of spectacular excess. More people became wealthy, and the rest of us wanted to become wealthy too. What was the mass take-up of the symbols of wealth (the designer shoes and handbags, posh restaurants and exotic holidays, the lavish home renovations), and the surge in credit card debt, than the race towards some sort of idealised life, like some page torn from the lifestyle supplements (to be memorised and metaphorically masturbated over)? There was this pull towards an imaginary place called Rich Land.

You've just read about how the marrow of our lives—our romances, and love affairs, our work and our play—has become warped and changed by the values of the Long Boom, infected by the 'values' of the Age of Entitlement. How the restless economy, the increasing speed with which modern life takes place, has changed us into restless human beings and how we have been spoilt for choice and then spoilt by choice.

How in the choice between living deeply or living widely the latter won out. And yet in the fatigue of living widely with all the spending and experiences this involves, no great collective wisdom has emerged.

But we're waking up now. There is a new reality we're taking the measure of and there is a real opportunity to change. We can and should assess how we're living our lives—the speed and breadth of how we live and the values that have been culturally dominant over the last fifteen years.

We are now looking at our levels of debt, the havoc we have caused to the environment, how we treat weaker members of society and asking if perhaps we can do a better job of things; if we can start again perhaps and salvage something that was lost in what was one of the most selfish eras in history. Remember the caravan analogy? 'When the front and back are stretched so far apart, at what point can they no longer be said to be travelling together at all, breaking the community between them?'[1] We allowed people to drop behind in an ever-widening gap, instead of moving together as one tribe; we did not even turn our heads to check on their progress. When we fall behind (as we may, it's not so hard to fall back these days), who will look out for us?

We have found ourselves not only in an economic recession but also, as one news report called it, in a social recession.[2] The spoils of the good times did not trickle down to the masses. Instead they led to a reconfiguration of society, where we broke apart the old structures that held things together like full-time permanent work, live communities and having moorings in one place, replaced by our scattered, diffuse connections and wanderings in places both real and virtual.

We can start to tackle this social recession and our own drift towards the tangential and the trivial: we can reframe the narrative. Where once it was all about Project Self, 'Me Inc.' and self-actualising, maybe we can look to the person next to us and not only ask how they are, but care about the answer.

The time is right. As Philip Larkin penned in 'Church-Going', 'someone will forever be surprising / A hunger in himself to be more serious'.[3]

The election of Barack Obama to US President was a sign of this new mood—a shift in values, a hunger in ourselves 'to be more serious'. In his inauguration speech, Obama said, 'we remain a young nation, but in the words of scripture, the time has come to set aside childish things. The time has come to reaffirm our enduring spirit; to choose our better history.'[4] Obama signalled an end to the global Age of Entitlement in his speech: 'And to those nations like ours that enjoy relative plenty, we say we can no longer afford indifference to the suffering outside our borders, nor can we consume the world's resources without regard to effect. For the world has changed and we must change with it.' Australia, one of the nations that enjoy relative plenty, take note.

More than that, there is something of Obama himself that embodies these restless times (his homes are an almost eccentric, seemingly haphazard combination: Kansas and Kenya, Indonesia and Hawaii, New York and Chicago). Yet anyone reading his book *Dreams from My Father* cannot help but see his need to stop, to settle somewhere, to belong and to engage with something much larger than his own experiences.

Obama writes about the influence of his grandfather's restless search for the American dream. His grandfather 'embraced the notion of freedom and individualism and the open road without always knowing its price ... Men who were both dangerous and promising precisely because of their fundamental innocence; men prone, in the end, to disappointment ... it was this desire of his to obliterate the past, this confidence in the possibility of making the world from whole cloth that proved to be his most lasting patrimony.'[5] The *New Yorker* considers Obama to have rejected the American dream, in particular the restless aspects of 'innocence, freedom, individualism, mobility' and remaking 'yourself in a new form of your choosing'. To Obama, these aspects seem 'credulous and shallow, a destructive craving for weightlessness'.[6]

Obama went back to where his grandfather started, the mid-west, and tried to create things for himself that had been abandoned: community, in his job as an organiser on Chicago's south side; religion, in his choice of a church home; family, in his stable marriage to Michelle. The *New Yorker* describes how these choices showed that Obama 'wanted to be bound'.[7] For the children of this restless life, there is a resonance in Obama's narrative—his journey from drift to meaning.

The powerhouse of Obama's campaign were the grassroots supporters and the volunteers, particularly the young, who Obama said 'rejected the myth of their generation's apathy'. This new political engagement in America, together with the rise in climate change activism and anti-globalisation protests across Britain and Europe in 2009, signals a new alertness, demands for checks and balances, and even a rediscovery of anger. In 2009, police across Britain braced for what they called a 'summer of rage' with the middle classes, affected by the financial crisis, returning to public protest.

There is a resurrection of the part of us that died on the streets after all that marching against the war in Iraq came to nothing. (What happened to our anger over all the WMD lies? Where did that go?) Finally we are waking up and freeing ourselves from that terrible shift towards the trivial; steadying ourselves after being blown about by the whims of a restless marketplace—a marketplace that in turn encouraged our restlessness, that kept us in thrall to the next, that didn't allow much space for peace, stillness or reflection.

We don't need to purchase our identities through our clothes or holidays or by owning furniture sanctioned by a company that places a high volume of advertising in fashion magazines. We don't need to have a thousand friends on Facebook to know the value of true friendship. We don't need to brand ourselves the way companies do when we put a profile on a dating site, or on a social network site. We don't need to create a brand at work that will appeal to the boss or a client. We cannot be broken into keywords or a core message or a slogan. We are so much better than all that: more imaginative and brave, stronger and more authentic.

More complex, confused, brilliant and deep. Our inner lives are infinitely richer than the material dreams that made us drift so restlessly for the past fifteen years.

Something happened to us when we were applying for the first homeowners grant, and watching with a lack of interest the TV footage of the refugees at detention centres who'd sewn their lips together, when we knew the government was lying to us but we didn't care because we were doing okay because we had our houses and our jobs, and the DIY in our backyards to take our minds off things. Something happened to us when our televisions and waistlines grew ever larger, when we became fluent in good years for wine, and lauded celebrity chefs and became obsessed with ghoulish plastic surgery, Botox and anti-aging voodooism, our attention span ever-shortening with the amount of Googling we did, with the amount of acquiring we did on eBay (paid for) and the music and movies downloaded (not paid for). When we began ticking off the countries we visited, when new experiences were collected like trinkets from Tiffanys, the cycle becoming so fast that there was no room for reflection. In all this, we sold ourselves short somehow.

We became people rich in all the experiences and technology and all the mellow leather and scientifically enriched moisturiser that credit can buy. But it didn't make us better at the job of being human; it just made us slicker.

I think of F Scott Fitzgerald at the end of his particular boom in the Jazz Age (Manhattan and the Cote d'Azur, and fur coats and champagne and dinner suits and limousines and falling drunk into the fountain at the Plaza Hotel) and his sad lament in *The Crack-Up* that 'I began to realise that for two years my life had been a drawing on resources that I did not possess, that I had been mortgaging myself physically and spiritually up to the hilt'.[8]

But we're waking up now. We can stop for a bit, right now—with the people we are with right now—stop, hold steady, take a breath, enter that still, reflective pool that stands right there (that has always been there) and dive deep down.

NOTES

Introduction
1 YouTube Fact Sheet, <www.youtube.com/t/fact_sheet>.

Love
1 Nic Fleming, 'Three-minute Speed Date Has Couple Rushing to the Altar', *Daily Telegraph*, 9 April 2004, <www.originaldating.com/articles/article10.htm>.
2 Tara Winter Wilson, 'The World-wide Web of Deceit', *Daily Telegraph*, 19 April 2007, <www.telegraph.co.uk/news/features/3632198/The-worldwide-web-of-deceit.html>.
3 Philip Sherwell, 'Adultery Business Cashes in on World's Recession Worries', *Daily Telegraph*, 3 May 2009, <www.telegraph.co.uk/news/newstopics/howaboutthat/5269426/Adultery-business-cashes-in-on-worlds-recession-worries.html>.
4 ibid.
5 Kate Perry, 'Want to Marry a Millionaire?', news.com.au, 24 April 2008, <www.news.com.au/business/story/0,23636,23586658-14327,00.html>.
6 Laura van Straaten, 'Online Dating Just Got Weirder', *Daily Beast*, 13 February 2009, <www.thedailybeast.com/blogs-and-stories/2009-02-13/online-dating-just-got-weirder>.
7 Robert L Mitchell, 'Online Dating: The Technology Behind Attraction', *Computerworld*, 13 February 2009, <www.computerworld.com/action/article.do?command=viewArticleBasic&articleId=9127711>. According to the *Computerworld* website, other popular sites include Match.com with 15 million members and Plentyoffish with 12 million members. In Australia, RSVP has 1.3 million

members with a thousand new members joining each day (RSVP website).

8 Mitchell, 'Online Dating: The Technology Behind Attraction'.

9 ibid.

10 ibid.

11 ibid.

12 ibid.

13 'Why Dating Sites Are Recession-Proof', Reuters, 23 February 2009.

14 News Corp chief Rupert Murdoch purchased MySpace for $300 million in 2005. With 50 million users globally, the acquisition was a sign that big business was keen to get some online dating action. Australian media company Fairfax bought RSVP.com.au for $39 million in July 2005.

15 James Maguire, 'Case Study: Match.com', e-commerceguide. com, 31 January 2003, <www.ecommerce-guide.com/news/ article.php/1577861 - e-commerce-guide.com>. Match.com is also linked to MSN, Excite, EarthLink, Netscape and BET.

16 ibid.

17 Philip Sherwell, 'Lonely Hearts Agency Pays Women to Date Men', *Sunday Telegraph*, 20 November 2005, <www.telegraph. co.uk/news/worldnews/northamerica/usa/1503474/Lonely- hearts-agency-pays-women-to-date-men.html>.

18 Match.com operates in twenty-four countries, in eight languages, spanning five continents (Mitchell, 'Online Dating: The Technology Behind Attraction').

19 Match.com, <www.abouttmcs.com/advertise/admatch.html>.

20 Stuart Washington, 'Online and Personal', *BRW*, 9 March 2006.

21 Robert L Mitchell, 'Online Dating: Your Profile's Long, Scary Shelf-life', *Computerworld*, 13 February 2009,

<www.computerworld.com/action/article.do?command=
viewArticleBasic&articleId=9127799>.

22 ibid.

23 ibid.

24 Damian Barr, 'The Growth of Gay Online Dating', *Independent on Sunday*, 19 February 2006, <www.independent.co.uk/news/uk/this-britain/the-growth-of-gay-online-dating-466871.html>.

25 Megan K Scott, 'Multitaskers Say One Online Dating Site Won't Do', ABC News Entertainment, 5 February 2009, <abcnews.go.com/Entertainment/wireStory?id=6812829>.

26 ibid.

27 ibid.

28 ibid.

29 Sathnam Sanghera, 'Internet Dating Is for Everyone (Except Me Of Course)', *Times*, 15 July 2008, <www.timesonline.co.uk/tol/comment/columnists/sathnam_sanghera/article4332971.ece>.

30 Rufus Black, 'Community in an Electronic Age', *Eureka Street*, 9 July 2006, <www.eurekastreet.com.au/article.aspx?aeid=1396>.

31 ibid.

32 Mitchell, 'Online Dating: The Technology Behind the Attraction'.

33 ibid.

34 ibid.

35 ibid.

36 Posted by Ricky on 2 August 2006, 10.05, *Sydney Morning Herald* online.

37 Brigid Delaney, 'Dating Games Without Frontiers', *Sydney Morning Herald*, 2 June 2004, <www.smh.com.au/articles/2004/06/01/1086058850840.html>.

38 Peter Munro, 'High-Tech Cupids for the Net Generation', *Sydney Morning Herald*, 22 May 2002, <www.smh.com.au/articles/2002/05/21/1021882055653.html>.

39 Sally Brampton, 'The "Past their Sell-by" Daters', *Telegraph*, 9 April 2006, <www.telegraph.co.uk/fashion/stellamagazine/3352695/The-past-their-sell-by-daters.html>.

40 ibid.

41 ibid.

42 ibid.

43 Julian Lee, 'When Two Busy People Click', *Sydney Morning Herald*, 11 June 2005, <www.smh.com.au/news/Technology/When-two-busy-people-click/2005/06/10/1118347602465.html>.

44 Delaney, 'Dating Games Without Frontiers'.

45 ibid.

46 ibid.

47 Maria Alvarez, '1 thing i kno, i luv u', *Telegraph*, 15 July 2006, <www.telegraph.co.uk/culture/3653998/1-thing-i-kno-i-luv-u.html>.

48 ibid.

49 Theodora Stites, 'Someone to Watch Over Me (on Google Map)', *New York Times*, 9 July 2006, <www.nytimes.com/2006/07/09/fashion/sundaystyles/09love.html>.

50 ibid.

51 Mitchell, 'Online Dating: The Technology Behind the Attraction'.

52 Adele Horin, 'How Porn Is Wrecking Relationships', *Sydney Morning Herald*, 19 May 2007.

53 Brigid Delaney, 'With Song in Their Hearts', *Sydney Morning Herald*, 21 January 2005, <www.smh.com.au/articles/2005/01/20/1106110880002.html>.

54 'Tempo Talk', *Sun-Herald*, 3 July 1988.

55 Katherine Glover, 'Coca-Cola Venice Sponsorship Sparks Protest', BNET Food Blog, 25 February 2009, <industry.bnet. com/food/1000497/coca-cola-venice-sponsorship-sparks-protest>.

56 David Fickling, 'Britain Is Home to Nearly 7 Million Bloggers', *Guardian*, 20 July 2006, <www.guardian.co.uk/technology/ 2006/jul/20/news.uknews>.

57 Neil Swidey, 'The End of Alone', *The Boston Globe*, 8 February 2009, <www.boston.com/bostonglobe/magazine/articles/2009/ 02/08/the_end_of_alone>.

58 ibid.

59 ibid.

60 James Harkin, 'No escape from the electronic loop', *Independent*, 5 March 2009, <www.independent.co.uk/ opinion/commentators/james-harkin-no-escape-from-the-electronic-loop-1637573.html>.

61 ibid.

62 Swidey, 'The End of Alone'.

63 *Daily Beast*, 27 February 2009, 12:59.

64 Sanghera, 'Internet Dating Is for Everyone (Except Me Of Course)'.

65 Patrick Wintour, 'Facebook and Bebo Risk Infantalising the Human Mind', *Guardian*, 24 February 2009, <www.guardian. co.uk/uk/2009/feb/24/social-networking-site-changing-childrens-brains>.

66 ibid.

67 ibid.

68 'Scalpel Junkie', *Daily Beast*, 27 February 2009.

69 Stites, 'Someone to Watch Over Me (on a Google Map)'.

70 Mark McKinnon, 'Twitter Jumped the Shark This Week', *Daily Beast*, 27 February 2009, <www.dailybeast.com/blog-and-stories/2009-02-27/twitter-jumped-the-shark-this-week/full>.

71 Lee Woodruff, 'Let's Stop This Twitter Madness', *Daily Beast*, 28 February 2009, <www.thedailybeast.com/blogs-and-stories/2009-02-28/lets-stop-the-twitter-madness/full/>.

72 Brigid Delaney, 'Meditation: The Key to Calm', cnn.com, 15 June 2007, <edition.cnn.com/2007/HEALTH/06/11/pl.meditation.main/index.html>.

73 Lorna Martin, 'Sex, Sand and Sugar Mummies in a Caribbean Beach Fantasy', *Observer*, 23 July 2006, <www.guardian.co.uk/travel/2006/jul/23/jamaica.theatre.theobserver>.

74 ibid.

75 Michel Houellebecq, *Platform*, William Heinemann Ltd, London, 2002, p. 146.

Work

1   Richard Sennett, *The Corrosion of Character*, Norton, New York, 1998, p. 16.

2   ThinkExist, <thinkexist.com/quotes/joan_didion/2.html>.

3   Sennett, *The Corrosion of Character*, p. 22.

4   ibid., p. 9.

5   Katharine Mieszkowski, 'The Revolt of the Wage Slaves', Salon.com, 31 May 2001, <archive.salon.com/tech/feature/2001/05/31/free_agent/index2.html>.

6   Daniel Pink, 'Free Agent Nation', *Fast Company*, 18 December 2007, <www.fastcompany.com/magazine/12/freeagent.html?page+0%2C2>.

7   *Human Capital Magazine*, <www.hcamag.com/hca_aus/detail_article.cfm?articleID=633>, accessed February 2008.

8   ibid.

9   Sennett, *The Corrosion of Character*, p. 23.

10 *Human Capital Magazine*, <www.hcamag.com/hca_aus/detail_article.cfm?articleID=633>, accessed February 2008.

11 Hugh Mackay, *Advance Australia Where?*, Hachette, Sydney, 2007.

12 BC Work Infonet, 'Making Career Sense of Labour Market Information: The Shift to Non-standard Employment', <workinfonet.bc.ca/lmisi/making/chapter2/SHIFT1.HTM>.

13 Fritz Williams, *Curriculum: New Work for a New Generation*, Detroit Educational Television Foundation, p. 16.

14 *Human Capital Magazine*, <www.hcamag.com/hca_aus/detail_article.cfm?articleID=633>, accessed February 2008.

15 BC Work Infonet, 'Making Career Sense of Labour Market Information: The Shift to Non-standard Employment'.

16 ibid.

17 ibid.

18 ibid.

19 Andrew Charlton, *Ozonomics*, Random House, Sydney, 2007; Sennett, *The Corrosion of Character*, p. 49.

20 Seek, 'The Future of Work', <www.seek.com.au/career-resources/plan-develop/future-work.ascx>.

21 Naomi Klein, *No Logo*, Knopf, Toronto, 2000, p. 231.

22 William Bridges, *Job Shift: How to Prosper in a Workplace Without Jobs*, Addison-Wesley, Reading, MA, 1995.

23 The Thinkers 50, 'Interview: Charles Handy', <www.thinkers50.com/?page=interview&ranking=14>.

24 ibid.

25 Ron Lieber, 'Don't Believe the Hype', *Details*, June 1997, p. 113.

26 David Boyle, *Authenticity*, Flamingo, London, 2003, p. 174.

27 Tom Peters, 'A Brand Called You', *Fast Company*, 18 December 2007, <www.fastcompany.com/node/28905/print>.

28 ibid.

29 Annette Sampson, 'Me Inc.', *Sydney Morning Herald*, 6 September 2005.

30 Brigid Delaney, 'A Pash Under the Mistletoe … Sorry, Too Busy Networking', *Sydney Morning Herald*, 5 December 2005, <www.smh.com.au/news/opinion/a-pash-under-the-mistletoe--sorry-too-busy-networking/2005/12/04/11336311 43107.html>.

31 Warrnambool's unemployment rate is 5.1 per cent compared to 5.3 per cent for Victoria, <www.business.vic.gov.au/busvicwr/_assets/main/lib60018/warrnamboolpresentation.pdf>.

32 Klein, p. 267.

33 Seek, 'The Future of Work'.

34 Sennett, *The Corrosion of Character*, p. 63.

35 David Leonhardt, 'One Safety Net Is Disappearing. What Will Follow?', *New York Times*, 4 April 2007, <www.nytimes.com/2007/04/04/business/04leonhardt.html>.

36 ibid.

37 Mark Coultan, 'Want a Pension and Health Care? Start Saving Now', *Sydney Morning Herald*, 29 June 2007, <www.smh.com.au/news/business/want-a-pension-and-health-care-start-saving-now/2007/06/29/1182624170262.html>.

38 Leonhardt, 'One Safety Net Is Disappearing'.

39 ibid.

40 ibid.

41 Brigid Delaney, 'Large Pay Rises Saved for the Few', *Sydney Morning Herald*, 30 April 2005.

42 ibid.

43 Richard Sennett, *The Culture of New Capitalism*, Yale University Press, New Haven, 2006, p. 4.

44 David Leonhardt, 'Reader Responses', *New York Times*, 4 April 2007, <query.nytimes.com/gst/fullpage.html?res=9D05EED9163FF937A35757C0A9619C8B63 – 88k>.

45 ibid.

46 Seumas Milne, 'This Is a Chance to Reverse Casualisation and Insecurity', *Guardian*, 31 January 2008, <www.guardian.co.uk/commentisfree/2008/jan/31/immigrationpolicy.politics1>.

47 ibid.

48 'Just in time' labour refers to a pattern of work that closely follows production.

49 Owen Boycott, 'MP's Bill Aims to Ease Plight of 1.4m Agency Workers', *Guardian*, 22 February 2008, <www.guardian.co.uk/money/2008/feb/22/workandcareers.tradeunions>.

50 Sennett, *The Corrosion of Character*, p. 48.

51 ibid., p. 50.

52 Ron Stodghill, Melissa August, Sarah Sturmon Dale and Maggie Sieger, 'Part-Time Recession', *Time*, 29 October 2001, <www.time.com/time/magazine/article/0,9171,1001078,00.html>.

53 Leah Shmerling, 'Irreversible Trend Towards Contract Labour', *Age*, 7 July 1998. In this article recruitment expert Geoff Slade says 'anecdotal evidence [suggests] that executives prefer contracting arrangements to full-time employment due to stress and pressure. Providing contractors are able to obtain on-going work, they are able to have breaks in between contracts. This brings lifestyle advantages.'

54 George Megalogenis, *The Longest Decade,* Scribe, Melbourne, 2006, p. 41.

55 Brigid Delaney, 'Doing It Their Way', *Sydney Morning Herald*, 26 April 2005, <www.smh.com.au/news/Business/Doing-it-their-way/2005/04/25/1114281505124.html>.

56 ibid.

57 Mackay, p. 98.

58 Adele Horin, 'Gen Y work towards a life, not a career', *Sydney Morning Herald*, 4 June 2005, <www.smh.com.au/news/

Adele-Horin/Gen-Y-work-towards-a-life-not-a-career/2005/
06/03/1117568376872.html>.

59 Mackay, p. 72.

60 Mieszkowski, 'The Revolt of the Wage Slaves'.

61 Andrew West, 'Enough Already', *Monthly*, December 2005 –
January 2006.

62 Sennett, *The Corrosion of Character*, p. 25.

63 The Thinkers 50, 'Interview: Charles Handy'.

64 *Today Show*, NBC, 26 November 2007.

65 Valerie Khoo, 'Variety Acts', *Sydney Morning Herald*, 19 March
2005, <www.smh.com.au/news/Employment-News/Variety-
acts/2005/03/18/1111085988222.html>.

66 Claire Adler, 'Mix and match', *Guardian*, 4 November
2006, <www.guardian.co.uk/money/2006/nov/04/careers.
graduates1>.

67 The Thinkers 50, 'Interview: Charles Handy'.

68 Adler, 'Mix and match'.

69 Clare Dight, 'Shop-floor Nous and Flexibility Hit the Spot',
Times, 8 March 2007, <www.timesonline.co.uk/business/
career_and_jobs/careers_in/article1483515.ece>.

70 Mary Braid, 'How to Connect with Generation Y', *Sunday
Times*, 20 May 2007, <www.timesonline.co.uk/business/
career_and_jobs/recruiter_forum/article1813031.ece>.

71 Khoo, 'Variety Acts'.

72 Sennett, *The Culture of New Capitalism*, p. 105.

73 ibid.

74 International Communist Current, <en.internationalism.org/
node/1137 – 50k>, accessed May 2009.

75 Sennett, *The Corrosion of Character*, p. 85.

76 Braid, 'How to Connect with Generation Y'. The business
pages of British newspapers reported on the impressive
portfolio career of former Director General Sir Digby who

will 'pursue a portfolio career with roles at Deloitte and JCB
and voluntary work for Cancer Research to add to his Ford
appointment'.

77 Michael Gove, 'Who Was Naked, the Princess or the
    Producers?', *Times*, 30 November 2005, <www.timesonline.
    co.uk/tol/comment/columnists/michael_gove/article597930.
    ece>.

78 Sennett, *The Corrosion of Character*, p. 26.

79 Sennett, *The Culture of New Capitalism*, p. 4.

80 Sennett, *The Corrosion of Character*, p. 10.

81 ibid., p. 24.

82 Delaney, 'Doing It Their Way'.

83 Cathy Booth Thomas and Thomas K Grose, 'High-Tech
    Nomads', *Time*, 26 November 2001, <www.time.com/time/
    magazine/article/0,9171,1001314,00.html>.

84 Fleur Britten, 'The Rise of the New Nomadics', *Times*,
    23 March 2008, <women.timesonline.co.uk/tol/life_and_style/
    women/the_way_we_live/article3570549.ece>.

85 Clive Hamilton, *Growth Fetish*, Allen & Unwin, Sydney, 2003,
    p. 152.

86 Thomas and Grose, 'High-Tech Nomads'.

87 ibid.

88 Dan Fost, 'Where Neo-Nomads' Ideas Percolate', *San
    Francisco Chronicle*, 11 March 2007, <www.sfgate.com/cgi-
    bin/article.cgi?file=/c/a/2007/03/11/MNGKKOCBA645.
    DTL>.

89 Britten, 'The Rise of the New Nomadics'.

90 Sennett, *The Culture of New Capitalism*, p. 4.

91 Chris Zappone, 'Fairfax Media to Cut 550 Jobs', *Age*,
    26 August 2008, <business.smh.com.au/business/Fairfax-
    media-to-cut-550-jobs-2008082642fu.html>.

92 Hamilton, *Growth Fetish*, p. 155.

93 Graham Greene, *The Third Man,* Heinemann, London, 1950, p. 1.

94 Delaney, 'Doing It Their Way'.

95 Andy McSmith, 'Polly Toynbee: Reborn, as a Lady of the Right', *Independent,* 26 November 2006, <www.independent.co.uk/news/people/profiles/polly-toynbee-reborn-as-a-lady-of-the-right>.

96 Elisabeth Wynhausen, *Dirt Cheap,* Macmillan, Sydney, 2005, p. 231.

97 ibid., p. 232.

98 Horin, 'Gen Y work towards a life, not a career'.

99 ibid.

100 David Uren, 'No Escape from Recession, Says RBA, as OECD Warns of 25m Jobless,' *Australian,* 1 April 2009, <www.theaustralian.news.com.au/story/0,25197,25272598-601,00.html>.

101 ibid.

102 ABC Radio, *PM,* 6 April 2009.

103 Gabby Hinsliff, 'Dreams Shelved as Recession Forces Britons to Put Lives on Hold,' *Observer,* 8 February 2009, <www.guardian.co.uk/business/2009/feb/08/recession-family-life-birth-rate>.

104 Matthew Franklin, 'Free Markets a False God, Says Kevin Rudd', *Australian,* 1 April 2009, <www.theaustralian.news.com.au/story/0,25197,25272773-5013871,00.html>.

105 Letters, 'Blair Taxed About the Filthy Rich', *Guardian,* 11 January 2008, <www.guardian.co.uk/politics/2008/jan/12/tonyblair.labour>.

106 Sennett, *The Corrosion of Character,* p. 25.

107 ibid.

108 Klein, p. 267.

109 Sennett, *The Corrosion of Character,* pp. 26–7.

Travel

1 F Scott Fitzgerald, *The Great Gatsby*, Charles Scribner's Sons, New York, 1925, p. 12.

2 The Senate Legal and Constitutional References Committee, 'They Still Call Australia Home: Inquiry into Australian Expatriates', March 2005, <www.aph.gov.au/senate/committee/ legcon_ctte/completed_inquiries/2004-07/expats03/report/ report.pdf>.

3 ibid.

4 ibid.

5 Philip Larkin, 'The Trees', *High Windows*, Faber and Faber, 1974.

6 United Nations, Department of Economic and Social Affairs, Population Division, 'International Migration Report 2006: A Global Assessment', New York, 2009, <www.un.org/esa/ population/publications/2006_MigrationRep/exec_sum.pdf>.

7 The Senate Legal and Constitutional References Committee, 'They Still Call Australia Home'.

8 The transcendental sense of a limitless and indissoluble bond between oneself and the external world that Freud believed to underlie religious sentiments (which he could not discover in himself), <http://www.encyclopedia.com/doc/ 1O87-oceanicfeeling.html>.

9 Malcolm Knox and Steve Toltz in conversation, Sydney Writers' Festival, Carrington Hotel, Katoomba, May 2008.

10 The Senate Legal and Constitutional References Committee, 'They Still Call Australia Home'.

11 ibid. The 2005 Senate report identified that more than two-thirds of long-term departures of Australian residents in 2002 were professionals, para-professionals, managers or administrative occupations.

12 ibid. The UK accounts for at least 25 per cent of Australians leaving on a permanent and long-term basis. Other popular destinations include Western Europe (particularly Greece), Asia, the USA and New Zealand. The report noted that the number of Australians emigrating to Asia has increased by more than 50 per cent in recent years.

13 James Meek, 'Super Rich', *Guardian*, 17 April 2006: 'One of the big tax advantages for super-rich British residents who aren't British-born is this country's unique "non-domiciled" tax rule, which allows tens of thousands of wealthy people to avoid paying tax on income earned overseas'.

14 James Button, 'Where the Bloody Hell Are They?', *Age*, 6 May 2006, <www.smh.com.au/news/world/where-the-bloody-hell-are-they/2006/05/05/1146335930554.html>.

15 Fleur Britten, 'Australian Fashion Gets Hip', *Sunday Times*, 27 July 2008, <women.timesonline.co.uk/tol/life_and_style/women/fashion/article4379587.ece>.

16 Steve Pavlovic, founder of Modular Recordings, in ibid.

17 ibid.

18 Ben Cubby and Brigid Delaney, 'It Works for Me', *Sydney Morning Herald*, 18 February 2006, <www.smh.com.au/news/national/it-works-for-me/2006/02/17/1140151815367.html>.

19 Wikipedia, 'Magic Circle (law)', <en.wikipedia.org/wiki/Magic_Circle_(law)>.

20 The Senate Legal and Constitutional References Committee, 'They Still Call Australia Home'.

21 Button, 'Where the Bloody Hell Are They?'

22 ibid.

23 ibid.

24 The Senate Legal and Constitutional References Committee, 'They Still Call Australia Home'.

25 ibid.

26 Highly Skilled, <www.highlyskilled.co.uk/index.php?No Parameter&Theme=default&Script=qualifying>.

27 Gretchen Lang, 'Foreign Postings Beckon to the Young', *International Herald Tribune*, 25 March 2006, <www.euro-career.com/webfiles/press/ITH2006.pdf>.

28 ibid.

29 Hamilton, *Growth Fetish*, p. 151.

30 ibid.

31 According to an HSBC survey of 2155 expatriates across fifteen countries, in Holly Ife, 'Australian Expats Third Wealthiest in the World', *Herald Sun*, 26 July 2008, <http://www.news.com.au/heraldsun/story/0,21985,24078300-664,00.html>.

32 ibid.

33 Mike Davis, *Evil Paradises*, The New Press, New York, 2007, pp. xiii–xiv.

34 David Jones, 'The Degenerates of Dubai', *Daily Mail*, 19 July 2008, <www.newser.com/archive-world-news/1G1-181688851/the-degenerates-of-dubai-contrasting-figures-a-veiled-emirati-woman-stares-at-a-scantily-clad.html>.

35 ibid.

36 Lucy Morgan, 'Common Indecency', *Guardian*, 15 July 2008, <www.guardian.co.uk/world/2008/jul/15/britishidentity?gusrc=rss&feed=worldnews>.

37 ibid.

38 ibid.

39 ibid.

40 ibid.

41 ibid.

42 BritishExpats.com/Discussion Forum/Living & Moving Abroad/Middle East/Dubai Brunch, <britishexpats.com/forum/showthread.php?t=524520 - 82k>.

43 Morgan, 'Common Indecency'.

44 Ian Gallagher, 'Revealed: The Lonely Bridget Jones World of the British Sales Manager Facing Jail in Dubai', *Daily Mail*, 2 July 2008, <www.dailymail.co.uk/news/article-1034629/Revealed-The-lonely-Bridget-Jones-world-British-sales-manager-facing-jail-Dubai.html>.

45 Nick Parker, 'Boozy Brits Go Wild in Dubai', *Sun*, 12 July 2008, <www.thesun.co.uk/sol/homepage/news/article1414337.ece>.

46 Jones, 'The Degenerates of Dubai'.

47 ibid.

48 Morgan, 'Common Indecency'.

49 Jones, 'The Degenerates of Dubai'.

50 ibid.

51 The International Monetary Fund has said it expects the UAE economy to grow only 3 per cent in 2009 after expanding 7.4 per cent in 2007 and an estimated 6.9 per cent in 2008. Vivian Salama, 'Dumping on Dubai: Have Hard Times Hit the Emirates?', *Time*, 31 March 2009, <www.time.com/time/world/article/0,8599,1888428,00.html>.

52 ibid.

53 Roula Khalaf, 'Don't Rule Out Dubai Comeback', *Financial Times*, 8 April 2009, <www.ft.com/cms/s/0/f098d4dc-2466-11de-9a01-00144feabdc0.html>.

54 Michael Schuman, 'On the Road Again', *Time*, 27 April 2009, p. 12.

55 Davis, p. xv.

56 Dan Milmo, 'Booming European Low-Budget Air-Travel Turns to Bust as Ryanair Predicts First Loss in 20 Years', *Guardian*, 29 July 2008, <www.guardian.co.uk/business/2008/jul/29/theairlineindustry.travelleisure>.

57 Dominique Lummus, 'But Mummy? Where Am I From?', Expat Focus, <www.expatfocus.com/mummy-where-am-i-from>.

58 ibid.

59 ibid.

60 ibid.

61 Button, 'Where the Bloody Hell Are They?'

62 The Senate Legal and Constitutional References Committee, 'They Still Call Australia Home'.

63 Swidey, 'The End of Alone'.

64 ibid.

65 Steven Swinford, 'Airline Squeeze Hits Holiday Homes', *Sunday Times*, 10 August 2008, <www.timesonline.co.uk/tol/news/uk/article4493293.ece>.

66 ibid.

67 ibid.

68 Philip Johnston, 'Emigration Soars as Britons Desert the UK', *Daily Telegraph*, 19 April 2008, <www.telegraph.co.uk/news/uknews/1569400/Emigration-soars-as-Britons-desert-the-UK.html>. The churn in the UK goes something like this: 'since … 1997, 1.8 million British people have left but only 979 000 have returned. Over the same period, 3.9 million foreign nationals have come to Britain while 1.6 million have left.'

69 Philip Johnston, 'Immigration Outpaces British Exodus', *Daily Telegraph*, 17 November 2007, <www.telegraph.co.uk/news/majornews/1569533/Immigration-out-paces-British-exodus.html>.

70 ibid.

71 ibid.

72 Austen Inverleigh, 'Amnesty for Illegal Immigrants', *Guardian*, 3 May 2009, <www.guardian.co.uk/commentisfree/libertycentral/2009/may/03/amnesty-illegal-immigrants>.

73 Andrew Marr, 'When the World Came to Stay', *Daily Telegraph*, 16 May 2007, <www.telegraph.co.uk/global/main.jhtml?xml=/global/2007/05/16/nosplit/ftmarr116.xml>.

74 ibid.

75 Philip Johnston, 'Immigrants "Swamping" Council Services', *Daily Telegraph*, 28 June 2006, <www.telegraph.co.uk/news/uknews/1522518/Immigrants-'swamping'-council-services.html>.

76 Schuman, 'On the Road Again', p. 12.

77 ibid. The UK government believes such moves could slash the number entering Britain from 26 000 a year to 14 000.

78 ibid.

79 Marr, 'When the World Came to Stay'.

80 The year was 2004; Angela Balakrishnan and Pui-Guan Man, 'Brain Drain Helping to Keep Third World Poor', *Sydney Morning Herald*, 21 July 2007, <http://www.smh.com.au/news/world/brain-drain-helping-to-keep-third-world-poor/2007/07/20/1184560038064.html>.

81 ibid.

82 According to the Australian Bureau of Statistics, Melbourne added about 49 000 people in the year to June 2006, Sydney 37 000, Brisbane 29 500 and Perth 30 000. Tim Colebatch, 'Melbourne Tops Nation in Growth', *Age*, 28 February 2007, <www.theage.com.au/news/national/melbourne-pushes-boundaries/2007/02/27/1172338625778.html>.

83 ibid.

84 Madeleine Bunting, 'The Middle Classes Have Discovered They've Been Duped by the Super-Rich', *Guardian*, 25 June 2007, <www.guardian.co.uk/commentisfree/2007/jun/25/comment.politics2>.

85 Lloyd Evans, 'A Slum for Half a Million', *Spectator*, 2 May 2007, <www.spectator.co.uk/the-magazine/features/29437/a-slum-for-half-a-million.thtml>.

86 Bunting, 'The Middle Classes Have Discovered They've Been Duped by the Super-Rich'.

87 The Senate Legal and Constitutional References Committee, 'They Still Call Australia Home'.

88 Richard Florida, *Who's Your City?*, Basic Books, New York, 2008.

89 ibid., p. 93.

90 ibid., p. 96.

91 Johnston, 'Immigration Outpaces British Exodus'.

92 The Senate Legal and Constitutional References Committee, 'They Still Call Australia Home'.

93 Clive Hamilton, 'It's Life, but Certainly Not as We Want It', *Sydney Morning Herald*, 30 December 2006, <www.smh.com.au/news/opinion/its-life-but-certainly-not-as-we-want-it/2006/12/29/1166895477172.html?page=fullpage#content Swap1>.

94 ibid.

95 ibid.

96 Florida, p. 18. Saskia Sassen suggests 'migrant women, especially, meet the demand for labour in the marginalised, flexible and devalued sectors of production and services in global cities', <www.focus-migration.de/Skilled_female_labou.6029.0.html?&L=1>.

97 The Senate Legal and Constitutional References Committee, 'They Still Call Australia Home'.

98 ibid., p. 18.

99 Davis, p. ix.

100 Schuman, 'On the Road Again', p. 12.

101 Leon Gettler, 'Just an Everyday Earner … Times 365', *Age*, 17 May 2006, <www.theage.com.au/news/national/just-an-everyday-earner-times-365/2006/05/16/1147545327257.html>.

102 Letters page, *Daily Telegraph* (NSW), 18 May 2006, p. 28.

103 ibid.

104 Davis, p. xii.

105 Florida, p. 99.

106 Katherine Spenley, 'Foreign, Friendless & Busy? Expat Contact Fills the Gap', AFP, 10 April 2003, <www.expatcontact.com/ ?id=2&ty=ge&sd=412>.

107 Florida, p. 14.

108 Spenley, 'Foreign Friendless & Busy?'

109 Wikipedia, 'Mark Granovetter', <en.wikipedia.org/wiki/Mark_ Granovetter>.

110 Spenley, 'Foreign, Friendless & Busy?'

111 Sennett, *The Corrosion of Character*, p. xx.

112 ibid.

113 ibid., p. 87.

114 Sennett, *The Corrosion of Character*, p. 88.

115 Hamilton, *Growth Fetish*, p. 152.

116 Gallagher, 'Revealed: The Lonely Bridget Jones World of the British Sales Manager Facing Jail in Dubai'.

117 Sennett, *The Corrosion of Character*, p. 83.

118 ibid., p. xx.

119 ibid., p. 161.

120 ibid., p. 151.

121 Lang, 'Foreign Postings Beckon to the Young'.

122 ibid.

123 Sennett, *The Corrosion of Character*, p. 85.

124 Joseph Schumpeter, *The Process of Creative Destruction*, Harper, New York, 1975.

125 Sennett, *The Corrosion of Character*, p. 20.

126 Matthew, 8:12: But the children of the kingdom shall be cast out into outer darkness: there shall be weeping and gnashing of teeth.

127 Joan Didion, *The White Album*, Simon and Schuster, New York, 1979.

128 Zoe Williams, 'Beat Rising Food Bills—Follow the Inflation-Proof Diet', *Guardian*, 13 August 2008, <www.guardian.co.uk/environment/2008/aug/13/food.consumeraffairs>.

129 Victoria Hartley, 'EON Raises Gas and Electricity Prices', *Guardian*, 21 August 2008, <www.guardian.co.uk/money/2008/aug/21/energy.householdbills21>.

130 Barbara McMahon, 'Australians Flee UK in Droves as Credit Woes Bite', *Guardian*, 17 May 2008, <www.guardian.co.uk/world/2008/may/17/australia.immigration>: 'Research by financial services specialist Link Recruitment showed that about 34,000 Australians annually are packing their bags and taking the long flight home, while those who might have considered moving abroad are staying put. In the past 12 months, the firm registered a 14% drop in applications from Australians searching for jobs in the UK.'

131 Robert Watts and Paul Ham, 'Aussie Migrants Waltz out of High Cost UK', *Times*, 29 June 2008, <www.timesonline.co.uk/tol/news/uk/article4232329.ece>.

132 ibid.

Conclusion

1 McSmith, 'Polly Toynbee: Reborn, as a Lady of the Right'.

2 Neal Lawson, 'Labour Party Has Presided Over a Social Recession', *Guardian*, 22 Febuary 2007, <www.democraticunderground.com/discuss/duboard.php?az=view_all&address=103x264641>.

3 Philip Larkin, 'Church Going'.

4 CNNPolitics.com, 'Obama's Inaugural Speech', <www.cnn.com/2009/POLITICS/01/20/obama.politics/>.

5 Barack Obama, *Dreams from My Father*, Text, Melbourne, 2008, p. xx.

6 Larissa MacFarquhar, 'The Conciliator', *New Yorker*, 7 May 2007.

7 ibid.

8 F Scott Fitzgerald, *The Crack-Up*, New Directions Publishing Corporation, New York, 1945, p. 72.